Risk, Crisis and Security Management

Risk, Crisis and Security Management

EDWARD P. BORODZICZ

John Wiley & Sons, Ltd

Other Wiley Editorial Offices

John Wiley & Sons Inc., 111 River Street, Hoboken, NJ 07030, USA

Jossey-Bass, 989 Market Street, San Francisco, CA 94103-1741, USA

Wiley-VCH Verlag GmbH, Boschstr. 12, D-69469 Weinheim, Germany

John Wiley & Sons Australia Ltd, 33 Park Road, Milton, Queensland 4064, Australia

John Wiley & Sons (Asia) Pte Ltd, 2 Clementi Loop #02-01, Jin Xing Distripark, Singapore 129809

John Wiley & Sons Canada Ltd, 22 Worcester Road, Etobicoke, Ontario, Canada M9W 1L1

Wiley also publishes its books in a variety of electronic formats. Some content that appears in
print may not be available in electronic books.

Library of Congress Cataloging in Publication Data

Borodzicz, Edward P.
  Risk, crisis and security management / Edward P. Borodzicz.
     p.   cm.
  Includes bibliographical references and index.
  ISBN-13 978-0-470-86704-4 (pbk. : alk. paper)
  ISBN-10 0-470-86704-3 (pbk. : alk. paper)
  1. Risk management.   2. Crisis management.   3. Industries—Security measures.   I. Title.
  HD61.B654 2005
  658.4′7—dc22

                                                                              2005004186

British Library Cataloguing in Publication Data

A catalogue record for this book is available from the British Library

ISBN-13 978-0-470-86704-4 (PB)
ISBN-10 0-470-86704-3 (PB)

Typeset in 10/15pt Sabon by Integra Software Services Pvt. Ltd, Pondicherry, India
Printed and bound in Great Britain by Antony Rowe Ltd, Chippenham, Wiltshire
This book is printed on acid-free paper responsibly manufactured from sustainable forestry
in which at least two trees are planted for each one used for paper production.

For Chun, Alice and Peter

CONTENTS

AIMS AND OBJECTIVES

The aim of this book is to provide a theoretical resource for students and practitioners interested in the relationship between risk, crisis and security management. The book will present a number of contemporary debates in this growing area of academic interest. The concepts of risk and security management are introduced in the context of a number of theoretical social science approaches to the subject. This book is designed to be of sufficient theoretical depth to satisfy the needs of the academic reader, particularly those studying electives and postgraduates, but also sufficiently accessible for the professional to derive practical benefit.

This book has two academic themes. First, to consider how risk, crisis and security may be linked themes. It is not the intention to overtly define these concepts; rather, to perform a role in establishing links between them. Risk is an established concept of academic interest in both pure and social science; it remains, however, a subject of intense social and political controversy. How we manage risk appears to dominate every debate from providing social services – such as health, transport and education – to the regulation of corporate activity. The risk and security industry has rapidly grown in recent years, largely as a consequence of increasing regulation and governance in many parts of the industrialized world. Demand for a readable text to facilitate the role of risk and security management functions in organizations has therefore increased considerably.

Academic debates about the theory and practice of crisis management are, in contrast, less well developed although equally controversial. This book aims to inform these debates by considering the relationships between risk, crisis and security. This book should be of particular relevance to those responsible for managing risk in a corporate context. Debates about where key decision makers should be sited in the organizational structure and hierarchy are currently unresolved. Demarcation lines between those responsible for risk, security and contingency planning functions in organizations appear to vary considerably in practice.

The second aim of this book is to review the role of simulation and gaming in responding to these phenomena. Much of the literature appears to be associated with managing emergencies and responding to disaster. Crises represent unique windows of opportunity, but when mishandled they are likely to result in disaster. A secondary theme to the work, then, is to consider how the effects of risk and security failures – in particular, crisis events – can be responded to more effectively. This book will review approaches to crisis response through simulation training. It is argued that many organizations, largely as a response to regulatory pressure, apportion too much emphasis on risk identification and avoidance and too little on response. The book reviews the scope for knowledge transference from areas of simulation and gaming to organizational crisis management. The work also considers contemporary developments in the area of simulation design, evaluation and scenario planning with potential utility for organizational crisis management and learning.

One key argument to develop from this work is to question the assumption that risk and security can ever be managed effectively. The nature and contexts of many difficult-to-manage crises act to continually remind us of this fact. Risk failure is an inherent property resulting from the operation of any organizational system over time (Perrow, 1984; Turner and Pidgeon, 1997). Many of the recent approaches to risk have been particularly important in deepening our understanding of the social and cultural complexity of risk in areas such as communication, perception, systemic analysis and decision making. In terms of managing and responding to these concerns, social and cultural perspectives have been less effective. Developing techniques for risk identification and protocols for managing failure is now a key issue of concern for virtually every organization. Recognizing and responding to crisis remains highly controversial.

The final section of the book will consider how simulations used to train for crisis can inform contemporary theory and practice. Primary disagreements among experts about application and the case for legislative control are also considered. This book will consider both the historical development of a theory of risk and review contemporary academic 'scientific' approaches. The book will also consider the extent to which current 'scientific' thinking may be market-led, particularly in the areas of crisis management, business continuity planning and security management.

The book will provide a valuable theoretical resource for students, theorists and practitioners interested in any area of risk, crisis and security management. The text should provide sufficient theoretical depth to satisfy the needs of the academic reader searching for an interdisciplinary introduction to the three subject areas, while being sufficiently accessible for the practitioner of security or risk management to derive benefit.

The main theoretical assumptions of the book should remain valid for some considerable time; it is acknowledged that many references to further information are liable to change over the course of time. The text is therefore supported with a website containing a variety of useful and updated information sources. Students and researchers would find the website useful as this will include study guides, sample questions, and relevant centres for excellence in the academic world. The website will also maintain links to other important websites, government bodies and professional associations with an interest in risk, crisis and security of potential use to practitioners. Changes in legislation and practice are now so profound and dynamic that it is almost impossible to keep up to date with current debates.

Chapter 1

THE NEW TOTEMS

the entire history of the human species is a chronology of exposure to
misfortune and adversity and of efforts to deal with these risks

(Vaughan, 1997)

Risk, the oldest questions

From the time of primitive 'oracles' to a contemporary world of science, risk has and
continues to perplex humankind. All societies, both traditional and modern, face choices
and decisions about how to confront risk and security. Where action can be deemed to
have consequences, then it is the degree of uncertainty in those consequences that can be
considered to be risk. Every time a choice is purposely made, risks are played off against
each other, on a particular social understanding of the world. For many traditional and
historic societies, this choice can represent fundamental survival strategies, from
methods of farming and a choice of crops or hunting to early systems of kinship and
social ordering. These types of choices and their associated risks can also be perceived,
at least among traditional societies, as fundamental to survival against the elements.

Equally for industrial and post-industrial societies, risk is a key question affecting
every sphere of lifestyle, from diet to transport and power generation. How we manage
risk and security is a central debate for policy makers and academics alike. Despite
some of the most dramatic technological advances over the last 150 years, we now
appear to live in a more dangerous world than ever before. National and international
terrorism have increased the security requirements for many already hazardous
activities, such as the freedom to travel. What we had begun to believe were safe western
civilizations are suddenly looking more dangerous. The people of London, New York
and Madrid have come to share the same security concerns as more exotic and tranquil
locations such as Bali. Concerns about 'health, safety, and security' in society have
brought risk to the forefront of contemporary debate (Hood and Jones, 1996). These
concerns have resulted in major shifts in social habits and practices.

Today, risk has become an omnipresent phenomenon. Risk is the hidden danger lurking beneath everything that we do; from the moment that the unborn child is established, to death, we are at risk from something. Our behaviour, diet, procreation, travel, homes and work are all subject to risk. There is no one single risk-free aspect to our lives. Sometimes these risks are easily apparent, for example, driving too fast or smoking tobacco. However, risks can also become obscured, due to conflicting or complex arguments surrounding safety. Debates about nuclear power, transport and the environment are by no means exclusive examples of activities where experts themselves disagree about the risks posed.

Risk is now of key interest to the business community who wish to limit potential corporate liability. This area of risk is concerned with fundamental threats to business operation and viability. The Kobe earthquake in Japan and terrorist bomb outrages against the City of London and Manchester in the UK highlight the diverse nature of risks posed in this area.

It would be wrong to presume that risk and security is a modern concern. The management of risk is probably among the oldest recorded human activities. Risk can be traced back to the early philosophers of both East and West; evidence for this can be found among early civilizations of the West. As Aristotle (384–322 BC) put it: 'It must be expected that something unexpected will happen.'

Similarly, concerns about the management of risk were a preoccupation among many early philosophers from the East. The Chinese 'I Ching' (book of changes) is one of the oldest recorded decision-making tools still actively used by many people today. Originally the I Ching was designed some 3000 years ago to assist ancient Chinese kings with difficult questions of strategy. Today, however, it has not only become a popular book in the East, but is rapidly becoming so in the West.

Many oracles have been recorded from traditional societies in anthropological literature: for example, Evans-Pritchard found the Azande people in Africa practised a 'poison oracle'. The oracle involved feeding *benge*, a poisonous substance, to baby chickens. The subsequent fate of the poisoned chickens would be used to assist in decision making about important issues (Evans-Pritchard, 1976: 44).

Similarly, concerns about security can be traced back to early civilizations (Button and George, 2000; Manunta, 1998a). Security is also commented on by the famous psychologist, Maslow, who argued that it is a fundamental requirement for life itself (Maslow, 1968). In fact it would be fair to say that for humans risk and security are part of life itself, as commented on by Vaughan at the beginning of this chapter.

Academic interest in risk among social scientists, however, may be traced back to the seventeenth century, when concepts of risk were developed concurrently with probability theory in mathematics (Hacking, 1975; Todhunter, 1865). This can be coupled with a growing capitalist philosophy, where justification for the ownership and creation of wealth could be affirmed in the risk-taking behaviour of entrepreneurs (Douglas, 1985). Capitalism brought new 'speculative' risks associated with entrepreneurial activity, for example, when and what type of business to engage in and who business should be conducted with (Douglas, 1985).

Insurance

Alongside this increased entrepreneurial activity emerged the insurance industry, specifically interested in quantifying what are sometimes called 'pure' risks. These are still referred to by insurers as 'acts of God'. Typically, acts of God include events such as fire, flood, storm damage, lightning and seismic activity.

For over a hundred years now insurers have attempted to identify and record personal and third-party loss using this method. Within a given population there is a statistical propensity for certain groups to suffer from adverse exposure to pure risk. Insurance actuaries calculate and aggregate these pure risks as a percentage figure for the population. These figures can then be used to quantify the level of premiums charged for insurance cover.

The development of insurance is often associated with shipping as a means to economically bind the British Empire.* Of interest here is an increasing distinction drawn by insurers between so-called 'natural' and 'artificial' failures. Fires, floods, earthquakes and high winds represent examples of what may be termed 'natural' disasters. In contrast, accidents and other types of technological failure constitute 'man-made' disasters (Waring and Glendon, 1998). It is argued here that this distinction between 'pure' and 'speculative' risk is problematic, and reliant on folk conceptions of a natural and non-natural world. Disasters, however, do not respect these distinctions. For example, if we were to consider a hypothetical flood, is this something caused by human mismanagement or nature? Floods could be argued to be a natural phenomenon, but the effects can cause drastic problems for human life. Who is to blame – the engineers

---

* The modern insurance industry is frequently cited to have begun in a small coffee shop in the city of London by a group of eighteenth-century ship owners and financiers attempting to control the risks posed by shipping cargoes around the world.

who failed to control the water, or the planners who allowed the development of homes and businesses on a potential flood plain? These are not questions that can be easily answered.

The methodology of actuaries is also questioned. Retrospective changes to health and safety legislation, advances in medical diagnostic techniques and social behaviour have all contributed to this. The heavy financial losses sustained by the 'names' at Lloyds of London are a poignant example of how the world has changed. The collapse of huge corporations, such as Enron, Anderson and Barings, demonstrates the way threats to organizations have become both complex and difficult to respond to. The recent publicity given to sufferers of asbestosis offers another illustration of huge retrospective claims being made against insurers, often 20 and 30 years after negligence has taken place.

Social changes have also cast doubt on the efficacy of an actuarial methodology. For example, increased poverty during times of economic recession has been linked to soaring crime rates, particularly burglary and car crime. However, by the time actuary records can be brought up to date and adjusted to reflect changed risk, many claims will already have been registered.

Both insurers and clients are reviewing levels of exposure and cover as the distinction between pure and speculative risks becomes blurred. They do this by either refusing corporate insurance altogether, or increasing the premiums to reflect the actual level of corporate exposure. In many cases insurers sell a new service, risk management consulting (Borodzicz, 1999a). In response, corporations must self-insure or find new proactive methods for managing exposure.

The greatest problem with insurance is that it only covers known risks, and particularly where methods of probability can be applied. The actuary model is very practical for delivering a degree of risk management by spreading the costs over a population. This process does not cope well with new or unknown risks, such as terrorism, new diseases, retrospective asbestosis claims, changing climates and new levels of socio-technical dependency.*

By the mid-twentieth century, risk assessment and management was firmly established as a scientific endeavour, particularly for the disciplines of engineering, physics and mathematics. A better understanding of the scientific properties of our world enabled designers to produce longer bridges, higher buildings, greater ships, faster and

---

* The subject of socio-technical dependency is covered in the next chapter in some detail.

larger aircraft and more sophisticated and complex communication systems. By the 1960s, the awaited control of nature by people gained further credence from politicians. UK Prime Minister, Harold Wilson, spoke of forthcoming social and material advances through the 'white heat of technology'. Supersonic space travel and the controlled use of nuclear fusion suggested that there would be few frontiers to human capability, at least other than those we imposed on ourselves. Risk was in this context and perhaps quite logically perceived by many in the scientific community as an objective understanding of physical properties. Questions of risk, safety and security were perceived as secondary to the need to develop and use technology. Many of the nuclear scientists involved in the early development of nuclear power stations, although quite aware of the risks involved, sincerely believed that these would be relatively easy to manage in comparison to the developmental difficulties preoccupying the time.

It is pertinent to ask what is it about the world that has changed so drastically in recent years. Risk, which used to be conveniently split into two types, 'speculative' (or entrepreneurial) and 'pure' (insurable), is proving more difficult to manage.

Many insurance companies are no longer prepared to expose themselves to pure risks without first questioning what efforts organizations have applied to prevention, but increasingly, what steps management could reasonably be expected to take in order to minimize the loss potential. A further factor here is the growing trend among extremely large organizations to self-insure and hence to absorb potentially serious business losses. The old proverb, 'the bigger they are, the harder they fall' may be an appropriate metaphor here.

The liability and negligence industry

> A generalised concern for fairness has started us on a new cultural phase. The political pressure is not explicitly against taking risks but against exposing others to it.
>
> (Douglas, 1994: 15)

Judicial processes and litigation trends have been highly influential in constructing contemporary social models of an acceptable risk. A massive legal industry has grown around the legal adjudication of risk (ironically, often surrounding the settlement of insurance claims). One criterion for a legal involvement in risk is to establish blame, guilt, liability or negligence. The 'no-win, no-fee' practice in America, and subsequently in the UK, has contributed to the generation of a huge and specialized legal industry associated with adjudicating such risk claims. The extension of this legal model is likely for many other countries. However, a judicial involvement in risk debates has not been without social and political controversy. In the UK and the United States, health care organizations must now divert significant resources away from their primary activities, in order to fund the ever-increasing legal bills associated with adjudications of blame and negligence. Distinguishing between failed and negligent medicine can be more expensive, and traumatic, than the treatment itself!

Similar problems occur with implementing and enforcing health and safety legislation, negligence claims and more recently corporate manslaughter cases, suggesting a need for an insightful review of the future legal role in risk. Laws and regulations in the risk area can pose particular problems where (as is the trend) organizations operate in more than one country.

Another mode of involvement for the judiciary is through large public inquiries following major disasters. The role of the judiciary in these contexts has been subject to some controversy. Public inquiries have a function to establish causality and blame; this can, however, pose a dilemma for those giving evidence. The need to tell it 'as it is (or was)' may be compromised when personal or corporate identities and liability are at stake (Borodzicz, 1997). This area of legal interest in risk has aroused some controversial debates. Questions such as who is to blame, who should be compensated and how can future disasters be prevented have highlighted the complexity of modern risk management.

Public inquiries are usually carried out in a highly formalized and even ritualistic manner. Public inquiries also need to satisfy a number of problematic and sometimes conflicting criteria. The need to establish as closely as possible the precise nature of events in question is a key purpose for having the inquiry. This is often problematic, however, due to conflicting accounts of reality as presented to the inquiry from those involved. Inquiries are also required to provide recommendations for future good or safe practice. This should on the one hand address the public need for catharsis; an angry or distressed public needs to be reassured that everything possible will be considered, so that similar events can be prevented. An inquiry's recommendations also need to be politically workable in that it should ideally be possible to turn these into guidelines, or even legislation. Risk, however, does not respect either legal or organizational borders. It is a feature of inquiries that recommendations are usually restricted to the particular organization in question or at best the national industry of this type. Other organizations may operate quite similar systems for quite different purposes; while these systems would be equally prone to failure, they would not necessarily be subjected to the same legislation or recommendations. A further feature of public inquiries, as suggested to Toft from his own research experience, is their quasi-legal and often quango-like nature:

> Some of the people closely involved with public inquiries as attendees, inter-viewed during the course of research, have argued that such inquiries are not always the formalised, objective, truth searching bodies of the common public perception. Public inquiries have no laid down formal procedures, are adversarial in nature, have no power to require organisations or individuals to carry out their recommendations, and may sometimes apparently have hidden agendas to address.

> (Toft and Reynolds, 1994: 199)

Inquiries, quite rightly, attempt to consult many experts in order to deal with this, but interpretations frequently differ substantially, and relate to specific (often unique) aspects of an incident grounded in a particular academic or professional context. The need to establish blame* may also cause a problem with the quality of accounts presented to the inquiry. Giving evidence might subsequently cause one to be blamed or held personally liable and create a dangerous conflict of interests for those being asked to 'tell it as it was'.

Despite these faults, public inquiries do produce a rich source of carefully collected data for analysis (Booth, 1995: 38; Borodzicz, 1997). Inquiries are also beginning to change in form, partly as a response to some of these criticisms. The inquiries into the Paddington and Southall rail crashes attempted for the first time to sideline liability in favour of fact finding.

With increasing litigation following many major incidents, organizations need to demonstrate to the legal establishment, and to society generally, that possible precautions are being taken in order to avert and where necessary manage potential hazards. The judicial process and litigation trends have shaped and continue to shape contemporary social models of acceptable risk.

---

* The legal industry has grown around the legal adjudication of risk issues, which designers of safety systems can no longer ignore without liability. One legal criterion is to establish blame, guilt, liability or negligence (Wells, 1995).

Governance, accountability and regulation

A variety of corporate legislation now exists, affecting the behaviour, performance and governance of organizational activities. How organizations should be governed, who should be responsible for this, and how they might be made more accountable are key issues of corporate governance.

In the UK over the last ten years, three reports have been highly influential in shaping corporate governance: Cadbury (1992), Hampel (1998) and Turnbull (1999). Each of these reports can be seen, fundamentally, as a reaction to a number of high-profile corporate disasters in the last two decades. Similar governance initiatives are being applied internationally: KonTrag (1998) in Germany and Sarbanes-Oxley (2002) in the USA are examples.

One school of thought here is that the focus of these initiatives is to drive up standards of regulation for the owners/shareholders of companies (Sternberg, 1998). Research carried out by Knight and Pretty (1996), for example, suggests a very high correlation between organizational disaster and share price. In summary, then, these reports can be seen as an extension of the economic model espoused by Friedman (1962), with an objective of maximizing shareholder value and return. In this case the model is extended to include senior managers or directors as 'quasi-owners'.

It is already clear that these reports are having a major effect on the overall regulation of publicly listed companies and those with a financial stake in them, particularly as they require organizations to consider their risks and come up with strategies for managing them.

A second school of thought suggests that customers and the wider community are stakeholders in organizations, particularly where the organization provides a valued social function, such as transport, health, education, utility providers and even local government. There is certainly evidence emerging to suggest that directors will increasingly need to be accountable for the failure of their risk management policies. The debates surrounding 'corporate manslaughter' (Wells, 1993, 1995) and 'corporate killing' (Bergman, 1993) follow a number of tragedies highlighting the often intense and highly emotional response from victims and the wider community. In this context, failures in accountability may be more difficult to define and redress, particularly when this must be established through the complexities of the legal system.

However, concerns about regulation are a pervading issue for this school. As put by Sternberg:

> Regulation is inflexible. In formalising and clarifying unwritten guidelines, it also typically lowers standards; compliance no longer requires a margin of safety, but can be obtained by satisfying the letter of the law.
>
> (Sternberg, 1998: 110)

Organizations defending accusations of negligence would have a variety of strategies available to them. For example, they may attempt to use institutional 'scapegoating' by arguing that individual staff actions in non-managerial positions were highly unusual in the context of normal operating conditions and or quite unreasonable in the normal performance of their work; although, under British common law, individual staff members prosecuted for failure to exercise due care might wish to use the absence of a corporate plan/procedures as a defence. Courts may be reluctant to prosecute individuals for negligence in the absence of clear indicators such as alcohol or drug abuse or direct contravention of organizational rules and practices.

Another approach might be to argue that a third party, responsible for supply and maintenance of equipment or advice, was at fault. In this case the sheer complexity of management systems involved makes the burden of proof very difficult to establish, if only because of the complexity of legal liability law. Despite various attempts to invoke the new law of corporate manslaughter, it has proved very difficult to prove criminal culpability following major disasters in all but a few cases.

These two schools could be seen as opposing ends of a spectrum; clearly, any large and complex organizational system involving both public and private interests requires some system of regulation. An interesting question about the extent to which good regulation of commercial risk management may be balanced against improved social provision arises here.

The debate about the effectiveness of different types of regulation is fairly well established. Posner (1974) referred to 'regulatory capture', a concept by which regulation of an industry will increasingly fail the regulated. Much of this debate revolves around the availability of information to both regulated and regulator. For example, it is sometimes argued that regulated organizations are able to withhold or use information commercially available to them in order to gain an advantage on the regulators. Regulation in this context can be seen as a competition for new information (Parker, 1998). One of the major problems with drafting regulatory contracts is that they can never include sufficient detailed guidance for the management of situations yet to occur. This may be managed through a degree of regulatory flexibility within the contract, although in practice effective implementation for situations of extreme risk has proved problematic (Borodzicz, 1996b, 1999b; Parker, 1998).

The subject of regulation will be discussed again in relation to debates surrounding regulation of security activities in Chapter 3 and business continuity management in Chapter 5.

The risk society

Some sociologists, political theorists and anthropologists have argued that social and political change contribute to the way risk is both perceived and managed in contemporary society. The German theorist, Beck, argues we are in a state of major transition from a class to a risk society. In his book, *Risk Society*, he argues that a fundamental arbiter of acceptable risk for the future will be the insurance industry (Beck, 1992). Such a view has become popular in Germany, where risk is increasingly viewed in the context of its link to industrial technology and environmental damage.

Beck argues that we are witnessing a major political change, away from a 'class-based society' to what he calls the 'risk society', and that this is due to the context of postmodernist influences (Beck, 1992). Beck postulates that modern conceptions of risk are (and have been historically since industrialization) mediated by the marketplace. This is formalized through what Beck describes as the 'calculus of risk'. Citing the French sociologist Francois Ewald, he argues that this 'calculus of risk' was invented through a complex mixture of private and public insurance against liability (Beck, 1992). The calculus of risk works on the basis of four central pillars: limitation, accountability, compensation and precautionary aftercare. The context for these are political, and can be identified within the domains of a liberal and socialist fair distribution philosophy. Ultimately, the boundaries of an acceptable level of risk are, for Beck, defined by insurance companies. Consider the following:

> Is there an operational criterion for distinguishing between risks and threats? The economy itself reveals the boundary line of what is tolerable with economic precision, through the refusal of private insurance.

> (Beck, 1992: 103)

Beck points out that insurance has successfully maintained itself to the present time. It has started to crumble in the face of the new, difficult to insure, techno-hazards such as nuclear power, biotechnology and an ever-mounting ecological destruction of the environment. Beck describes these as the 'residual risks' of modernity.* Residual risks are beyond the realms of insurance, either public or private, but not beyond the comprehension of a society which displays its anxiety politically as an increasing scepticism for established expert dialogues (Beck, 1992).

Beck can be viewed politically (and perhaps criticized for this) within the context of a growing ecological lobby. Beck's polemic is powerful and persuasive, but short on recommended praxis for dealing with the immediate problems of crisis management. However, Beck does argue for a much longer-term analysis of the social and physical manifestations of economic trends. More in the style of the old grand theorists, Beck claims that we are moving into a risk society as part of the postmodernist shift away from a class-based society. This transition is gradual, as was the case with the earlier shift away from a feudal society to a capitalist class-based society identified by Marx.

In questioning the desirability of certain industries, Beck is making a similar political point to the organizational theorist Perrow discussed in the next chapter. There are certain high-risk industries whose social acceptability may be problematic under any circumstances. However, Beck's overtly political message goes further than Perrow's, in questioning a social need for blind economic growth coupled with an endless expansion of technology. Beck's arguments might also be considered important for risk communication theorists.† This is the agenda of both Beck and also an increasing greening trend in political thinking originating back to the works of E.F. Schumacher's economic model (Schumacher, 1973).

Contemporary society has shifted away from a position where people are concerned about having enough to eat – instead we are now becoming more concerned with the risks associated with particular foods (Beck, 1992). Scares about modern food production techniques are highlighted by salmonella food poisoning in poultry and eggs, BSE from infected cattle and swine fever in pigs; and the now widespread practice of vegetarianism in Europe suggests one strong example of the link between perceived risk, health and behaviour.

---

* Many theorists suggest a transition to a knowledge-based economy, often described as 'post-modernist' or 'post-industrial' (Bauman, 1991; Beck, 1992; Giddens, 1991; Fukuyama, 1999).
† 'Risk communication' attempts to address the differences in perceptions of risk takers by understanding the social and cultural contexts in which risk takes place. This perspective is discussed more fully in Chapter 2.

Chapter 2

THEORIES OF RISK AND ORGANIZATIONAL FAILURE

Risk, an interdisciplinary perspective

Risk has become an area of major debate for contemporary social theorists. One helpful metaphor for landscaping 'risk' is offered by Hood *et al.*, in the Royal Society study group report. They argued that risk can be characterized as an 'archipelago', a group of islands where each represents a particular subdiscipline or associated area of expertise (Hood *et al.*, 1992). It is argued here that risk has grown so large as to now represent a major discipline in its own right. Risk, academically at least, is well developed in both the physical sciences (e.g. engineering) and, more recently and increasingly, in the social sciences (e.g. psychology, sociology, anthropology, politics, management, economics, finance and business studies, and criminology). Risk analysis in the former areas is seen largely in quantitative terms, by placing an assessment figure on the relationship between the frequency or probability of a potential physical failure and its seriousness. This approach leads to management concerns about how best to avoid, eliminate or reduce potential threats, and to decision making about the costs and benefits of risk 'management', 'control', 'retention' or 'transfer'.*

This chapter is broadly grouped into three disciplinary areas of research: psychology-, social- and culture-oriented approaches. While each of these disciplines are presented in turn, it is pertinent to note this by no means represents an exclusive system of categorization. These theoretical perspectives could equally have been presented in

---

* These concepts will be discussed again more fully in Chapter 5.

other ways, for example, by type of research methodology, chronology or classified in terms of interdisciplinary research.

The approaches to risk management in this chapter provide a useful resource for anyone trying to understand how perceptions of risk have changed in the social sciences over the last 30 years, with a focus changing from calibrating the actual probability of individual risks to understanding the psychological, cultural and social context in which it occurs.

This chapter begins by introducing two influential risk perception approaches: cognitive/behavioural decision making and psychometrics. The social context of entrepreneurial risk taking, previously discussed, influenced much of the earlier psychology-oriented research. Risk perception originally focused on the identification and measurement of a variety of features in the human decision-making process. Risk, for these theorists, can be perceived as a real entity – measured, and reduced to its simplest elements. In other words, by reducing risk to a number of basic elements, understanding is gained through detailed and repeated analysis of the decision-making process.

In contrast, approaches to risk in the social sciences have focused more on the social and cultural contexts in which risk is both perceived and managed. The focus for these approaches is to look at the context in which risks occur. These could be communication, systemic or cultural.

A sociological analysis of risk suggests an equally complex appraisal. Sociological approaches to risk research have broadened considerably in the last 20 years, mainly as a complement, but also as a critique and response, to the more quantitatively based research in psychology. These can now be grouped together into a number of main areas of theoretical study: risk communication, systems approaches, risk homeostasis and socio-technical or isomorphic learning approaches.

The theme of safety culture, sometimes also called organizational safety culture, is another theoretical approach. A number of theorists are now working in this area from a variety of disciplinary backgrounds, but this should be seen as distinct from cultural theory.

Cultural theory offers another distinct theoretical lens through which risk may be viewed. As a theory, cultural phenomenon is seen as dependent on everyday social involvement with family, friends and peers. Risk, for cultural theorists, must be viewed within the concept of 'identity' for the individual. Cultural theorists argue that the strength and context of an individual's relationship to social groups, and the social structure or nature of such groups, will define how risk is perceived. 'Is risk management a science or an art?' (Bernstein, 1996: 6).

Risk perception

Early risk perception work aims to quantify risks using a bottom-up process. A latent presumption of this approach is to assume that all risks can be removed or at least reduced to an acceptable level. Psychologists found many popular social views on risk to be at variance with those of experts. This led to a psychometric approach aimed at understanding social trends in risk perception so that re-education could be targeted as appropriate.

The study of *perception* has been a dominant theme in contemporary psychology. Psychologists typically concern themselves with how the human mind becomes aware of, learns from and deals with the environment. In psychology, risk has largely been studied, at least among the early theorists, within the context of a *cognitive* research paradigm. Cognition is the mental process or faculty by which humans acquire knowledge through perception, reasoning or intuition. The study of risk by many psychologists still largely reflects this cognitive approach.

Psychologists view risk as a both real and objective concept, suitable for study by means of quantitative analysis (measurement).* Psychologists try to understand risk by isolating some aspect of the phenomenon (a variable), and then simulating this in a laboratory context as an experiment. These social experiments usually require a group of subjects to undertake a risky decision-making task. The decisions made by subjects can be gauged against known probable outcomes for the decisions in order to give a measure of risk judgement.

An alternative method of measurement is to collect and analyse social data using surveys and questionnaires. The genre for such research has typically been to attempt to measure a 'perceived risk' against a calibrated 'actual risk', within a certain population of individuals. In order to identify and measure the types of risks which concern people, these studies would typically attempt to measure how strongly a given sample population feels about a particular risk or group of risks. This method is described as a *psychometric* approach. However, the reality of doing both approaches has proved quite difficult, because risk perception has been found to depend as much on context and culture as physical reality (Starr, 1969: 165; Slovic *et al.*, 1980; Otway and Von Winterfeldt, 1982).

---

* This view that all social phenomena are quantifiable and therefore measurable is less strictly adhered to by many psychologists today.

Cognitive/decision-making strategies

The earliest 'cognitive' approaches to decision making were developed by Kahneman and Tversky (1979). These theorists questioned the notion of humans acting as rational beings (this is a western philosophic notion of human rationality dating back to Aristotle). Instead, and arguing against an Aristotelian legacy, Kahneman and Tversky suggested that humans may often make certain types of irrational choices or preferences with a degree of regularity (Gardner, 1987: 360).

The classic method for exploring such theories was to provide a sample group of subjects with a simulated decision-making process. Subjects were required to choose between a range of gambling options under experimental conditions. The results of these experiments could be recorded and analysed. Kahneman and Tversky established certain pre-defined conditions, where people are likely to make certain preferences as opposed to others. It was found that subjects' decisions often displayed a logic having little to do with rational choice-making (Kahneman and Tversky, 1979).

Much of this work has been applied to risky decision making by another psychologist, Lola Lopes. Like Kahneman and Tversky, she also used gambling scenarios for her lab-based approach to research. Lopes argued that it was important to make explicit within her work the definition of risk used:

> Technically, the word risk refers to situations in which a decision is made whose consequences depend on the outcomes of future events having known probabilities. Choices among the different kinds of bets in games like roulette and craps are good examples of choices made under risk.

> (Lopes, 1987: 255)

Lopes' work is significant in considering the types of motivation influencing choice. This approach attempts to understand the semantic value of the decisions made by subjects. Lopes also introduced a secondary issue, called 'risky choice'. Risky choice, she argues, affects behaviour, and begins to provide consideration to contextual factors influencing decision making.

One advantage of this experimental approach is to allow the application of various stimuli to respondents, and observe the response. In other words, a variety of perceived risk scenarios can be contrasted with actual risk. Lopes theorized that for situations where the probability ratios were already known or could be calculated, there would be a variance in the ways different people would react to a variety of predetermined risk scenarios. Lopes also found two dispositional factors responsible for mediating an actor's response. These were the extent to which subjects could be measured as risk-averse, 'pessimists'; or risk-seeking, 'optimists' (Lopes, 1987: 256). By screening subjects in advance of testing, a marked statistical difference was found by Lopes in the level of risk taking between the risk-'seeking' and -'averse' groups.

Decision-making theories can be described as reliable, at least in terms of laboratory tests. Decision-making experiments appear to produce replicable results. However, this research may be questionable in terms of validity when applied to everyday risk management contexts. Slovic for example, is critical of how this type of empirical research can relate to the reality of decision makers who operate in conditions where data sources are often limited, and judgement strategies may be mediated by criteria such as 'trust' or 'intuition' (Slovic, 1987: 281).

Can choices made in a gambling context inform us about decision making under risk? We need to consider the applicability of gambling analogies for the study of risk situations where there are no pre-defined probabilities. Gambling as a phenomenon may be more appropriately considered within its own social context as a risk-taking behaviour and therefore prove to be a misleading experimental design for other types of risks. Gambling situations may also invoke certain risk-taking features, but these are not necessarily synonymous with risks in other contexts, particularly outside of the laboratory.

A laboratory may constitute a social setting (Latour and Woolgar, 1986), hence any attempt to measure risk in this setting may necessarily still rely on social rather than objective constructions of reality. The process of taking any phenomenon out of a naturalistic setting and into a laboratory may be of questionable scientific validity (other than to prescribe the researcher's own perceptions of risk on to the subjects).

Not withstanding this critique of experimental studies, there is also an array of social and cultural features to be considered in the use of gambling settings as a representative analogy for other types of decision making under risk. For example, gambling is not simply a case of winning and losing, but must be viewed within the context of its meaning within a 'gambling culture', where rationality may not be the most significant (or only) factor affecting choice. Pessimists (the risk averse) and optimists (the risk seeking) need to be viewed in terms of their need to take a chance, or gamble, as a way of seeking personal satisfaction.

Loss making may also have very different meanings and repercussions to the gambler or to the expert decision maker operating within a crisis situation. The losing of large sums of money may actually spur the gambler to try harder, by increasing the optimism about an eventual win on the grounds of probability, or the psychological need for a spectacular win. It can also been argued that gambling is a social problem. It is, therefore, reasonable to assume that a gambler's sense of identity to the units being put at risk may relate closely to the nature of their relationship to it. In other words, it is questionable whether a bad decision costing say, 20 lives, could be viewed in a similar context to losing £20 or £30.

Another problem with the decision-making methodology is that subjects asked to gamble in a laboratory may act differently in a natural environment. It is difficult to establish how seriously the subject is treating the task in hand, or the level of ability and motivation to understand between subject and experimenter. A further problem with decision-making models is that they do not take account of the range of risks and weightings which individuals attach to them. This was investigated by another group of risk perception theorists using a psychometric approach.

Psychometric studies in risk

A psychometric study is one where the psychological variables are collected and measured from individuals in a sample population (hence the term *psycho - metric*). The design of such tests would typically involve statistical analysis, in order to indicate how a representative sample of a population perceives particular risks.

Psychometric approaches also attempt to consider the qualitative characteristics of hazards. Early studies in the psychometric tradition were concerned with the extent of people's expressed preferences towards particular risks, and how this might relate to actual fatalities. These approaches also developed at a time when there was increasing social and political pressure to investigate public perceptions of known hazards. One aim here was that the public could be better informed, and where necessary re-educated when it was found that their perceptions were at a variance with, or conflicted with, expert views.

An important study was carried out in 1978 involving educated, but non-expert, subjects. Subjects were required to judge the fatality rates from a number of known hazards, ranging from natural disasters to common fatal diseases. These judgements were then plotted against known actual death rates. The survey indicated that subjects had a tendency to overestimate the death rates for low-frequency hazards, such as smallpox vaccinations and floods, while underestimating the death rates for high-frequency hazards, such as strokes and heart disease (Lichtenstein *et al.*,

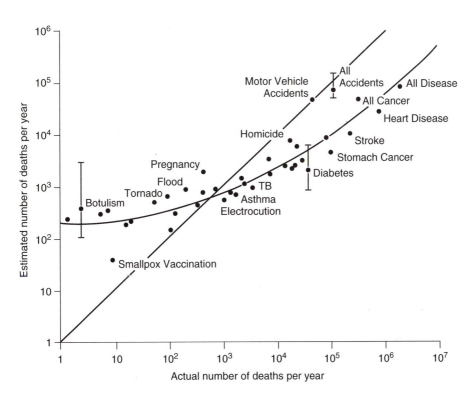

Figure 2.1   Relationship between perceived and actual risks
Source: Slovic, P., Fischoff, B. & Lichtenstein, S., Facts and fears: understanding perceived risks. In R.C. Schwing & W.A. Albers (eds), *Societal Risk Assessment*. Plenum Press, New York, 1980

1978). This study was important in enabling theorists, for the first time, to measure the match between human perceptions in relation to a substantive measure of risk (Figure 2.1).

Risk perception was, however, to prove a much more complex issue than simply assessing death rates. As early as 1969, Starr identified a distinction between voluntary and involuntary risks. He argued that one's perception of risk could be affected by the extent to which it was considered to be self-imposed, in contrast to risks exerted by an outside influence beyond personal control. Involuntary risks were for Starr defined as, 'imposed by the society in which the individual lives' (1969: 165).

There have since been a number of similar attempts to understand what Slovic more recently described as the 'personality' of hazards (Slovic, 1992). Many of the early attempts to do so suffered from having small sample sizes (Pidgeon *et al.*, 1992). However, two major works are worth considering here, one carried out by Otway and Von Winterfeldt and another by Slovic *et al.*

Otway and Von Winterfeldt argued that a variety of 'negative hazard attributes' influence people's risk perception (Otway and Von Winterfeldt, 1982). These have been summarized by Pidgeon *et al.* in the 1992 Royal Society Report:

1. Involuntary exposure to risk.
2. Lack of personal control over outcomes.
4. Uncertainty about probabilities or consequences of exposure.
4. Lack of personal experience with the risk (fear of the unknown).
5. Difficulty in imagining risk exposure.
6. Effects of exposure delayed in time.
7. Genetic effects of exposure (threatens future generations).
8. Infrequent but catastrophic accidents ('kill size').
9. Benefits not highly visible.
10. Benefits go to others (inequity).
11. Accidents caused by human failure rather than natural causes.

This study was significant in highlighting the complexity of the social features likely to mediate perceptions of risk. Any risk measurement, therefore, needs to be sensitive to the system of understanding in which that risk is viewed. This also suggests that some apparently irrational folk views may actually constitute a logical framework for constructing perceived reality.

The other important survey, carried out by Slovic *et al.* in 1980 using factor analysis techniques,* analysed the types of hazards most feared. Slovic's study was important for two reasons. First, the study was comprehensive, collecting a large population sample for its data. Second, Slovic *et al.* looked at the perceptions of 90 different hazards in relation to three factors mediating the perceptions of risk. The study locates different hazards on a three-dimensional axis by plotting 'dread risks' (factor 1) on the horizontal axis against 'unknown risks' (factor 2) on the vertical axis, against 'frequency and extent of exposure' (factor 3) on the third axis (Slovic *et al.*, 1980). The result of Slovic's research was to produce a highly detailed diagram (Figure 2.2) suggesting the complexity of popular risk perception among the population.

––––––––––––––––

* Factor analysis is a statistical method for studying the interrelations among various scales. The object is to discover what the scales have in common and whether these commonalties can be ascribed to one or several factors that run through all or just some.

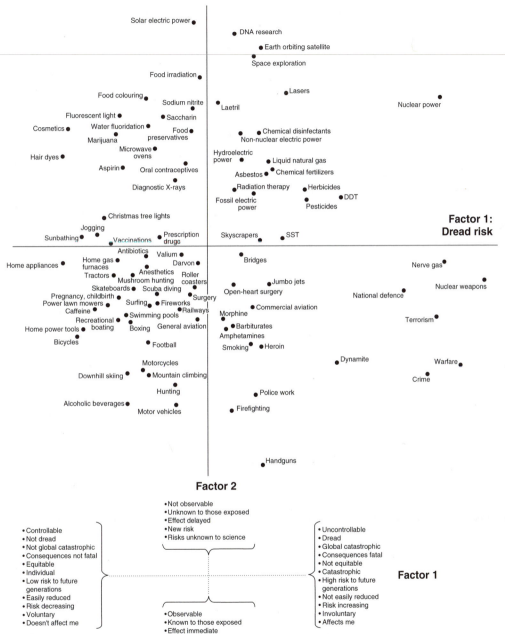

Figure 2.2   Unknown versus dread risks

Source: Slovic, P., Fischoff, B. & Lichtenstein, S., Facts and fears: understanding perceived risks. In R.C. Schwing & W.A. Albers (eds), *Societal Risk Assessment*. Plenum Press, New York, 1980

Both Slovic *et al.* and Otway and Von Winterfeldt found a complexity of factors mediating our lay perceptions of risk. Of fundamental importance, risk perceptions could be measured and the results replicated. Using statistical analysis techniques, different studies could be used to contrast risk perceptions in the population. A whole range of psychometric studies were now possible, in order to measure specific risks among certain groups in the population.

The problem with this type of psychometric approach is that once questionnaires are prepared, respondents are restricted to giving their views only on the basis of hazards mentioned. Other risks, which respondents might also consider to be real and tangible hazards, would not necessarily be considered.* Therefore the relationships between unquestioned risks and the other questioned factors would never be known. It is arguable that, to an extent, this criticism can be addressed by good questionnaire design and the use of pilot studies prior to conducting full surveys. It is also arguable that more axes could be created, for example, economic, social or political dimensions of risk. The effect of these further axes in terms of practical research might also be to make data sets unmanageable. The complex structure of popular risk perception, as highlighted by these psychometric studies, demonstrates that the tip of a highly complex social and cultural iceberg had been found.

Systems theory

The use of systems theory dates back to the work of the biologist Von Bertalanffy in the 1920s. Bertalanffy developed the idea that organic systems, despite outwardly variant manifestations, display common internal similarities. Bertalanffy was concerned with plants, but the application of this theory has been extended to many different applications in diverse areas of study in the pure and social sciences.

The earliest references to socio-technical approaches in organizational management date back to pioneering work at the Tavistock Institute which looked at problems

---

* The use of a short interview alone to ascertain a complete account of perceptions is perhaps methodologically naive. Popular knowledge that experts agree on the dangers of many other hazards, such as smoking or HIV infection, has had marginal influence on behaviour. It is argued by Parker that this is because these expert approaches take little account of human need as a motivating factor (Parker, 1987).

caused by organizational change in the British coal industry (Trist *et al.*, 1963). The industry, at that time, was undergoing a transition from private to public ownership. Staff in the coal industry were experiencing a high degree of workplace-related stress and an alarming number of trained employees left the pits at a time when miners were much needed. A great deal of this work stems from the writings of a medical practitioner who practised in a colliery district between the wars. This work has been described by Trist *et al.* (1963) as the 'first evidence in favour of a general theory of organizational health and work effectiveness'.

The term 'socio-technical system' was applied to individual production units in an original mining study carried out by the Tavistock Institute (Trist and Bamforth, 1951). Trist *et al.* argue that a number of benefits arise from considering organizations as 'open technical systems' which both influence and respond to the wider environment (1963).

Theorists interested in organizational failure and disaster management have highlighted the relevance of systems theory. They argue that major incidents can be recognized fundamentally as systemic failures. Further, that these systems comprise both human and technical elements and that failure in either of these systems can result in a crisis. These theorists also argue that such system failures predominantly represent human or technical failures of operation within organizational systems (Horlick-Jones, 1990).

However, and more fundamentally, it has increasingly been argued that both social and technical systems are inclusive systems of operation. This means that any analysis of system failure should take account of both human and technical types of error as these are mutually reliant upon each other for the operation or failure of the overall system. The late Professor Barry Turner was highly influential in arguing that both humans and human organizational systems form the background precondition to most disasters.

> ... it is better to think of a problem of understanding disasters as a 'socio-technical' problem with social organization and technical processes interacting to produce the phenomena to be studied.
>
> (Turner, 1978: 3)

Evidence for Turner's view can be found in the results of many public inquiries which have argued that the way many disasters are perceived should be reconsidered (Toft and Reynolds, 1994: 3). The conclusions of many contemporary theorists on the subject have suggested similar findings: 'The majority of accidents are, in some measure, attributable to human as well as procedural and technological failure' (Cox and Tait, 1991: 93).

In his book, *Man-Made Disasters*, Turner proposed a model for understanding systemic failure in organizations. Turner's model is based on an understanding that accidents are latent failures of socio-technical systems. These failures occur after a period of incubation has taken place. In other words, the relationship between the social and technical features of a system may incubate over a period of time producing an environment where an accident can be triggered by some small precipitating event. This, Turner argued, is not apparent from a separate review of technical and social systems of operation in isolation, because this would not reveal the intricate nature of links and mutual reliance of the two systems.

Turner's model for understanding socio-technical disasters operates in six stages and has been summarized by Toft and Reynolds (1994: 11–12). The first stage operates from the inception of the organization. Culturally defined beliefs about the world and codes of practice are brought together to form a system of operation, or an agreed code of practice. This system of operation may be formed at the beginning of an organization's life, or subsequently, as the result of some change in the organization's function. A fundamental feature of the first stage is a potential system failure, although this is difficult to perceive, that is programmed in to the system's operation. Also typical for this stage is an independent risk assessment of technical and social systems in isolation, and failure to consider interaction between the two systems. Latent risks not perceived from this stage will be transferred to the second stage, incubation.

During the second stage, the system will function, with minor problems and events arising, but these will not be treated seriously as they do not fit in with the organization's world view of a hazard. In other words, those members of an organization with the responsibility for its safe running and operation do not have in the context of the organization's safety culture any history or reason to suspect that these problems are in fact latent incubating system faults. When minor problems become apparent they may be perceived as normal operational difficulties, rather than the system faults which violate the integrity of the system itself.

The third stage of Turner's model is the appearance of some precipitating event which, owing to its impact, raises the perceptual awareness of decision makers involved in stage two. Attempts will be made to respond to the problem within the context of previously held assumptions about the system's mode of operation. However, the system will fail to respond to these interventions and lead to stage four – system failure or breakdown, with possible catastrophic effects and a violation of the previously held world view of the system's decision makers.

Stage four of the model can be recognized as the onset of disaster. This will typically constitute an 'ill-structured' crisis scenario which does not conform to previously held assumptions of safety by members of the organization. An ill-structured event is a situation of disorder that might arise from the errors and/or failings (e.g. poor or inefficient plans, inappropriate application of resources) which go unseen within the pre-crisis incubation period. As Turner puts it, an ill-structured scenario is one:

> where problems use symbolic or verbal variables, have vague, non-quantifiable goals and lack available routines for their solution, relying instead on ad hoc procedures, a variable disjunction of information is more likely to be found – disasters may be regarded as arising from attempts to handle ill-structured problems, the full implications of which were not realised before the event.
>
> (Turner, 1978: 52)

Stage five of the model is the rescue and salvage operation. The need to recover and re-establish operation of the system will be compromised at this stage by the nature of the ill-structured situation. The element of ill-structure in the handling of the crisis exists when, given the nature of the event, the application of preconceived emergency plans or procedures are inappropriate, in conflict, require cross-service coordination, or even exacerbate the situation. This stage of incident response will therefore require a level of 'flexibility and improvisation' in the response, which is not characteristic of a normal mode of operation (Turner, 1994).

Stage six, the final stage of Turner's model, is the learning phase. In this stage, those responsible for the operation of the system come to terms with what has happened. Normally this is carried out through an official 'inquiry process', with the aim of both establishing the cause of the problem and making recommendations for future system operations.

Two features are central to Turner's theory. First is the understanding that social and technical systems can be an inclusive system of operation. This means any analysis of system failures should take account of both human and technical types of error, as these are mutually reliant upon each other for the operation or failure of the overall system (Turner, 1978; Toft and Reynolds, 1994). Second is the structural failure of foresight. Theoretically, if it is possible to create systems of operation then it should be possible to predict the failures. However, one problem with this is the complexity of modern operational systems. Identifying the number of permutations of possible system failures may be difficult if not impossible.

Isomorphic learning

Toft and Reynolds have argued that *isomorphic learning* can be made possible by examining intrinsically similar systems of operation across industries as a whole (Toft and Reynolds, 1994: 4–5). Toft and Reynolds suggest that disasters are typically low-frequency events when viewed in the context of any one organization or field of activity. It is therefore unlikely that any one organization would be able to predict such events on the basis of an examination of its own operational history. However, when incidents are viewed in the context of a whole industry employing similar practices, a number of similar failures can be observed to be recurring in different organizational contexts. In other words, although disasters may be rare events for any one organization, they may be quite high for an industry.

The reason for this similarity, Toft and Reynolds argue, is due to the isomorphic nature of the systems themselves. Toft and Reynolds suggest that many managers in organizations using quite similar socio-technical systems in their operations to those of other organizations could benefit from such isomorphic foresight. Therefore, for an industry to be able to learn from the experience of managing these types of risks, individual organizations need to be able to learn from the experiences of each other. Cumulatively, Toft and Reynolds would argue, these same disasters keep recurring because what little is learnt from them is passed on only to managers in the organization concerned. Toft and Reynolds argue that the best method for transmission of such isomorphic information is through the use and implementation of a good organizational 'safety culture'. This should be based on both official inquiry findings and further qualitative research.

The literature would appear to suggest that there is still much more potential for isomorphic learning as suggested below by Walsh and Healey:

> The occurrence of a disaster usually overwhelms those affected by it when there has been no planning or preparation. Even in situations that are repetitions of previous calamitous events, people often seem to be unprepared. The annual flooding of certain rivers offers a prime example of this category. Residents will repeatedly be devastated, but each time be no better equipped than the time before.
>
> (Walsh and Healey, 1987: 10.1)

In terms of the recommendations of public inquiries and safety practices generally, a substantial amount of reinvention of good safety practice is continually taking place.

If isomorphic learning constitutes hindsight in this context, then how should this form of learning be brought about? Toft and Reynolds (1994) are arguing here that some form of communication needs to take place between those who learn from disasters and those who manage the risk of disaster.

Toft and Reynolds illustrate their argument by referring to a number of case studies of disastrous situations which appear to confirm not only Turner's incubational model, but also that such tragedies might also be used to prevent similar tragedies occurring in the future (Toft and Reynolds, 1994: 104–116).

Diagrammatic analysis

Another way we might try to understand socio technical systems failure is by attempting to model the aetiology of events in diagrammatic form.

Turner's systems approach is particularly useful here in providing a socio-technical structure for doing this. Turner's model complements a sociological analysis of disaster life cycles by analysing the events leading to socio-technical system breakdown in a practical way. This is done by constructing a 'schematic report analysis diagram' (SRAD). SRAD diagrams graphically present complex events in a pictorial form based on the qualitative data collected from a case study or inquiry following an incident. The reduction of so much information into a small diagram will require some compromising of data quality by way of simplification and representation. This should, however, be considered in the context of the advantages of this method. Figure 2.3 is an example of an early SRAD diagram produced by Turner following a mining accident in a Cambrian colliery. This diagram shows how it is possible to condense a substantial inquiry report into one simplified representation.

Initially, SRAD diagrams were developed in order to demonstrate the aetiology of socio-technical system breakdowns. Turner, initially, was concerned to point out that disasters do not simply happen, but are usually incubated during a socio-technical operation of the system. One advantage of producing such diagrams is that they can be used to contrast with other events. The use of diagrams in case study research can also serve to highlight omissions in the final recommendations to inquiry reports (Borodzicz *et al.*, 1993a).* A diagram can provide a clear overview of an event, thus providing an easily intelligible format in contrast to a lengthy public inquiry or case study reports characteristic of formal investigations. It is important, however, that

---

* See Appendix, Case study 3: King's Cross underground fire.

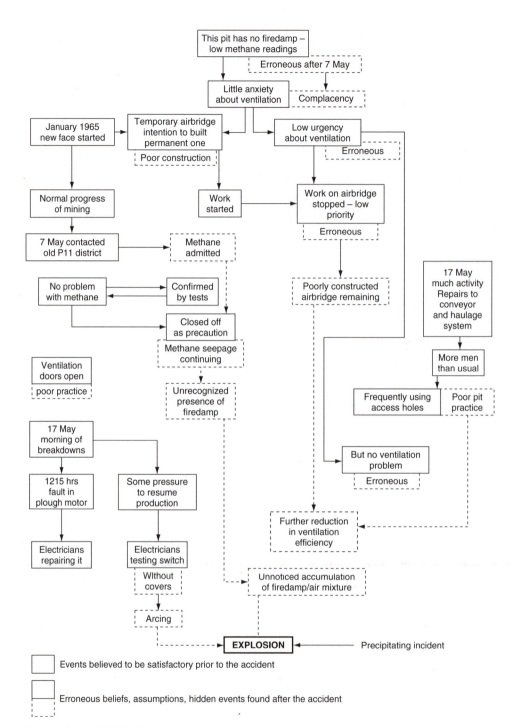

Figure 2.3 SRAD diagram depicting events leading to an explosion in a Cambrian colliery

Source: Reproduced from B. Turner, *Man-Made Disasters*. Wykeham, London, 1978: 98

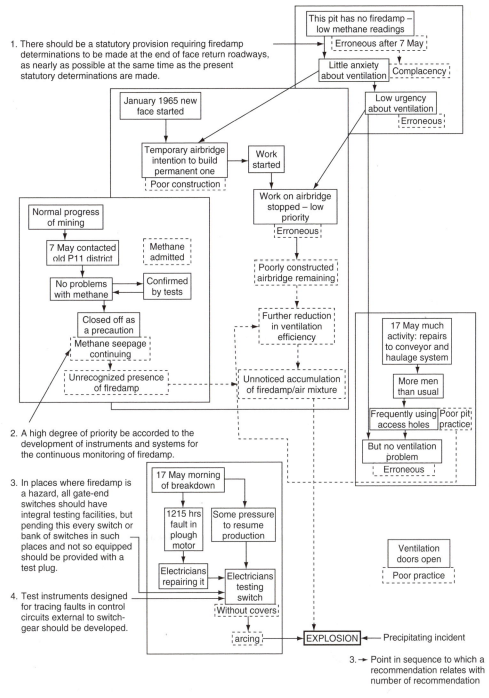

1. There should be a statutory provision requiring firedamp determinations to be made at the end of face return roadways, as nearly as possible at the same time as the present statutory determinations are made.

2. A high degree of priority be accorded to the development of instruments and systems for the continuous monitoring of firedamp.

3. In places where firedamp is a hazard, all gate-end switches should have integral testing facilities, but pending this every switch or bank of switches in such places and not so equipped should be provided with a test plug.

4. Test instruments designed for tracing faults in control circuits external to switch-gear should be developed.

Figure 2.4 Revised SRAD diagram depicting event chains

Source: Reproduced from B. Toft and S. Reynolds, *Learning from Disasters: A Management Approach*. Butterworth-Heinemann, Oxford, 1994: 36

the diagrams are wherever possible created by researchers who are detached from an inquiry's recommendations as a methodological precondition for this.

Diagrams can also facilitate the identification of 'information (data) gaps' in the accounts presented to an inquiry. Events could, for example, be clustered in order to relate the main inquiry findings to the original chart for comparison as has been done in Figure 2.4 by one of Turner's students, Brian Toft. Toft and Reynolds suggest that three sets of 'event chains' can be identified from this second chart (Toft and Reynolds, 1994: 34).

Turner's work has subsequently been highly influential, and developed in a number of ways by theorists operating in an interdisciplinary perspective. Brian Toft, for example, has also developed this work further in the context of 'isomorphic learning' in organizational systems.

Perrow's 'normal' accidents

For another theorist, Charles Perrow, organizational systems are the background precondition to most disasters. For Perrow, it is not the humans but the system itself which is to blame. Perrow, in his book *Normal Accidents*, argues that catastrophic accidents are an inevitable feature of advanced technological society (Perrow, 1984). For Perrow, the creation of 'high risk' systems are a function of humanity's technological attempts to control nature. Perrow argues that these systems are likely to fail when two or more components or processes malfunction in some previously unanticipated way. A simple example of such a failure might be a malfunction in a fire alarm, which then causes the sprinkler system to deactivate as well. Perrow suggests two separate features of a system are of pertinence in assessing its likelihood of failure: the extent to which there is tight 'coupling'* and/or 'interactive complexity' in the system. In other words, the greater the number of tightly coupled or mutually reliant components, the more likely it is that there will be serious failure when two or more linked components fail. Such accidents, resulting from tightly coupled or complex interactive system failures, Perrow calls 'normal accidents'.

---

* This point relates to the case studies presented at the end of the book. Significant risks were not only found to be defined differently between expert and lay groups, but also between expert groups operating in multiservice response.

If interactive complexity and tight coupling – system characteristics – inevitably will produce an accident, I believe we are justified in calling it a normal accident, or system accident. The odd term normal accidents is meant to signal that, given the system characteristics, multiple and unexpected interactions of failures are inevitable. This is an expression of an integral characteristic of the system, not a statement of frequency.

(Perrow, 1984: 5)

Perrow argues that interactive complexity and tight coupling are independent dimensions of a systems propensity to fail. Two issues appear to be problematic with Perrow's assertion. First, both of these features may in fact be part of the same thing (complexity), rather than independent as Perrow implies. The second issue is the practical problem of differentiating between these dimensions in relation to their application to real issues.

Perrow makes a distinction between 'loose' and 'tightly' coupled systems. Loosely coupled systems have similar failures but these would not directly be dependent on each other as part of a process. For example, if the failure of the fire alarm coincided with that of a water supply, the result might be very similar to the first example. However, these multiple failures would not be linked in any way, or within the scope of the operators' abilities to control them.

Perrow also highlights 'operator error' as a frequently attributed component to many accidents. The majority of accidents may appear to be caused by operator problems; however, these need to be considered within a context of operators' working conditions and environment. Operators can be confronted with multiple technical failures or inaccurate information systems. In these circumstances, Perrow argues, the fault lies not with the operators, but within the system they have to operate. 'Time' is a critical feature of Perrow's normal accident theory. The presentation of misinformation to operators during a critical time period can cause a series of system failures to proceed without effective control.

The organizational structure in which system failures take place may also contribute to the overall risk. Tightly coupled systems tend to be rigidly controlled from the centre of operations. Operators in such systems are trained to adhere strictly to prescribed rules and procedures (which ironically have been created for safety reasons) but these can act to limit the amount of innovative and flexible responses available to operators when confronted with risky situations.

Perrow argues that some of these risks are acceptable technological ventures, while others should be avoided altogether, as simply too dangerous to hazard. Statistical probability should not be the sole guide to risk acceptability. Technological risks need to be considered in terms of their ramifications if, rather than when, they occur. Perrow questions the risk acceptability of many modern high-technology industries, suggesting the number of possible coupling errors is simply incalculable. The acceptability of risky systems is likely to remain a high-profile and emotional political question. However, in the short term at least, the number of such systems (and consequently their failures) is likely to increase. Therefore the immediate need for improved preventative measures and the ability to respond to incidents is likely to remain.

Risk communication

Risk communication, while still in its developmental stage as an academic field, has largely emerged from earlier work in the area of risk perception (Pidgeon *et al.*, 1992). This happened for two reasons. First, there was concern about the passing of quantitative information about risks to lay folk from expert analysts. Ordinary people would find it increasingly difficult to understand the types of highly technical information which experts are very good at producing. And this is often further complicated by the use of an abstract and difficult to comprehend argot (language) in which such information is often presented (Slovic, 1992; Covello *et al.*, 1986; Covello, 1991).

Risk communication represents a quite different sociological approach to the study of risk. Risk communication theorists concern themselves with the dialogue (or, rather, the lack of it) between expert and lay folk (Irwin, 1989, 1995; Wynne, 1989). The crux of such work on risk communication is a critique of the distinction which has been drawn between expert and lay decision makers in much of the psychological and sociological work on risk. Expert approaches, it is argued, are based upon a misconception of 'science'. The idealized view expressed here is one of an objective scientific community in which subjective factors (social, cultural and psychological ones) either do not, or at least minimally, influence the decision-making process.

In contrast to experts, lay perceptions of risk are tied, at least ideally, to a particular set of social, cultural and psychological factors. Lay perceptions are frequently characterized as being constructed on the basis of irrational and non-objective models of reality which become validated on the basis of folk theories of risk and danger.

Risk communication theorists suggest that these polarized views of both expert and lay folk have historically been reinforced by human science research into risk management, which itself has largely been carried out within the context of a scientific paradigm in turn inherited from the natural sciences. Much of the risk perception work in psychology is also viewed by risk communication theorists in this way.

In terms of risk management, the benefits of a risk communication approach must be considered within the context of a general reduction in social conflict, brought about through an enhanced process of mutual understanding. This will moderate the differing expectations of both lay and expert decision makers by establishing realistic goals which can hence be achieved through dialogue (Irwin, 1989, 1995).

Not unrelated to the issue of dialogue, risk communication has also evolved in the context of mounting political dilemmas related to the siting of large-scale hazardous installations during the 1960s and 1970s (Krimsky and Plough, 1988). Work in risk perception has indicated that conflicting perceptions of the acceptability of such hazards are dependent on varied public frames of reference, hence much of the initial work in risk communication was designed to improve understanding between these conflicting groups (Borodzicz *et al.*, 1993b). Risk communication in this early phase was perceived as a tool for public education. Public questioning of political and expert assertions was attributed by some risk experts to irrational folk world-views based on a mistrust of expertise and progress (Wynne, 1992).

However, more recently there has been mounting concern among communication theorists about the pluralistic nature of risk. As a consequence, the approach to the subject has more recently focused on gaining a greater understanding of the variety of ways in which risk can be perceived. This is in contrast to the attempts to calibrate or compare folk and expert models of risk as 'irrational' and 'objective' models of risk. In other words, while various aspects of risk can be measured, from a risk communication perspective, these measurements will have little or no validity if considered apart from the meaningful interpretations of risk that social actors construct for themselves. The result of this has been to question the validity of any one conception of 'risk', instead suggesting that it might be more useful to examine how conceptions of risk are constructed (Wynne, 1992).

Some risk communication theorists have even suggested that experts cannot agree among themselves as to what constitutes a risk. For example, in a case study of the *Exxon Valdez* oil spill, it was found that a situation of 'multiple realities' existed among the expert decision makers responding to the event.* In particular, there was

---

* The notion of establishing blame, guilt or negligence and impartially investigating the 'multiple realities' of various actor accounts poses a dilemma to any major inquiry. Such a view of expert difference is congruent with Browning and Shetler's 'post-modern' analysis of communications between response organizations during the *Exxon Valdez* oil spill in Alaska. Browning and Shetler argued that fundamentally competing expert perceptions and treatments of such scenarios are due to a state of 'multiple realities' existing at a qualitative, stratified and cultural level of variance between organizations (Browning and Shetler, 1992).

some considerable confusion among the response staff about whether the crew should have been airlifted from the stricken vessel so quickly. It was argued by some response staff that the vessel could have been diverted from its collision course with the rocks if there had been a crew on board (Browning and Shetler, 1992).

The sociologist Brian Wynne suggests that a serious dialogue between expert and layman has yet to be embarked upon, if risk communication is to become an effective framework for establishing rationality in risk management. Wynne argues that both expert and lay conceptions of risk must be viewed within the deeper social assumptions within which they were embedded. Such assumptions, argues Wynne, are a necessary precondition for the expert construction of a 'technical risk analysis' (Wynne, 1989). In other words, Wynne is arguing that the social models one has of the world will define how we construct that world in our minds; this in turn will define what we consider to be a safe or dangerous phenomenon. This model of risk could utilize both technical and folk metaphors for its construction.

Wynne illustrates his argument with some interesting case histories. One example is the 1960s controversy over the use of the pesticide 2,4,5-t also known as 'Agent Orange'. The scientists who developed the pesticide tested it under laboratory conditions and concluded that, provided it was properly used as directed, it would pose no health threat to either agricultural workers or other countryside users. Yet despite this, the National Union of Agricultural and Allied Workers vigorously lobbied for its banning. Wynne points out that there are two traditional ways of conceiving this situation; either the workers were 'being irrational, imagining harm where none existed' or the scientists were 'cooking the scientific books under discreet political pressure either to keep 2,4,5-t on the market, or to maintain their own prior credibility (or both)' (Wynne, 1989: 37).

While Wynne would not wish to discount these factors totally in explaining the controversy, the problem lay in each group's misinterpretation of the other. The scientists had projected their controlled sterile environment on to the farm workers who would have to use their product, but the reality was quite different. The farmers would often work in less than optimal conditions; instructions on the sacks of 2,4,5-t might frequently be illegible; protective equipment and the correct mixing solvents and spraying equipment might not be available. Hence the expert and lay conceptions of the world were used as parameters for the construction of each other's reality.* As Wynne puts it:

---

* This point relates to the case studies presented at the end of the book. Significant risks were not only found to be defined differently between expert and lay groups, but also between expert groups operating in a multiservice environment.

The point of general importance shown by this case is that different parties – the scientists and the workers – defined different actual risk systems, or risk analytic problems, because they built upon different models of the social practices creating or controlling the risks.

(Wynne, 1989: 37)

Risk communication is a process which requires careful consideration; establishing goals for people with differing expectations may act to increase rather than decrease tensions. Risk communication, therefore, may act to distort information in order to achieve a particular outcome, hence there is a need for an independent assessment to be built into such processes. One key recurring criticism made by risk communication theorists is the reliance of official risk management bodies on definitions of risk which are presented in purely technical (or expert) terms (Irwin, 1989: 19).

Risk homeostasis

One of the most interesting and controversial theories of risk to come out of the social sciences is *risk homeostasis theory*. The origins of this model go back to two key authors: Peltzman's risk compensation theory (Peltzman, 1975) and Wilde's work on target risk (Wilde, 1976, 1994), now commonly referred to as the risk homeostasis theory.

The proponents of this theory accept that it is feasible to either reduce or even remove risks altogether, but suggest that this very process will make us increase or accept other risks in return, in order to rebalance the total risk. In other words, while much can be done to ameliorate or control certain risks, the threat remains that the more we do to contain one type of risk, the more blind (or accepting) we become to others. This process is what is described here as 'risk homeostasis' (Adams, 1995).

A useful analogy to understanding risk homeostasis is found in human biology. Normal human body core temperature is 37 °C. This is maintained despite large variations in ambient temperatures. Similarly arguments can be posited for blood levels, heart rate and breathing. Our bodies, like many other types of organisms are in a constant state of homeostatic restoration.

> If blood is lost in an injury, the body produces just enough new blood to
> re-establish homeostasis. If heavy exercise increases lactic acid in the muscles,
> the body increases the heart rate and the breathing rate, along with many
> other adjustments, so as to bring the level back to normal.
>
> (Filley, 1999)

Filley (1999) argues that whole populations are able to exhibit homeostatic qualities, citing breeding as an example in animal populations. If this also applies to human groups in organizations, then this may radically affect the way we think about how to manage risk in society. Regulating risk in one area may mean populations shift behaviour to compensate in another.

Another useful analogy offered by Filley is a 'mechanical' one. Systems such as a boiler thermostat can regulate the temperature of water in central heating systems: 'feed back is the name given to systems that use information from the output of the system to regulate the behaviour of the system' (Filley, 1999). In reality, the system is only momentarily at equilibrium; instead, it is always just above or below the required temperature within a predefined range.

A lot of the discussion about risk homeostasis has been within the context of driver risk taking on the roads. The introduction of seat belt regulation in the UK and many other countries was widely hailed as a positive step towards the management of risk in a road safety context but, as has been pointed out by Adams, the net effect of this change in legislation should be considered in its meaningful context to those affected. This does not only include vehicle drivers. It can be argued that drivers feeling safer as a result of being strapped into their seats may well drive faster and take more chances which may adversely affect other road users such as pedestrians and cyclists* (Adams, 1988, 1995).

---

* Risk homeostasis (from the Greek *homeo*: stay the same, and *stasis*: state of affairs, condition) theory was originally argued by Wilde (1982). As a model, risk homeostasis theory is designed to be generalizable to all forms of risk; however, it is usually considered in the context of road users. The main thrust of risk homeostasis theory is that there is a constant level risk; if this is increased or reduced through intervention, it will be compensated for overall in the population by a change in driver behaviour.

Although the propensity to take risks is widely assumed to vary with circumstances and individuals, there is no way of testing this assumption by direct
measurement.

(Adams, 1999b: 24)

Hence, to restate the earlier point about risk measurement, while it may be quite
possible to measure the decrease in driver injuries, this is only possible because the
variable being measured is whether a seat belt is worn or not. The driver's enhanced
feeling of safety wearing a seat belt may affect the driver's speed and style of driving;
the implications of this on other road users' safety may be negative.

Another interesting observation followed from the changeover to driving on the
right in Sweden. It was reported that road deaths reduced by 17% in the first year
(*Guardian*, 26 January 1996).

A three-year study of cars with anti-lock braking systems (ABS) is another example
cited by Wilde (1994). ABS was fitted to half of the fleet of a taxi company in Munich.
Although the drivers were not aware that they were being observed as part of an
experiment, they did know if the vehicles they drove were fitted with ABS.

Among a total of 747 accidents incurred by the company's taxis during that
period, the involvement rate of the ABS vehicles was not lower, but slightly
higher, although not significantly so in a statistical sense. These vehicles were
somewhat under-represented in the sub-category of accidents in which the
cab driver was judged to be culpable, but clearly over-represented in accidents
in which the driver was not at fault. Accident severity was independent of the
presence or absence of ABS.

In another part of their investigation, the researchers installed accelerometers
in ten ABS and ten non-ABS cars, without the drivers' knowledge. These sensors
measured the G-force of acceleration and deceleration once every ten milliseconds
for a total of 3276 hours of driving. It was found that extreme deceleration, that
is, extremely hard braking, occurred more often in the vehicles with ABS.

(Wilde, 1994)

Similar risk homeostatic arguments have been made for a disturbing range of other
applications, including speed limits, airbags, and the so-described 'child-proof' bottle
tops for medicines and dangerous cleaning products.

There is no 'technological or regulatory fix' that will simply take the risk out of the equation. Adams makes the point in relation to road safety that the best way to improve accident rates in cars might be to fix a spike to the steering wheel pointing at the driver (Adams, 1995).*

Risk homeostasis has not been without its critics, who refute the whole basis for the theory and at best, argue it is only a hypothesis.

> These so-called theories that purport to explain human behaviour in the face of risk are nothing more than hypotheses with a large body of empirical evidence refuting the studies that allegedly validate them.
>
> (O'Neill and Williams, 1998)

The debate about the validity of risk homeostasis is beyond the scope of this work. The theory does, however, raise fundamental questions for governments and regulators. Improvements to the safety of both technical and human systems may increase the propensity for risk taking in other (or new) areas of activity. Laws and regulations need to be drafted carefully if they are not going to have unintended consequences. It is likely that this needs to take account of both the complexity and organizational safety culture within the system. Risk initiatives should also consider how good safety might be rewarded through the organizational culture.

Culture

Use of the term 'culture' in relation to risk has been influential with two groups of theorists in the social sciences. The first group has considered culture in relation to organizational influences in the risk management process. This theoretical approach is described as safety culture. The term 'culture' has also been used by a second and quite distinct group of theorists, who claim to be anthropologically inspired in the way they understand risk. The second group has been highly influential in developing an approach called 'cultural theory'. Before considering these theories further, it would be

---

* It is worth noting that Adams would also support the cultural theory model presented at the end of this chapter.

pertinent to briefly consider the development of an anthropological understanding of the term 'culture'.

There are perhaps two common ways of understanding the term culture. The first views culture as a way of describing a particular autonomous group or population. This has often proved problematic due to the difficulty in defining the boundaries of such populations. The second common understanding of culture views it as a system of ideas, values and behaviours associated with one or more social groups. These are sometimes considered as 'subcultures', for example, 'black American subculture'.

However, culture has proved a particularly difficult and elusive concept for theorists to understand. One reason for this is that culture will reveal different features of itself, depending on who is looking and how. A further problem is that, while theoretical descriptions of culture may portray a static entity, culture is more likely to be a dynamic phenomenon, liable to constant influence and change. It is not surprising, then, that concepts of culture within the anthropological literature have been highly controversial; over the past 150 years many definitions of culture have been posited. By the middle of the twentieth century, the concept of 'culture' was already no stranger to controversy. For example, Kroeber and Kluckhorn listed nearly 300 further definitions of the term culture as early as 1952 (Kroeber and Kluckhorn, 1952).

The earliest and most famous of a long line of definitions of culture was produced by the anthropologist Edwin B. Tylor in 1871:

> Culture or civilisation, taken in its wide ethnographic sense, is that complex whole which includes knowledge, belief, art, morals, law, custom, and any other capabilities and habits acquired by man as a member of society.
>
> (Edwin B. Tylor, 1871, in Gardner, 1985)

Consider this rather static conception of human culture with a more recent and politically oriented version by Edward Said, whose area of study was Oriental cultures and their historic relationship with our own: 'Cultures are permeable and, on the whole, defensive boundaries between polities' (Said, 1989).

Much of the controversy surrounding the nature of culture has focused on the features which should be included in that complex whole, and the parameters which identify it as a *society* or group. In other words, if culture were a box full of things, then how big is that box, and what are its contents? Tylor's use of the term 'acquired' is also important because it indicates that one's attributes as a cultural actor are derived from social membership rather than biological birthright. Therefore, culture must also have some means of recreating itself through common practices. Culture, then, may not be a static entity but, as Waring argues: 'a complex and dynamic property of human activity systems' (Waring, 1992).

For theorists interested in understanding risks, culture has proved an equally controversial concept, particularly for organizations.

Safety culture

Safety culture was developed by theorists interested in the use of qualitative methods in psychological research (Henwood and Pidgeon, 1994). Safety culture theorists also argue that expert decision makers may operate within the context of an organization's cultural factors. Safety culture theorists advocate that a 'risk' or 'safety culture' operates at an organizational level (Pidgeon, 1991; Dake, 1991c; Turner, 1991; Booth, 1993; Waring and Glendon, 1998).

It is argued that safety culture provides a method for perceiving the risk management processes in hazardous operations and this can be used to analyse the preconditions for many major socio-technical disasters (Pidgeon, 1991; Turner, 1991). One theorist has even suggested that the concept 'safety culture' is one of the most important advancements in risk management to have occurred in recent times (Lee, 1993: 21–23).

The origins of the term 'organizational safety culture' can be traced to literature relating to the western nuclear industry's response to the Chernobyl disaster. In this case, a poor 'safety culture' among employees in the then Soviet nuclear industry was deemed to be a contributory human factor to the accident (OECD, 1987; Pidgeon, 1991).

The extent to which a 'risk' or 'safety' culture can be equated with the general use of the term 'culture' in the social sciences may be pertinent; particularly so, as there has been some debate about what actually constitutes a safety culture. For the OECD, safety culture was perceived to be a set of administrative procedures including training, emergency plans and attitudes to safety which cannot be regulated. In contrast, the human sciences approaches to culture have largely drawn upon anthropological literature which, although quite pluralistic in description, generally describes the phenomenon of culture as 'systems of shared meanings or beliefs'.

In this context it is hardly surprising that the application of culture to such an amorphous phenomenon as safety should prove problematic to define. The OECD criteria for a safety culture can at least be seen as distinct from more recent approaches in its absence of the concept of shared meanings or beliefs. In contrast, Pidgeon defines the term:

> We might therefore, by this account, advance a working definition of culture as the collection of beliefs, norms, attitudes, roles, and practices shared within a given grouping or population.

> (Pidgeon, 1991: 129)

For Pidgeon, the 'grouping' or 'population' unit is clearly the organization, and the emphasis of his work is not to define what should go into or out of the conceptual box called 'safety culture', but to recommend how and why a good safety culture might be brought about. In contrast, this more recent and somewhat deterministic definition of safety culture is offered by the human factors study group:

> The safety culture of an organisation is the product of individual and group values, attitudes, perceptions, competencies, and patterns of behaviour that determine the commitment to, and the style and proficiency of, an organisation's health and safety management.
>
> Organisations with a positive safety culture are characterised by communications founded on mutual trust, by shared perceptions of the importance of safety and by confidence in the efficacy of preventative measures.

> (ACSNI, 1993)

Perhaps the real problem is not so much to define, but to recognize a safety culture and assess its qualities and parameters. In this respect the study of safety cultures may pose similar problems to that of traditional cultures in the anthropological literature. Similarly, it may be argued for the safety culture found within an organization, that it will only reveal itself for analysis when faced with a crisis scenario. This is because it is only at this point that those shared assumptions and beliefs are tested and sometimes painfully exposed as inadequate. This also suggests that a 'safety culture' may be an interesting theoretical construct for the study of crises.

If the safety culture of an organization determines the extent to which foresight can be both generated and ultimately acted on, then it is by changing that safety culture that many unknown risks can be identified and avoided. Safety culture theorists also argue that, by improving the safety culture of an organization, economic efficiencies will also accrue. Hence, expenditure on promoting a positive safety culture may be more fundamental than simple insurance against disasters; it could represent sensible economic management. An organization with a good safety culture will benefit from enhanced profit and safety in both the long- and short term (ACSNI, 1993).

> Official inquiries into safety disasters such as Chernobyl, King's Cross, and Piper Alpha specifically pinpointed cultural characteristics as important both to understanding why the disasters occurred and as indicators for other organisations in reducing the likelihood that they would experience similar events.
>
> (Waring and Glendon, 1998)

Safety culture represents an innovative applied approach to the study of risk and decision making, in attempting to depart from the methodologically reductionist paradigm of decision making and attitude measurement prevalent in psychology. Instead, proponents of this approach concentrate upon the cultural context in which the decision making takes place in organizational settings. A safety culture approach is also important in opening up the potential for study by means of naturalistic inquiry, thus moving away from the experimental gambling analogy scenarios and psychometric measurements which have come to characterize much psychological research in this subject.

Studying safety culture requires a certain degree of ethical detachment which practitioners within a culture may be unable to attain easily. Immersed within the safety culture of their own organization, the native is unable to distinguish outside of an apparently 'natural' world view. This may include a variety of emotive sympathies which have been forged in the enculturation process. In contrast, the qualitative methodology of an ethnographic or grounded theory case-study researcher is ideal for observation and analysis of such data, where the researcher is ideally an outsider to the organization under study, and confronting the culture for the first time. A further benefit of a safety culture approach is that it facilitates interdisciplinary studies with other social scientists studying risk. One interdisciplinary approach has been with sociologists, who advocate a systems theory approach to studying risk, discussed earlier (Pidgeon and Turner, 1997).

Cultural theory

Cultural theorists have divided previous definitions of culture into two groups: those which perceive culture to be a *set of mental products*, and those which define culture as *a way of life in terms of interpersonal relationships and attitudes*. Rather than trying to differentiate between these, or considering what should go into or out of the conceptual box called culture, cultural theorists attempt to simplify the world by reducing human culture to three terms, *social relations*, *cultural biases* and *ways of life*, the latter being the product of combinations of the former (Thompson *et al.*, 1990).

Culture, then, at least for cultural theorists, can be seen in the context of two attributes: cultural biases (group), which are portrayed as shared beliefs, values and myths typifying the cosmology of a 'group'; and social relations (grid), which can be described as a pattern of interpersonal relationships.

Mary Douglas defines 'group' as 'the experience of a bounded social unit', while she defines 'grid' as that which 'refers to the rules that relate one person to others on an ego-centred basis' (Douglas, 1970). Michael Thompson *et al.* (1990) describe a 'grid' thus: 'Groups are patterns of relationships that are, as it were, independent of the individual who happens to be taken as the reference point.'

For cultural theorists, risk, like any other phenomenon, is socially constructed, being influenced by people's involvement in the course of their everyday interactions with family, friends and peers. Hence any concept of 'identity' for the individual has to be seen in the context of the strength of that individual's relationship to social groups, and the social structure or nature of such groups.

Cultural theorists claim that, from an anthropological perspective and with the aid of a highly elaborate theory, there are four universal predispositions which will mediate the nature of any individual perception and response to risk. These categories are: 'hierarchical', 'individualist', 'egalitarian' and 'fatalist'. There is a fifth category of 'autonomists' or 'hermits' (Douglas and Wildavsky, 1982; Thompson *et al.*, 1990; Dake, 1991a, 1991c). It is argued by cultural theorists that these predispositions would be prescribed by the extent to which one is oriented to either 'group' or 'grid' positions.

Where there is a low level of orientation to both group and grid dimensions, the individualist predisposition is likely to be found. Individualists are likely to accept a high level of risk on the understanding that this represents entrepreneurial opportunities. However, when orientation to both dimensions is high then a contrasting hierarchical predisposition is likely to occur. Hierarchists would be less inclined to accept risks, and then only if part of an institutionally sanctioned process. This contrast between individualists and hierarchists can be seen as opposing ends of a traditional social science continuum, analogous to the *laissez-faire* market and the regulated Weberian democracy (Frosdick, 1995: 45).

However, where grid influences are weak but group is prominent, then an egalitarian predisposition is likely to occur. For the egalitarian, risk is an omnipresent threat of disaster caused by the actions of significant others. This perpetual threat is also the case for the fatalists, who are in contrast high grid but low group. The difference between these groups is that fatalists accept the risk on the grounds that there is little that they can do about it anyway.

The particular disposition adopted will be dictated by the individual's embeddedness within a 'social group', and the extent to which this relates to 'other individuals through a system of rules' (Douglas and Wildavsky, 1982).

Central to cultural theory is the understanding that permutations of 'group' and 'grid' influences can only be reduced to these four categories (Thompson *et al.*, 1990: 84; Frosdick, 1995: 45–47). These categories, argue cultural theorists, will define how any one individual perceives and interacts with their world. Further cultural theorists maintain that these categories represent human universals, and therefore do not respect social, cultural or psychological boundaries. In other words, it is claimed by these theorists that these disposi- tions appear *throughout the human species in every type of human society* (Figure 2.5).

Both the group and grid constructs are theoretically measurable. Hypothetically, one should be able to measure the extent to which one is incorporated into a bounded unit (group influences), and also the extent to which one is externally exposed to circumscription (grid influences). The reality of measuring group and grid phenomena is highly problematic, and the theory appears to offer little consideration to the like- lihood that some people may vary in their predispositions depending on social context. For example, one may be an absolute hierarchist when dealing with superiors at work, but a total individualist when driving a car. Up until now, attempts to ascribe category status have usually been restricted to pseudoscientific terms, such as 'high, low or

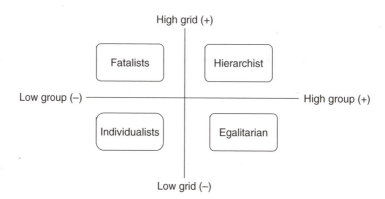

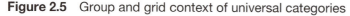

Figure 2.5   Group and grid context of universal categories

Source: S. Frosdick, Organisational structure, culture and attitudes to risk in the British stadia safety industry. *Journal of Contingencies and Crisis Management* 3(1) (1995). Reproduced by permission of Blackwell Publishing Ltd

strong' (Thompson *et al.*, 1990); this can make precise measurement of the theory difficult.

This lack of preciseness is due to the fuzzy nature of a category such as 'group', the key to which lies in the labelling and identification of a particular group of people. In particular, how they would be contrasted as distinct from another group. However, cultural theorists do attempt to define the term 'group'. It is not clear how this would relate to a number of other culturally constructed groupings such as tribe and race or ethnic and political allegiances. Such groups have all exhaustively been shown to be highly malleable ways of categorizing the world, often based upon folk conceptual models for perceiving and ordering the world rather than scientific validation. As Worsley (1984) puts it: 'We need to question whether these taxonomies are merely academic exercises, or do they reflect distinctive underlying political praxis?'

Cultural theory as a concept has aroused some controversy among risk theorists. This may be due in part to a critique of early psychological approaches to the study of risk. More fundamentally, cultural theory has a tendency to be tautological, in that it provides a way of perceiving the world which questions all other ways of looking. This means that as a theory it can only be fully understood if believed in and vice versa. It could therefore be argued that cultural theory represents a belief system about risk, in the same way that cultural theorists argue for other theoretical approaches to the subject.

Further, to suggest that all social life can be reduced to four personality types, with a fifth catch-all category, may be questionable. The highly prescriptive segregation of individuals into ideal types may also constitute an oversimplification of the way risk is in reality understood in the population.

Quantitative analysis of cultural theory has been attempted by a few theorists with mixed results. Work carried out by Dake for his PhD thesis suggests that some significant correlations could be found to validate the five categories. This was done by constructing attitude scales for the measurement of cultural biases which correlated with 36 societal concerns. Of these concerns, a significant result was found for 19 out of the 36 (Dake, 1991).

In contrast, a study by Sjoberg found that the results of Dake's study could not be replicated (Sjoberg, 1995). Sjoberg explains this failure to replicate by suggesting that Dake's work suffered from a number of methodological shortcomings; in particular, the limited sample size used by Dake for the analysis. Commenting on Dake's work, Sjoberg suggests:

> The samples are said to be representative but they were clearly too small for that. Furthermore, no information is given about refusal rates. No details

about the response scales used for measuring the cultural biases are given in the thesis or the subsequent publications; both replication and interpretations of the results are thereby hampered.

(Sjoberg, 1995: 9)

The value of a cultural theory of risk may be questionable. How would, or could, such a theory be used to reduce or manage risks in a practical way? As a conceptual approach to understanding risk perception, cultural theory offers an interesting context within which other theories may be contrasted, but there are few examples of cultural theory being used to directly influence risk management in practice.

A brief review of risk

A number of preliminary conclusions can be drawn from this chapter regarding risk and the social sciences. Perhaps of fundamental concern here is that there are a number of ways in which risk can be both perceived and managed. The different perspectives which have been presented here are therefore not exclusive; for example, economic risk modelling has not been included.

Much of the risk perception work would appear to suggest some recurring social features. First, it would appear that people find unusual or unknown risks particularly terrifying, at least much more so than familiar ones. Despite this terror factor, it is the familiar risks which claim the most lives. Second, voluntary risk appears to be preferable to imposed risk. The issue of choice is familiar to many of us who regularly choose to engage in risky behaviour, for example, smoking. In contrast, the siting of a potentially hazardous installation near to our homes may provoke considerable concern. Third, people find it difficult to either comprehend or believe probability. The apparent irrationality of popular risk perception suggests that people have a problem with cognition or trust of official data sources.

A sociological analysis of risk suggests an equally complex situation. For systems theorists, this is to suggest that familiar accidents may be barely noticed; in contrast, unfamiliar ones may provoke a crisis. Any crisis will be particularly difficult to deal with if it appears to set a precedent for a system's operational history. Utilizing a systems perspective, both foresight and isomorphic hindsight may be used to improve the safety of a system's functioning.

For risk communication theorists, experts and lay folk value risks differently. This is because experts count lost lives while the general public focuses on a number of other factors, in particular fairness and controllability. There are a number of potential benefits which may arise from adopting a risk communication perspective. These are providing information and education, bringing about behavioural change, providing instruction for a disaster and providing a resolution of conflict. The central feature of risk communication is not to produce some grand solution, but to increase dialogue and cooperation by establishing realistic aims for people of differing expectations.

The use of 'safety culture' and 'cultural theory' as a way of understanding risks represents a more recent theoretical approach to the subject. The practical application of these theories is still problematic; adequate definitions of terms such as culture, safety and risk continue to offer a formidable academic challenge. However, in terms of understanding and changing the way people train for, perceive and manage risks, culturally oriented approaches may be of considerable utility.

Perhaps the most fundamental and disturbing conclusion that can be drawn from current approaches to risk is that even under optimum conditions, risks are still very difficult to eradicate. It is, therefore, the subject of Chapter 4 to review the effects of failed risk management. Before doing this, we are now going to look at risks of a different kind.

Chapter 3

SECURITY: THE NEW CORPORATE TOTEM

The focus of risk so far has concentrated on failures caused by human error, irrationality, systems failure and poor communications. Another major and growing area of risk failure is security. Security differs from other types of risks discussed so far, in aiming to protect systems, organizations and society from those with an *intention to commit harm*. The 'intention to harm' may be provided by terrorists with political, nationalist or extreme religious beliefs, or by organized criminal gangs who simply want to profit from an illegal activity. Threats are also posed by opportunistic criminals, employees and even rival organizations.

One area of security activity with which we are all familiar is guarding or private policing. Many areas of Western society today are in effect policed by private armies of security guards; shopping centres, car parks and banks are perhaps most prominent. The UK is certainly not alone in having debated the importance of regulating this activity.

For the management of risk within organizations, security is also a key area of significance. The effects of high-profile and tragic events such as 11 September 2001 in New York have had wider implications for corporate activity beyond the Twin Towers themselves. The effects of terrorism in the financial areas of the UK, particularly London and Manchester, suggest that distinctions between accident and design in risk are false, and may even lead to risk myopia. However, away from high-profile terrorist events, the effects of other types of security failures may constitute a more serious risk to the viability of commercial activities. The lessons learnt from risk perception in the last chapter indicate that it is the spectacular and most shocking risks that galvanize our attention, while the more mundane pose the significant threats.

Security is a rapidly expanding and essential feature of corporate activity. There is virtually no major organization, public or private, without a team dedicated to managing issues of security.

Security: a problem of definition

Although security has emerged as an academic area of study and research only recently, debate about the constitution of a discipline and profession of security has aroused much contemporary debate (Borodzicz, 1996a). Security could be seen as risk management in practice; one theorist, Sally Lievesly, has even argued that security is the wrong term altogether, preferring, in contrast, *'risk engineering'* (Lievesly, 1995). Again security praxis is beginning to respond to social changes, partly through legislation and regulation (particularly in health and safety and guarding), but also through the privatization of modern policing practices and the emergence of a huge private security industry.

The term 'security' originates from the Latin *se-curus*, from *cura* meaning 'to care'. Generally the term security can be considered in two contexts, either *freedom from danger*, or a show of *force* (or strength), able to respond to or deter threats. It is usually the latter that is most obvious to us in terms of a visible presence.

This latter model is congruent with a traditional military model maintaining a particular social ordering from internal or external adverse influence, through the use of 'force'.* A popular although narrow perception of security is thus portrayed by uniformed staff found protecting shopping centres, banks, offices and entertainment venues. In this context, security is a form of private policing for commerce.

A more inclusive view of security might involve the management of health and safety, auditing, crisis and contingency planning, CCTV, whistle-blowers, reputation risk, workplace bullying and harassment, employee screening, counterfeiting, the purchase of security intelligence and bodyguarding; in fact, anything interfering with the functioning of an organization, its profitability or viability. This wider view of security is perhaps more akin to a corporate risk management function, allowing organizations or individuals to carry on their business 'free from danger'.

A large and growing part of the security market that is often ignored by the security literature is 'personal security' for individuals and their families. The growth of many gated communities and the purchase of security activities and products by individuals is also rapidly increasing. These may range from simple locks and lighting (often a condition

---

* It is fair to say that this may be an oversimplification of a modern use of 'force'. Terms such as 'stealth' and 'capability' typify modern military dialogues on international security. Armies rarely face each other on the battlefield these days. It is more likely that the military would be asked to feed the enemies of the enemy than fight the enemy directly.

for obtaining home insurance) through to sophisticated alarm systems for our homes and vehicles. Virtually everyone with access to the Internet now requires some form of cyber-security device. Another area where individuals would purchase security is through the procurement of private detectives.

At a theoretical level, corporate security is still a relatively new issue for academic scrutiny, to an extent seeking a disciplinary base (Nalla *et al.*, 1995; Borodzicz, 1996b). Despite its academic infancy, the subject of security confronts theorists with a number of puzzling questions about the practical management of corporate and social life. Despite the proliferation of security activities, little consensus exists among theorists about practical application, theory or training. Security remains one of the most unregulated and misunderstood areas of corporate life, with reliable data about the precise size and nature of the industry difficult to assess (Button and George, 1994, 2000). Two reasons suggested below may account for this.

First, much of what is described as 'corporate security' is often obscured by secrecy. For example, the actions of private investigators would be expected to have an obvious confidential element but, equally, people involved in the management of organizational risks may have commercial reasons for not publicizing their work. Similarly, information about the precise activation and monitoring of CCTV systems is not something organizations would necessarily want to publicize. An illustration of this was the highly secretive preparations made for the millennium bug. A perceived weakness by one organization may be viewed by rivals as a good business opportunity to exploit.

Corporate security is not confined to sinister back-room plots and attempts to detect corporate subversion. Corporate security managers may be responsible for risks and accidents unconnected with deviant or criminally motivated behaviour as described in the last chapter. Virtually every organization now has both a risk and security function, although how these are differentiated from each other is almost unique to each organizational context.

Second, much of the work defined as corporate security is often categorized or demarcated as something else. Security in this context represents a rapidly growing industry of practitioners involved in a number of quite diverse tasks. These range from situational crime prevention to highly elaborate corporate plans for the management of crisis and disasters, internal (and external) audit, health and safety functions, insurance buying and cyber-security. For example, one subfield of auditing, 'forensics', is an area normally associated with the application of scientific knowledge to assist courts and the legal system. A wider definition might include the use of scientific methods more generally for the detection and prevention of crime. With further investigation, it is possible to discover a whole range of subdivisions into areas as diverse as psychology, accounting and information technology.

Ten years ago most very large accountancy firms might have had one or two employees in forensic accounting/auditing; today this is a recognized and expanding area of the accounting discipline with specialist courses, conferences and journals. Sources within the accounting profession appear to be taking forensic auditing quite seriously. A campaign in 1996 by the Audit Faculty, called 'Taking Fraud Seriously', was supported by a conference with leading speakers from academia, the legal profession, business, the police and of course the accountancy profession. Corporate security managers were not at the conference. This is curious considering one of the principal findings: a fragmented approach to fighting corporate fraud is estimated to cost a staggering £10bn a year (Bingham, 1997).

A more complex conception of security is provided by Post and Kingsbury (1991), who suggest we should not try to define the term as this will, inevitably, not account for substantial overlaps with other areas of study. Post and Kingsbury instead suggest considering security within a theoretical discourse in terms of eight categories or features.

Eight categories of security

1. Historical or narrative of past events

Post and Kingsbury (1991) argue that history may be said to constitute a narrative of past events. Security knowledge, therefore, represents an accumulation of facts gleaned from societal growth and development. Consider the historical legalistic approach where security derives from law. There are two sources of pertinence here: the *individual* and *social*. The former refers to the right for all (individuals) to be seen as equal and independent in terms of health, liberty and possessions. This view is congruent with the works of John Locke.

At a social level antecedents for this can be clearly seen in tribal life totems, taboos and customs which constitute the regulation of early civilization. Freud's work on *Totem and Taboo* (1950) is a key influence on Post and Kingsbury's thinking here. In more complex and contemporary societies, this is achieved through *codes of practice, laws* and *rules*.

2. *Psychological*

Psychologists are normally interested in the study and interpretations of the human mind. Of interest here is the concept of perception and learning as an influence on definitions of security, but also the behavioural characteristics of either groups or individuals.

This can be seen in three ways:

a. Rather than trying to catch thieves, understand why and how they commit crimes and put up barriers – *target hardening*.
b. Security is *protective not punitive*. Security's ultimate reliance is not achieved through power or the fear of it, but on an understanding of the ethos of society.
c. Security function is about creating a pattern of *operational relationships* resulting in a climate free from danger.

3. *Sociological (or anthropological)*

Again there are three main ways in which a sociological study of security might be identified. First, 'security' is viewed as a theoretical aspect of *human social behaviour*. Second, conceiving security through a broad analysis of *human society and cultural groupings*. Both of these conceptions in fact relate to an overlap of psychological and anthropological understandings of the world. Third, 'security' is considered through *human organizations and institutions*. However, while corporate security relates primarily to organizations and institutions it is difficult to view these in isolation from human society and culture more generally.

4. *Functionalist or procedural social control*

The term *functional* is used here in terms of application. For most people involved in security activities, the scope of their activity is defined in terms of narrow procedural roles. In other words, security is there only because it serves a clearly identified and functional purpose. The danger with such a prescriptive approach is the extent to which the world is in a constant state of flux. Hence many of today's security issues could not reasonably have been identified in a preventative capacity, as a major failure is required before a problem is identified and role developed to respond.

5. Management – organizational context of security

This model draws primarily on the work of French theorist Henri Fayol. Fayol argued that management activity is divided into *five major functions*: *planning, organizing, command, coordination and control.*

- *Planning* – (originates from the French term *prevoyance*, 'to foresee', but also assumed to include forecasting) is the management function associated with setting goals and deciding how best to achieve them. This might also involve encouraging innovation and change in the workplace.
- *Organizing* – is about providing the material and human resources and building the structure to carry out the activities of the organization. Through organizing, managers will determine which tasks are to be carried out, the order in which they are carried out and the basic organizational structure for doing this. Organizing is also about staffing jobs with individuals who are best suited to them.
- *Command* – is about maintaining activity among personnel and getting the optimum return from all employees in the interest of the whole organization. Command is essentially about leadership, providing direction and motivating employees to put forth the substantial effort that is required.
- *Coordination* – unifying and harmonizing activities and effort in the organization to facilitate working success.
- *Control* – the process of regulating organizational activities so that actual performance conforms to expected organizational standards and goals. Control is also about verifying that everything occurs in accordance with plans, instructions, established principles and expressed command.

As one of the founding fathers of modern management, Henri Fayol's definition of 'security activities' is clearly based around the organization as the unit of analysis:

> Safeguarding property and persons … against all social disturbances liable to endanger the progress and even the life of the business. It is, generally speaking, all measures conferring upon the undertaking and the requisite peace of mind upon the personnel.

(Fayol, 1916)

6. Normative – standards and norms

A normative definition of security is about defining norms and standards and then endeavouring to protect them. This can take two forms:

- *Protective security* – defending and preserving property for the rightful owner
- *Detective security* – the art of detecting crime; this of course only works when the crime is detected at the planning stage.

Another definition encompassing this normative view could revolve around the term 'acceptable organizational standards'. An example of this is offered here by David Paine:

> Security being those measures which are necessary to maintain a state of well being within a facility and to prevent loss, damage or compromise due to crime, espionage, sabotage, fire, accidents, disasters, strikes, riots.

> (Paine, 1972)

7. Structural – security portrayed in terms of interrelationships

A structural view of security views it in terms of an organization's parts and the control of interrelationships. Security in this context is about social control to protect a way of life through the arrangement and configuration of an organization's elements.

The extent to which an organization's structure can be controlled to bring about security is, however, questionable. Turner's systems theory approach to risk management, discussed in the last chapter, might suggest that all systems are simply incubating failures waiting to happen. Interrelationships might again be viewed in the context of Perrow's model. 'Tight coupling' and 'interactive complexity' of security procedures would act as a precondition for a normal accident (systems failure).

8. Descriptive – different typologies of security

A descriptive level of security allows various definitions and meanings. These could be based on 'context', 'environment' and 'utility'. In this sense, everything contained in the previous seven features will to some extent define the scope and application of security. However, common elements can usually be found, for example, using terms like 'prevention of' or 'protection from' or 'freedom from' a variety of conditions, events and problems.

Post and Kingsbury's eight themes described above provide a useful series of lenses through which security might be observed. It is clear that security might be viewed as a subpart of risk, or even 'operational risk management'; however, within security management is a range of issues requiring multidisciplinary approaches.

Another way we might define security is by considering the content of security courses as taught in higher education establishments. A number of new postgraduate courses have emerged on the international arena in the last decade. Of interest here is the way that security, as an academic discipline, has been both defined and presented to students by these courses. One of the most revealing exercises is to simply mine the postgraduate prospectuses of contemporary university departments for the range of security-related courses on offer. Generally these fall into three types, although there is some overlapping.

The first type of course in security management specializes in *technical security management*. Prospective students for these programmes are expected to have a basic university education in the pure sciences, typically engineering, before taking such a course. These courses focus on issues such as target hardening, cybercrime, and electronic surveillance and alarm systems. The emphasis here is on security devices, usually through physical means.

The second type of course is usually offered by military and police training institutions. These emphasize (perhaps predictably?), the *military and policing aspects of security*. This type of course is embedded within the notion of highly disciplined and task-oriented human systems of organization, not unlike military ones. While such an approach will clearly have its appeal biased towards those looking for a second career from the police or armed forces, this is not in itself an academic argument for a theory of security congruent with the needs of practical application. These types of course focus on transferring military and/or policing skills to the civilian context. One definition that appears to fit this model is Manunta's 'APT' model. Manunta (2000) argues that security is the function of three components: an asset (A), a protector (P) and a threat (T). Put mathematically, these three components for any situation (Si) can express security (S) thus:

$$S = f(A, P, T) \, Si$$

This model is useful in reducing the security problem down to its basic components. The problem is that these components are likely to be defined differently depending on who is defining and when. If one compares this to the risk communication argument in the last chapter, it is clear that in a situation of 'security communication' multiple realities might exist. Manunta himself would be the first to acknowledge the problem of defining security. But his definition is important in being the first to be grounded in philosophical reasoning.

The third type of academic approach offers study programmes based in the social and political sciences. These types of study programme typically combine elements of *criminological theory, management, law and risk*. Academia has responded to the marketplace with a number of postgraduate courses in this area (Manunta, 1998a).

However, the extent to which syllabi are determined by academic and theoretical rigour, as opposed to an industry demand for qualified security professionals, is an issue. A large number of security professionals and managers are in second careers; many of these bypassed the university system at university entrance age, opting instead for a life in uniform (Borodzicz, 1996a). The option of postgraduate education for these people will be largely restricted to distance learning programmes for which these types of courses are most ideal. While a growing number of security professionals now enter the industry with first degrees, and then specialize in security, these are still very much the minority. Other factors may also act to compromise the content and mode of delivery of postgraduate education available in order to allow for flexible, distance or e-learning modes of study. Many courses are dependent, in the majority, on accepting students without any formal academic qualifications for postgraduate study. The value and equivalence of flexible learning programmes remains an issue for the security industry to reconcile.

The problem is compounded by a poor selection of academic material available on the subject of security. For the student seeking an authoritative academic guide to the subject, there are few places where written material can be found. Most academic departments would specialize in only one or two areas of security; there is a need to concentrate specialisms together. This also reflects the lack of accredited and independent research subjected to rigorous academic peer review. Specialist academic journals, normally a guide to the virility of theoretical research in any subject area, are in short supply.

Academic institutions are responding to a strong industry demand for security theory. In this knowledge vacuum, an apparent professionalism is offered by university training. While degrees are eagerly grasped by a growing minority of employees wishing to professionalize their activities within the security industry, the majority of security staff today remain untrained.

Regulation of security

In Chapter 1, regulation was considered in relation to corporate governance. Clearly it is desirable that organizations entrusted to manage our safety and security should be regulated to ensure high standards of operation.

The case for regulation is a very clear one. Until very recently it has been possible to set up a security business in many parts of the world, including the UK, without being vetted. This has resulted in many cases where criminal elements have penetrated the industry. Poor (or no) standards of performance and a lack of accountability for security operations is another major problem. For certain sectors of the security industry – for example, manned guarding and doormen – the need to employ persons who do not have a criminal record is a matter of pressing ethical and moral concern.

Another reason for regulation is sheer size and importance of the industry. A survey by Button and George estimates that £300m each year is spent on private security by the British Government. Despite this volume of security procurement, there is no central controlling strategy for this process (Button and George, 2000: 175).

The sheer size and scope of the contemporary security industry places consumers in a difficult position. Measures of professionalism and competence are often difficult to identify from those employed within the industry. Attempts by so-called industry associations to internally regulate security activities have at best been piecemeal in their success. Calls for government regulation of the security industry might in this context be well intentioned; there is certainly a need to stop convicted criminals and those with dubious motives from setting up in business.

The problems are what to regulate and who is to define good practice. There is an urgent need for security management theorists and practitioners to engage in this debate with some vigour.*

The case against regulation largely revolves around two criticisms. First, a *general ideological commitment to deregulation*. The argument here is that there has already been too much regulation of just about every sphere of our lives and that further regulation is going to be counterproductive. Health and safety, for example, is quite well provided for in the UK under the HASWA (Health and Safety at Work Act). Despite this, there has been a very poor record by the HSE (Health and Safety Executive) in

---

* A really good discussion about the case *for* regulation of the private security industry can be found in Button and George, 2000: 175–184.

bringing about prosecutions. The cost of regulation is another negative factor. Security is already a relatively low-status activity, at least in terms of remuneration for employees at an operational level. The cost of registering and checking staff sufficiently at this level is not unproblematic. The cost of regulating more complex forms of security is more difficult to calculate and dependent to a degree on how security is defined.

The second and perhaps more poignant concern with regulation is that in order to effectively regulate any activity, one would require a satisfactory definition. Security represents such a broad church of activities it is hard to imagine how any one body could be competent enough to carry out the task.

> The Socratic problem 'What is Security?' is under-estimated and under-researched. Different answers are given, which are of value at the tactical and specific level. There is general agreement and a surfeit of information on the physical and formal aspects of security. Standards, technical details and codes of practice are available. Systemic procedure planning, training and methodology are covered in great detail by many sources. None of them appears to address the general concept of security. We need to understand what we do mean by 'security' before addressing the problem: How can we attain it?
>
> (Manunta, 2000)

It goes beyond this work to attempt to resolve the issue of security regulation. It is important, however, that regulation does not bring about a state of 'security homeostasis'.

Security as a criminological/policing function

The notion of illegal practices in the workplace is now an established theme in criminology. Corporate crime has been documented for most of the last century within criminological discourses. It was quickly recognized among social theorists that the economically powerful were in a position to be 'harmful to the progress of capitalism' through the manipulation of markets, stocks and securities (Bonger, 1905, 1969: 142). Much of this early debate was not about removing capitalism per se but dealing with individual cases of greed and ethically doubtful practice. A more general approach to work-related crime was not to emerge until the middle of the twentieth century. The founding father of this approach was Edwin Sutherland who produced a series of papers and a book in his attempt to outline a general theory of work-related crime

(Sutherland, 1940, 1945, 1947, 1949, 1983; Croall, 1992; Nelken, 1994; Slapper and Tombs, 1999).

A report in the *Independent* newspaper on corporate crime highlighted the extent of the problem as being twice as costly to society as ordinary types of crime. For example, UK fraud in 1985 was reported to cost £2113m, twice that of theft, robbery and burglary combined. The situation regarding employees seriously injured or killed in the workplace is similar (*Independent*, 22 September 1999).

Corporate crime and negligence is a growing area of concern. It is easy in a competitive world for expediency to take precedence over security in modern organizations. Organizations are in a constant state of flux as they constantly reconfigure themselves either to be more efficient than rivals or to offer different levels of service. This drives a need to develop new and ever more complex corporate operations and hierarchical complexities (Chryssides, 1993). Difficulties in determining and maintaining responsibilities for security in this context are self-evident.

The role of private security in crime prevention and policing is frequently evident. Guards routinely patrol many of the public areas of our life. When the physical presence of security is not overtly found, covert artefacts of this practice can usually be detected by careful observation: small secret cameras and recording devices in shopping malls (CCTV), electronic screening equipment, and door entry identification systems in addition to the array of intruder alarms and cash-carrying vehicles popularly associated with security. 'Crime risk security' is no longer exclusive to government and political power; it is an established commercial service industry available to those who can afford it.

This visible presence is frequently associated with the rise of the private security industry as fundamentally a crime management function. The popular perception of an increased private security role has been further bolstered by media attention to the contracting out of a number of Home Office functions – for example, the incarceration and transportation of convicts – and many other aspects of policing.

Security at an operational level has replaced the labourer as one of the twenty-first century's greatest employers of unskilled staff. A survey carried out by APEX, a trade union for the industry, claimed that there were over 100 000 security personnel in the UK (Button and George, 1994). These figures are likely to have increased substantially since then. In the UK, the industry is likely to have outpaced even the national police force.

Security employees are often poorly motivated and underpaid. At one extreme, there are cases of unscrupulous ex-offenders who set up protection companies in the very areas they used to operate (in many countries, anyone with a telephone and office can start a security company). At the other extreme are huge and highly differentiated international security organizations, arguably beyond the practical control and regulation of any one national government.

The issue here is one of competence and professionalism in the absence of academic consensus. A further issue is the ability of a number of unscrupulous practitioners to operate without control in the absence of government regulation. With regulation the situation could be more dangerous still, as organizations might be forced to comply with 'minimum standard' rules and procedures.

In a criminological/policing context, security is always seen as fundamentally a reaction to criminally motivated stimuli. This implies that prevention must rely on the removal of criminal intent, or at least total 'situational' prevention (Clarke, 1980). The following definition of security given below supports this: 'Security risks concern the hazards of criminal activity against any or all of: persons; property; organisations; the state' (Waring and Glendon, 1998: 40).

However, policing and criminology are concepts grounded within a social and ethical context. A key issue for corporate security, if it is to be recognized as a criminological issue, is the extent to which it can offer a social and ethical service to society. There is very little compelling evidence to support this. The role of corporate security managers is to support the aims of the employing organization, not the society that forms the organizational context. Where the aims of the organization are morally questionable, or just plainly myopic, then the corporate security manager will be placed in a very difficult or impossible ethical position.

With an increasing international trend towards the legislation of corporate governance, security managers will find it even more difficult to maintain a professional distance between themselves and their employers. If it is problematic to maintain an ethical corporate security function within one social system, then it will be even harder to achieve this on an international basis. While security may be seen as a social tool for the management of crime, it is also an optional risk against the organization itself.

Security as risk and loss management

The ancient philosophers of China, Greece and Egypt referred to in Chapter 1 were certainly not alone among members of early civilizations to have been concerned about security. Some form of security must have been the very basis for these early civilizations to exist. Many early attempts to manage risk have left us with elaborate and mysterious oracles, some still in popular use today.

The research on risk perception by psychologists suggested that people find unusual or unknown risks particularly terrifying, at least much more so than familiar ones. An irrational element to human risk perception may have similar implications within the corporate security industry. Corporate security has become obsessed with low-frequency, high-impact events, such as extreme acts of terrorism and major catastrophes and crimes. This might also be viewed as irrational when considered against the frequency and cumulative level of losses sustained in the management of mundane events, such as fraud, staffing problems or internal theft.

The relationship between risk and security is perhaps more than simply a linguistic turn. Certainly, security can be seen as an element of risk management in a holistic sense (Borodzicz, 1996a). A link between risk and security management in British postgraduate study programmes has been noted (Borodzicz, 1996a; Manunta, 1998a). From a corporate risk perspective, security can be viewed pragmatically as just another hazardous exposure. While security management may be viewed as a cost against the operation, it also represents a significant threat if not treated seriously.

Treating corporate security as a loss prevention activity may facilitate a more inclusive appraisal of corporate exposure. This could acknowledge criminal threats, but also allow for a wider security agenda. Such losses could be the result of either internal or external crime, but they could also arise from an accident or natural calamity – for example, a fire, flood or earthquake – with no association to criminal behaviour.

A theoretical approach to security should aim to identify losses in order to establish appropriate security procedures. An implicit assumption of loss prevention is that prevention is to a degree quantifiable (if only by statistical probability). In practice, attempts to quantify risk have been and remain problematic.

Security as a management activity

The absence of consensus among criminologists and risk theorists suggests, for the time being at least, responsibility will still remain a management activity.

For commercial activities, corporate risk and security management are likely to be a significant factor affecting viability, profitability and even share price (Knight and Pretty, 1996). Perhaps the most serious risk that can be posed to any organization is survival. Organizations need to train specialist groups of high-profile decision makers to manage organizational survival within the context of ill-structured and often dangerous crisis events. Much of the orthodoxy found in emergency training relies on the operation of highly structured plans and procedures based on a priori risk assessment and evaluation. In contrast, the needs of unstructured crisis scenarios are for flexible and innovative interventions based on factors which could not have been envisaged on an a-priori basis (Turner, 1994; Lagadec, 1995; Borodzicz, 1999a).

The case for considering security as a management activity is perhaps even stronger than that for criminology or risk. Security represents a significant capital cost in most major projects. A road bypass project at Newbury, Berkshire, in the UK, was estimated to cost £100m; a staggering 20% of this was down to the management of a group of environmental protesters at the construction site. Security failures at high-prestige projects are not exceptional. The Channel Tunnel fire, for example, occurred despite high levels of security management input and at considerable capital cost to the project. There have been two further European tunnel fires in the Alps resulting in loss of life and injury, and again with significant implications for revenue and the local infrastructure.

> ...the circumstances of recent years, the increasing professionalism and the demands of cost effectiveness alike have created the need for the safeguarding of assets, personnel, and even the profitability of the organisation against theft, fraud, fire criminal damage, and terrorist acts. To achieve these objectives, formulation and implementation of strict rules and policies by employers are required.
>
> (Wilson and Slator, 1990)

A further reflection on security failure is that the media are often allowed to highlight the extent of the problem. There have now been many highly publicized breaches of security conducted by reporters from the media gaining access to aircraft at British airports. Often this would take place just hours after giving completely fictitious personal details on job application forms (BBC *News*, 1999).

One of the greatest potential management assets – staff – are another source of concern for corporate security managers. Few employers check the information contained on job application forms methodically, yet it is common practice for people to enhance these. Cases of so-called whistle-blowers are also becoming increasingly common, as staff speak out against unethical or illegal practices witnessed at work (Adams, 1992; Vinten, 1994; Rayner, 1997). The cost of preparing for and defending tribunals and legal adjudication in such cases can be considerable, even where the organization is not subsequently even found to be at fault.

Most contemporary theorists would agree that management does not represent an exact science, but rather a theory-driven practice, based on four principal activities: planning, organizing, leading and controlling (Mintzberg, 1980). While these activities are real, they are also difficult to measure or appraise in a systematic way. In contrast, corporate security is often misperceived to be a highly prescribed task (enforcement) with a strict and inflexible emphasis on rule conformity.

Frequently the business of security, at least in the corporate context, is compart-mentalized: personnel or establishment deals with health and safety issues; finance deals with financial risks; there will be an appointed fire and first aid officer; and building maintenance will deal with risks to the physical structure of the organization. In this context, security is left to deal with the legitimacy of whatever goes in or out of the door. In the aftermath of a major incident, such compartmentalized responsibility can have a negative effect on an organization's ability to learn from and recover from disasters: 'Don't tell me what is going on because if I know, I might be held accountable' (Crainer, 1993).

The problem here is one that could benefit from both a greater understanding of the risk systems involved and an improved level of meaningful dialogue (risk communication) between these apparently discrete parts of the organization. Separate risk analysis means that different parts of the organization become managed as sub-systems in their own right; little attention is therefore paid to the interaction of these sub-systems together. The only risks which are taken seriously are those which threaten the integrity of the sub-system; these are themselves defined by experts in that sub-system. Such discrete risk analysis will be unlikely to take account of the effects of system failures, which may interact with other system failures in the total organization.

The diversity of functions and responsibilities of corporate security are simply too great to make any inclusive codified practice feasible. In this context there is a strong case for including security within the realms of management. One of the few research exercises that have addressed this topic – Nalla *et al.* – argues for a greater emphasis on business and communication skills as of paramount importance to the security function: '. . . findings suggest security practitioners clear emphasis on business and communications skills in the graduate curriculum' (Nalla *et al.*, 1995).

Similarly, Davidson proposes:

> Security management has developed to the point where it deserves recognition as a free-standing management science. To that end, it clearly needs specialised professional training and universal recognition as an academic discipline.
>
> (Davidson, 1989)

In this context it is probably more pertinent to ask why security is not more commonly associated with management. This is partly due to the demographic make-up of many of the professionals who work in the corporate security industry. Most are in their second career usually following service in the police or armed services. Previous uniformed experience, although of limited academic value, is probably still the most widely accepted qualification within the industry. Where these individuals are educated, it is likely that this was in the fields of criminology or policing. At the time of writing, very few British management schools offer corporate security management at a postgraduate level. It is hard to imagine any other important area of corporate activity so thoroughly ignored by management theorists.

This legacy also has implications in terms of the organizational structure and culture of the security industry. Uniformed services tend to be structured; many of the staff have brought this method of operation with them as cultural baggage. Hence when they set up security arrangements they will do this in a way seeming most obvious to them.

The extent to which some commercial firms of security agents appear to be almost entirely made up of staff who originate from the same regiment or police authority is perhaps an indication of the extent of the problem. There are also a number of areas where security services are engaged in the same or similar activities to those recently or still carried out by government agencies. For example: private prisons, intelligence gathering and dissemination, and personal protection. These are all areas dominated by staff with a history of uniformed service first careers. The extent to which this cultural baggage shapes the way we perceive and manage security cannot be discounted.

Security as a management totem

The German social theorist, Ulrich Beck, argued that society is in a state of transition to a new state of modernity typified by reflexivity and complexity (Beck, 1992). For Beck, a radical change in the nature and complexity of production processes and logistics is responsible for postmodernity. The British sociologist Anthony Giddens has also been highly influential in promoting a view of postmodern society as based on the influence of huge global corporations which transcend all the traditional barriers of culture, knowledge and power (Giddens, 1991).

Beck and Giddens argue that social changes and uncertainties constitute evidence of a significant global shift on a scale not previously encountered. One theorist has argued that a failure to manage this process is evidence of our failure to even become 'modern', let alone 'post modern' (Latour, 1993). In a global society, no one can be sure whose rules we are following. Seventy companies now control more than half of all global sales (Dicken, 1992). Much of this business is conducted through virtual electronic markets. The imposition of national regulations may have little effect on a company's global security policy. The effect of any one criminal justice system must then be viewed within a context of globalization.

In this context, society, politicians and theorists need to re-engage in a debate about what should be secure, how and by whom. Society has failed to understand the complexity of defining and maintaining security. Risk is popularly conceived to be that which can be identified on an a-priori basis, and therefore preventable to at least a fair degree of confidence. Reality is not quite so neat and tidy; security operatives are often called on to make difficult decisions based on incomplete or erroneous information. Even legal conceptions of acceptable risk will be restricted to inter-pretations of action and behaviour based on legal definitions of reasonable corporate behaviour.

For Bauman (1991), coming to terms with the postmodern world means acknow-ledging that uncertainty and confusion are features of the modern condition. Bauman offers a metaphor of gardening to illustrate his position. While attempting to secure order and control the gardener must acknowledge that variety and complexity are a necessary element in the dynamic management of the garden. Total security, while theoretically possible for any venture (as shown by Manunta's APT model), will stifle the very complexity which makes commerce possible in the modern global market.

In the absence of consensus, it is left to the professionalism and experience of individual managers rather than theory to facilitate effective corporate security. Professionalism, however, can be established only through a deeper understanding of the social conditions under which security failures occur. The reality of the organization for many security managers is one where there are indeed many improvements but always an exponentially greater number of associated risks. For example, technological advances and new forms of travel enable us to travel more often, safely and further. However, a level of residual risk is involved and it is the increased frequency that must be multiplied by the residual risk. The same can be said for strategic risks relating to security. The sheer complexity of most modern organizations means that the management of security failures and the implementation of contingencies are far from rare (Reason, 1997).

There is a danger of turning corporate security into a contemporary management totem in the strict anthropological sense; in other words, it is something good to think but not necessarily a real or achievable thing. For traditional societies the totem represents a collective belief system that could domesticate and manage the unpredictable relationship between humans and the unknowns of nature (Radcliffe-Brown, 1952: 131; Kuper, 1987: 57).

For most organizations, corporate security has become one of these totems. A popular conception of totems is that they are tall wooden or stone effigies, erected by primitive peoples in order to practise ancestor worship. Much of the recent thinking in anthropology suggests this to be an erroneous view. Totems, anthropologists tell us, are things that are good to think; they embody the deepest essence of cultural values (Levi-Strauss, 1962; Kuper, 1987). Totems are a way of structuring the natural (unpredictable) world so that it can fit with the cultural one. Definitions of good and evil, deviance and social order are cultural constructions rather than physical artefacts.

Corporate security according to popular perception is a way to manage these phenomena; its application, therefore, represents the synthesis of our cultural views. The central argument made here is that totems, far from being primitive artefacts based on unsophisticated beliefs, are modern-day statues representing the frontiers of the social and physical sciences. Security represents the frontiers of a number of disciplines; this is precisely why attempts to produce a cohesive, all-encompassing and regulated profession are and will for the time being remain ill-founded. Security consultants promise much, but when we scratch the surface we discover the same old prickly chestnuts which preoccupied many contemporary management theorists: planning, organizing, leading and controlling.

It is suggested here that a concept of security, which suggests a complete freedom from risk of every kind, will for the foreseeable future continue to represent a utopian ideal. If we make a choice, it is usually on the basis that we have calculated that this will benefit us, but putting that choice into operation will involve sustaining risks. The application of security, then, can be described here quite simply as a number of craft practices, dedicated to the management of operational risk. The complexity in this definition lies in the number of context-specific ways in which risks might be perceived and managed. There are no 100% tried and trusted methods; at best we can look for examples of good and bad practice, but these are usually indicative of how well the response fitted the context.

Despite the question of appropriate syllabus, an academic input into contemporary security practice is necessary. Effective security will have implications for a vast range of practical management activities. This poses a dilemma: the extent to which security management syllabi should be designed as generalized forms of management training, or be specifically designed for particular types of security issues. It is argued here that corporate security syllabi should contain an element of both. Corporate security then, like risk, is applied management.

Beyond the totems

In comparison to risk management, academic approaches to the study of security as an academic discipline are in their infancy. This is perhaps surprising considering the size and importance of security as a rapidly expanding global industry. The security industry is beginning to change in function and application. The traditional task of the security manager was to prevent loss of property, usually incurred as the result of some form of either internal or external crime; however, this rather narrowly defined role has broadened considerably to include health and safety, risk assessment and risk management components. The simplistic conception of security – controlling physical access to the organization and controlled movement of property – may have been adequate 20 years ago. Today this would include a much larger range of risks, such as fraud, terrorism and disaster contingency plans.

Risk assessment, prevention and management in this context poses an altogether more complex set of requirements and skills, not traditionally associated with the security manager. The types of crime traditionally encountered by the security manager can to an extent be measured and therefore targeted to reduce losses; in contrast, the types of losses incurred through more complex forms of risk failure are more difficult to measure or predict. The effects of such losses to an organization's operations can be crippling, if not terminal.

Another reason for increasing awareness of risk among security managers is that insurance companies have become reluctant to act as a safety net for poor risk management. There are a number of reasons for this. First, insurance companies will increasingly suggest to their clients that they either take steps to improve the management of risk or seek alternative arrangements for cover.

A second reason is that the modern security manager needs to provide the employing organization with a value-for-money service. Simply reacting to breaches of security on an a-posteriori basis may have been adequate in the past two decades. The contemporary security manager needs to identify risks in a proactive and demonstrative way, otherwise the security contract may simply go to someone else.

There is also a need for greater security involvement in the management of an organization, possibly at the board level. Arguing for greater resources in order to prevent future catastrophic losses will for most organizations be an alien concept. Unfortunately the following reactive situation described by Wilson and Slater is all too common:

> Security is easily established as a board level agenda item in the aftermath of a disastrous incident or in the knowledge of something catastrophic which has happened to a local or closely related firm.
>
> (Wilson and Slater, 1990)

Today's security manager must demonstrate sensitivity to subtle shifts in organizational activities. Subtle changes to products and markets can radically alter the pattern and types of risk exposure. Most organizations, periodically, need to diversify, cut costs, enter new markets, change to new production processes. Such changes will alter the types of socio-technical systems that an organization operates. It is important that these changes are reflected in appropriate changes to the safety culture. If not, the staff who operate the system will be unaware of potential hazards and may report them as routine system problems.

For the security manager to play a greater role in the management of an organization's activities, various social and cultural issues within the organization will need to be addressed. This will require an upgrading of status for the security team, but also a change in the way security is culturally perceived within the organization and society generally. Such change requires action from both those within the security industry and at a governmental level.

It is therefore suggested that if the security manager is in future to play an important role in risk prevention, management and ultimately loss control, a number of key changes need to take place in the industry.

First, the security industry needs to move away from the ex-policeman's (and it is usually men) second career image. The security manager needs to be perceived as a risk professional in their own right, who has been specifically trained and equipped for the job they do as part of a career-long process. This is partly being addressed in the UK by training for national vocational qualifications (NVQs), and university-accredited training courses. These offer those entering the security industry without formal qualifications a series of nationally recognized certificates for on-the-job training and classroom-based teaching in stages.

Second, governments need to actively regulate the industry, so as to enhance both the real and perceived level of professionalism. For example, in Belgium, police officers are not allowed to join a security company until a period of five years has elapsed following their police service. It is clearly important that security companies can carefully vet the people who join them, and even more so that the government can vet those who set up security companies and consultancies. Such regulation has still to occur in the UK for many aspects of security. It is, therefore, difficult for potential clients to distinguish between real security companies with grounded expertise and those that simply claim this. The procedural skills of the ex-police officer are not necessarily those required of the modern security manager or even the modern police officer!

Setting up in-house security services is equally problematic; there may be much 'reinvention of the wheel' as already tried and tested risk management procedures are developed. These might subsequently have been easier to identify if there had been greater cooperation available within the industry to capitalize on the isomorphic system learning highlighted by Toft and Reynolds (1994). As suggested by Toft and Reynolds, intrinsically similar systems of operation will have similar risks; for criminals these systems offer similar opportunities. An adequate risk communication context should be developed in order to capitalize on this knowledge between security organizations.

Third, increased academic credibility is necessary for managers in the security industry. If the security manager is to be perceived as of sufficient status to be part of senior management within an organization, then this should be commensurate with expertise and qualifications. One would expect the manager of the legal or accounts divisions within an organization to be trained to a professional academic level; they are responsible for making decisions with large financial consequences. Why then do we not train security managers to the same level of academic professionalism? The security manager is responsible for the management of safety in complex socio-technical systems with large, if not terminal, financial as well as human consequences.

Many of the courses available in higher education are perceived as conversion courses for uniformed types looking for a second career to boost their pension. Bright young people will not be attracted to the security industry without a change in image.

More theoretical work needs to be carried out on security management as a discipline in its own right, and an increased level of dialogue between practitioners and academics is required. We need to ask ourselves two questions. First, if there were a theoretical approach to the subject of security, then what should be included in such a theory? Second, what would constitute a profession of security?

It is argued here that theoretical risk management perspectives will need to be part of any contemporary theory of security. However, it is also suggested that a profession and an academic approach are related, at least so far as each represents the theory and practice of contemporary security management.

Despite the capabilities of modern science, the ability to completely control the means of production secure from hazard is still and will remain problematic. It is argued here that while debates will continue about how we should define security as a theoretical concept, the practice of corporate security is and will remain fundamentally a management function. In this respect security is no different from any other form of risk management process. Security, like any other applied management issue, is about the management of finite resources in the face of an infinite range of threats and demands.

At a theoretical level the subject poses a serious and philosophical question about our very being. While it may not be possible to manage security effectively, it has become a necessary condition for postmodern corporate life that we believe we can.

No academic or practitioner alone can be expected to have a detailed competence in the entire breadth of the field. This raises a serious question about establishing expertise and professionalism in security. If security is management rather than management science, then it must be measured by subjective rather than objective means. As Bauman puts it:

> Postmodernity is modernity coming to terms with its own impossibility; a self monitoring modernity; one that consciously discards what it was unconsciously doing.
>
> (Bauman, 1991: 272)

It is now time for the disciplines of management and security to engage in a debate about fundamental issues affecting the very being of corporate life – a challenge most modern management schools have so far failed to take up.

Chapter 4

CRISIS

Problems cannot be solved at the same level of awareness that created them.

(Albert Einstein)

The focus in this chapter moves away from risk management and prevention to dealing with the consequences of risk failure in the form of emergencies, crises and disasters. The social and psychological approaches to risk, reviewed in the last chapter, can be seen to have increased our understanding about why things go wrong and what should have been done to prevent this. In contrast, dealing with the physical and social effects of risk failure have proved far more problematic. Understanding why things go wrong does not necessarily help us to manage them. Hindsight knowledge is of little use to decision makers unless it can be available at the time of deciding. The systemic models of Turner and Perrow appear to suggest an inevitability for organizational failure. The homeostatic model (Adams, 1995) suggests that an unconscious or instinctual need to create risk will always balance out against those that are eliminated. Problems with risk, irrationality and the complexities of social communication and regulation again point to the need for more resources applied to response, rather than prevention.

The focus of risk management in corporate contexts has moved forward, particularly following initiatives in corporate governance and health and safety practice. However, there is a lack of practical understanding about crisis events and how these should or could be controlled. Organizations are becoming increasingly complex and interdependent, in a world of 'just in time' processing and rapid communications. Prevention, where possible, is always better than response after things have gone wrong. In the complex world we now inhabit, a failure to be able to respond to failure is of equal concern.

Typological terminology?

Theorists and practitioners often use a variety of terms to discuss dangerous events. It is argued here that while these terms are frequently used, there is often very little distinction made between them and this may have important implications for the way we train decision makers to manage risk. When looking at the literature on this subject, one finds a number of interchangeable terms used by authors to describe a variety of scenarios with a potential for escalation. It is argued here that *emergencies, crises* and *disasters* may represent distinctly different types of phenomenon and that this conception may have important implications for both analysis of events and training. This chapter will, therefore, consider both the context and practical implications of a distinction in terms.

The terms 'emergency', 'crisis' and 'disaster' are methodologically problematic, if only because of the pluralistic accounts of reality offered by the many informants attending public inquiries. The liturgy of disaster and crisis management is less well-defined theoretically and finds its expression as a reactive response to incidents, usually in terms of 'best practice'. It has proved difficult to establish quantified measures of risk management for these types of incidents. In this context, understanding the complex relationship between risk, crisis and a disaster as a single defined area of study is argued here to be of significance.

The term 'crisis' has aroused considerable debate among risk theorists. It is argued here that the moment of crisis could be described as a differentiating feature between emergencies and disasters. A risk could give rise to a crisis, which in turn could become a disaster. The concept of crisis (which it is argued here is not the same thing as an emergency) is a relatively unexplored academic concept, although the analysis of human behaviour (the so-called 'human factor') in crisis precipitation and crisis resolution is now receiving substantial attention from academics and practitioners.

In contrast, disaster management (often, and perhaps wrongly, called 'emergency planning') comprises much of what is normally taught under this label. Disaster management is largely concerned with the practical problems of emergency activity, 'picking up the pieces' when the unwanted and unexpected has occurred. Fundamental to more recent academic approaches to disaster management is an acknowledgement that an incident may be termed a disaster while still containing many ongoing crises and emergencies. This is because social actors involved in responding to disasters may be dealing with different response issues simultaneously.

Understanding these different types of events may be helpful for those who have to train key decision makers. If emergencies, crises and disasters are different phenomena, then it would appear logical that appropriate training may also need to be different. Further, identifying the appropriate people to train within organizations may also need to be reconsidered for such distinctive events.

Most theoretical positions found in the academic literature focus on preventing or minimizing risk before a crisis occurs, or the analysis of events following tragic disaster. It is, however, much more difficult to find theoretical positions on the issue of crisis management itself. While prevention is a laudable aim, and clearly much of this theoretical work needs to continue, the phenomenon of crisis is still very much a theoretical black box waiting to be opened.

It is pertinent to point out here that much of the literature and research has and continues to perpetuate a split between prevention and response. Much of the work on health and safety, risk analysis and assessment tends to be linked to compliance either with state- or industry-required standards. In contrast, work on crises and disasters focuses on a social science research context. These two professional communities have little in the way of a dialogue between them. This is particularly surprising considering that neither community could exist without the product of the other.

Even without considering terrorism and crime, practical examples of crises are all too familiar: fires and explosions in complex nuclear or chemical plants; accidents in the transportation and storage of hazardous products (or ourselves); and tragic fires which sweep through ever more adventurous building structures. Many social scientists are in general agreement that there is an increase of crisis incidents with a potential for disaster of this type. Although theorists may differ in their explanations for this increase, the focus of their interest tends to be on the reasons why disasters occur and post-incident management.

Some theorists have argued that more attention needs to be given to understanding and managing situations of crisis. The late Professor Turner identified a mismatch in the relationship between social (or human) and technological systems, leading to dangerous situations of 'ill-structure' and disaster (Turner, 1978). The French sociologist, Lagadec, also raised the issue of crisis as an increasingly dangerous phenomenon:

> Major crises – from *Challenger*, Bhopal, Tylenol or Chernobyl to *Exxon Valdez* and Braer – are no longer exceptional events. Indeed the risk of crisis is even becoming structural as large networks become more complex, more vulnerable and more independent . . . crises continue to become more frequent and destabilising.
>
> (Lagadec, 1993: 45)

Lagadec is not alone here:

> Crises become more numerous, visible, and calamitous, organisations have no choice but to accept them as inescapable reality that must be factored into their planning and decision making.
>
> (Lerbinger, 1997)

Theorists and practitioners are faced with a dangerous plethora of events and terminology. 'Major incident', 'emergency', 'crisis', 'disaster', 'accident', 'catastrophe' and 'abomination' are all examples of terms used to describe events capable of rupturing our social world and devastating our physical one. What these terms mean, and how we should respond, remains problematic. However, without a model to understand the phenomena that we are describing, event response and theorizing is made more difficult.

Historically, disasters were popularly conceived of as 'freak' events, 'acts of God' (Toft and Reynolds, 1994: 1) or 'abominations' (Douglas, 1970). In contrast, scientific approaches to the study of disasters appear to suggest that all disasters should have causal agents and, further, that these could be identified and therefore prevented. The notion of a causal agent suggests that blame may be identified. For public inquiries, an exhaustive amount of time and expense may be focused on establishing causality and responsibility (Toft and Reynolds, 1994).

Some system for ordering event phenomena would enable academics to make comparisons between events. How one would conceptualize phenomena described as emergency, crisis and disaster and how this material should be categorized poses a number of problems.

First, the apparent uniqueness of disasters suggests that a general rule of categorization may be difficult to stipulate in advance. The almost infinite ability for technological advancement in the context of ever more complex social structures continues to pose many new forms of scenario for emergency decision makers to deal with. The evidence for this alarming trend is displayed in the form of new and difficult to deal with socio-technical incidents, which have a potential to rapidly transform into tragic disasters. What may often begin as an apparently small or routine emergency may quite dramatically turn into a major disaster, because it was impossible to envisage how the event would (or could) manifest. This apparent uniqueness, then, is caused by difficulties in predicting the timing, nature and social and geographic context of the event.

Obtaining reliable data about incidents – in other words, learning through the experience of significant others – is often complicated by a number of conflicting accounts of events. Disagreements between those involved in responding to major incidents are notoriously difficult to reconcile and have become the subject of much media attention during public inquiries.

Such events are difficult to categorize. There is a considerable body of literature devoted to dealing with emergency, crisis and disaster management. Rarely, however, are these concepts either defined adequately or even distinguished from each other (Borodzicz, 1997).

Major incidents will place different demands on different agencies at different times. Hence, a defined disaster for one agency, may, in contrast, still be an ongoing crisis or emergency for another. For example, in responding to an air crash once survivors have been removed, the police, coroner and civil aviation authorities will be involved in disaster recovery. However, for social services, this situation would constitute an ongoing crisis in the management of resources for survivors and the community. Such illustrations suggest that the nature of the liaison occurring between social workers, the health authority, emergency planning officers and those voluntary agencies which deal with the human tragedy following a major event are *dynamic* and in a state of *mutual construction*. This unique mix of response requirements for each crisis event is problematic in terms of highly structured response plans.

Crises occur in a number of different contexts, making comparisons extremely difficult. For example, can we model business, political, health and terrorist crises in the same way? Clearly, establishing comparable levels of decision making between highly structured emergency response organizations poses a problem, particularly if the hierarchies and decision-making points in the response organizations are different. However, to make this type of comparison among commercial and political organizations may suggest that an overall theoretical model of crisis is somewhat elusive.

A number of attempts have been made to model the phenomena we know as disasters, but this has proved difficult, due to the amorphous nature of disasters and the varied and unpredictable contexts in which they occur (one such model is offered in the King's Cross case study). Understanding the perceptions of disasters for those who respond to them does appear to be important, at least in terms of the quality and scope of response. Particularly for crisis management, there is a need for training to go beyond a structured system of well-choreographed and ritualized drills for fire and bombs to highly destabilizing shocks to the fundamental organizational systems. This can only take place when we understand the difference between crises and other types of events.

Modelling by type

One way we might choose to model an emergency, crisis or disaster is by type. We could categorize such events by the type of activity affected. Air travel, for example, might be contrasted with maritime travel. Floods and earthquakes might receive a similar distinction, as would fires and explosions. Another popular distinction by type is often made between so-called 'natural' and 'man-made' disasters.

The problem with a classification system based on type is that many contemporary incidents may easily fit into more than one category. This is because the effects of many catastrophic events can be highly complex and causality may not be easily established. For example, if we were to take all shipping accidents and attempt to compare them, we would expect an exclusive category to contain incidents which all exhibit certain similarities or patterns of events, at least in terms of causality and effect. The problem here is the range of different incidents in a would-be category. Not all marine accidents cause loss of life; some may be responsible for environmental damage through the spilling of crude oil or other chemicals; others may be caused by fire (which may itself constitute another type of incident altogether).

Modelling by response

It is argued here that a clear distinction should be made between emergencies, crises and disasters and that this distinction is of critical importance for developing response requirements. This distinction is not apparent in much of the literature, and even when attempts are made by theorists to define or distinguish these terms, this is often in the form of a plurality of context-specific descriptions making sociological comparison difficult. It is hoped the definitions offered here provide a useful contribution to this debate.

Terminology is problematic. The terms 'emergency', 'crisis' and 'disaster' are often used by theorists, policy makers and practitioners when describing different situations. In addition, a number of other terms – for example, 'mass emergency', 'major incident' or 'catastrophe' – can also be found in the literature. This point is commented on by Professor Quarantelli, in the introduction to a debate entitled, 'What is a disaster?':

> So a main reason we need clarification is because otherwise scholars who think they are communicating with one another are really talking of somewhat different phenomena.
>
> (Quarantelli, 1995b: 224)

A failure to distinguish between emergency, crisis and disaster raises important questions for the validity of any synthesis between theory and practice. For this reason a working definition of the terms is given below. In a wider context, these terms are likely to remain problematic; therefore, it is argued that further work towards the definition of these terms is both a desirable and necessary feature of future research.

Emergencies

Emergencies can be defined as situations requiring a rapid and highly structured response where the risks for critical decision makers can, to a relative degree, be defined. A key feature of emergencies, as understood here, is that for those who manage such situations, conceptualization (or *mental modelling*) both appears and is sufficient to identify an appropriate and effective strategy.

In organizational terms, an emergency could represent a situation of danger that can be responded to using the normal contingencies and procedures as laid down typically in a management plan. For example, in the case of a fire emergency, buildings would be evacuated and staff would be moved to a pre-designated safe area.

Much of the existing academic literature on emergency management has been criticised for focusing too closely on the role of principal emergency response agencies (police, fire and ambulance) in the context of a highly structured response to incidents (Drabek, 1986; Dynes, 1994). It is argued here that if emergencies constitute highly structured situations, then much of this type of training may in fact be appropriate. However, for managing ill-structured scenarios, highly structured training may be more questionable.

Crises

Crises are also situations requiring a rapid response (for this reason they are all too easily misconceived as emergencies). In contrast, the risks for critical decision makers here are difficult to define owing to an ill-structure in the situation. It is typical for such situations that the effect of a response either is, or appears to be, unclear.

A working example here might be the same as given above for an emergency, but this time there is some added complicating factor (either social or physical ill-structure); this makes a structured response more difficult or even dangerous in its application. These factors could be numerous. For example, the fire has affected a vital manufacturing plant which produces a valuable component required for all of its products; or the building contains a dangerous chemical (or mixture of chemicals) which may cause an explosion; or the fire has been deliberately started by a deranged person who is threatening to kill the occupants or rescuers. A crisis, therefore, may not be immediately apparent to those decision makers responding to the situation. Crises may also go on to cause disasters and continue to occur long after the onset of a disaster.

The concept 'crisis' has not been very well researched. However, there is now a debate emerging among some contemporary theorists about response and management of crisis situations. A growing number of academic journals, conferences, seminars and workshops on the subject of response and management of crisis appear to support this assertion. The fact that many of these have emerged only recently may be an indication of the urgent need for further academic research on the concept of crisis.

Turner's systems work is helpful here in providing a theoretical context within which distinctions could be made. For example, crisis could be argued to correspond to stage four of Turner's model (see Chapter 2) for understanding socio-technical disasters, although the outcome need not progress to disaster as was suggested by the model. By concentrating on the positive features of response, much can be learnt from successfully managed incidents. This presents an opportunity for isomorphic learning as outlined by Toft and Reynolds (1994).

A number of theorists have acknowledged crises as distinct phenomena: 'There are a number of distinctive characteristics of a crisis' (Heinzen, 1996: 16). For Heinzen, there are four key characteristics. First, the crisis constitutes a series of events rather than the management of a single entity. Second, the crisis may be caused by a disaster (although no definition of disaster is provided by Heinzen). Heinzen does, however, acknowledge that the 'disaster' may not necessarily be a physical one. Third, the crisis has a diffuse origin making it difficult for decision makers to gain a macro view of events. Fourth, it is unclear what action needs to be taken (Heinzen, 1996: 16–17).

Many of Heinzen's points are congruent with the definitions given here and those offered by contemporary theorists. Crisis situations do pose a special problem, because despite giving the appearance to decision makers of an emergency, there are few signals to suggest a more serious underlying threat. Lagadec makes this point using the analogy of triggers: 'What is missing is the characteristic feature of an emergency: a clear trace that would justify triggering the warning procedures and mobilising resources' (Lagadec, 1995).

Lagadec also argues the need for training specifically geared towards crisis management. One reason he gives to support this is the value of training to bring about a crisis among decision makers. Lagadec comments on the reluctance of private industry, governments and NGOs to consider crisis decision making as evidence for this (Lagadec, 1993). This view is also congruent with the Dutch theorist Uriel

Rosenthal's definition of crisis as: 'a serious threat to the basic structures or the fundamental values and norms of a social system' (Rosenthal, 1996).

For both Lagadec and Rosenthal, the crisis can be found to operate at a social and cultural level by challenging the status quo. The crisis in this context could be perceived to be an affront to current knowledge and socially accepted notions of expertness. In contrast, some theorists have attempted to define crisis by distinguishing it from a disaster. For example, Goemans (1996) states: 'A crisis is different from a disaster in a number of ways.' Goemans then goes on to differentiate the two terms, using exactly the same four criteria as outlined for Heinzen above.

The central argument offered here is that crises are ill-structured situations both in terms of technical, social and cultural contexts. The greater the degree of ill-structure, then the more difficult the incident becomes for recognition and management; more agencies become involved and hence more social agendas become juxtaposed. It is this spiral which can lead to disaster.

Ill-structured crises are those which slip through the procedural net; this is why they are often misconceived to be acts of God, or totally unique abominations. This is not the case. Ill-structured crises and disasters are the rational result of operational systems, communications and organizational culture interacting to produce the circumstances required by a triggering mechanism. Crises may appear to be unique and tragic disasters due to their low frequency and high impact. However, in reality this is no more improbable than the chef's failed soufflé, because both the eggs were not fresh and the oven thermostat did not function properly. The good chef with skill may continue to get good results if only one part of the process is below standard, but it is the combination effect which will cause the inevitable disaster.

> The disaster must not be seen like the meteorite that falls out of the sky on an innocent world; the disaster, most often, is anticipated, and on multiple occasions.
>
> (Lagadec, 1982: 495)

Disasters

A *disaster* can be defined as a cultural construction of reality. Disaster is distinct from both emergency and crisis only in that physically it represents the product of the former. Disasters are the irreversible and typically overwhelming result of ill-handled emergency and crisis. 'Disasters do not cause effects. The effects are what we call a disaster' (Dombrowsky, 1995: 242).

Fundamental to the understanding given here is that specific socio-technical systems affected by disasters will have been indelibly challenged, possibly leading to inquiries at the highest social and cultural levels (the public inquiry in the UK is an example of this). This can be deemed similar to the definition of disaster given by Turner as an overturning of the cultural norms for dealing with hazards (Turner, 1978).

Responding to what is described as a disaster may typically involve dealing with a number of smaller ongoing crises and emergencies. Disaster is perhaps the most difficult phenomenon to define due to its apparent amorphous nature. In this case, using the analogy given for emergency and crisis, the disaster would have caused destruction and or serious loss of life. Response staff would be dealing with the failure to manage emergency and crisis.

A number of different context-specific ways of perceiving disaster have been proposed by contemporary theorists. The relevance of Turner's systems theory model has already been discussed in some detail and suggests an example. This approach argues that disaster is the collapse of cultural precautions for dealing with socio-technical phenomena in some systemic way (Turner, 1978; Horlick-Jones, 1995).

Another method for defining disaster in the literature is as an overwhelming situation; this could be in terms of human costs (lives lost) and financial loss or damage to social structures. This can also be expressed as insufficient resources to deal with the situation; for a commercial organization this might mean terminal insolvency. In this context, the disaster can be seen as 'social vulnerability' (Gilbert, 1995) or a 'lack of capacity' (Dombrowsky, 1995). Event quality also suggests a similar method for conceptualizing disaster. In this context it is again event typology, or severity, which can be used to gauge the disaster (Kroll-Smith and Couch, 1991; Dombrowsky, 1995; Gilbert, 1995).

Of concern is that many theorists still freely conflate the terms emergency, crisis and disaster in their work. It is perhaps easier to distinguish between emergencies and disasters in that the former at least presents a more structured and less overwhelming decision-making task. However, it is argued that problems of definition highlighted here represent a deeper form of misunderstanding. If one were to take a neo-relativist position, a disaster is nothing more than the social construction of symptoms from emergency and crisis.

In this respect disaster becomes reified as a cultural 'myth' given the status of physical phenomenon (Baudrillard, 1988; Horlick-Jones, 1995). To reify disaster as anything more than this would attribute disaster with the status of agency – a Hobbesian

Leviathan which must be resisted, or what Giddens refers to as the 'dark side of modernity' (Giddens, 1991).

Responding to crisis

The term 'crisis' needs to be understood if it is to be effectively addressed in a training environment. Crises typically develop fast, confronting decision makers with large quantities of conflicting or erroneous information. Conversely, a crisis may bring about a complete lack of available information to decision makers. Decision makers may even have to operate with less information than the media. It is certainly not unusual for a crisis to receive heavy and close monitoring by the media. With modern communication facilities, the media are often more up to date than the decision makers who are attempting to respond. For example, live pictures of the events of 9/11 were broadcast as the situation unfolded. The image of the crisis portrayed by the media may have to be dealt with at the same time as the crisis itself; sometimes this can even pose the greatest difficulties (Booth, 2000). Structured and inflexible plans, ironically developed for safety reasons, can in this context become one of the major focuses for the media.

It is, therefore, very important for trainers to understand the concept 'crisis' as distinct from 'emergencies' or 'disasters', particularly when designing training exercises (Borodzicz, 1997, 1999a, 1999b).

Emergencies are situations requiring rapid applications of an organization's existing policies and procedures. Simulated emergencies are, therefore, tests or drills used to practise or evaluate the behaviour of key personnel in their performance. In this context both the problem and solutions are not problematic so rules and procedures can be adhered to without question. Simulations are of value here in providing an experiential learning context for the players. Highly disciplined, often militaristic models of training are effective for emergencies, as decision makers need to select an appropriate and rehearsed training strategy and apply it with skill and precision. These exercises are also of use to test the use of equipment and facilities.

In contrast, crisis events will require players to make significant changes to the operating procedures while responding to the crisis event. This may even mean changes to the appointed crisis team itself! The Chinese definition of crisis provides an interesting and useful analogy; viewed as a 'turning point', the crisis presents both 'dangers' and 'opportunities' (Capra, 1975). Hence, crises become a turning point for those responding because of the potential opportunities. The Chinese word for crisis is formed by joining together two different characters. The first character, 'danger', is followed by a second, 'opportunity'. It is worth noting that the Chinese word for 'crisis' is not a new concept; in fact this written form dates back over a thousand years. Within the Chinese conception, solutions to the crisis may well require an unorthodox response while presenting new opportunities for the organization. This approach is congruent with the portrayal of crisis by Sundelius (1998), who argues that decision makers must take up 'opportunities' for reform, innovation and leadership.

How we conceive dangerous events will remain problematic. In this chapter we have discussed one methodology for doing this, by viewing events from the perspective of response. Typology and severity do provide an apparently pragmatic methodology. While these ways of managing the data can provide a pragmatic approach to classifying data, it is questionable whether these criteria will assist in understanding and managing the aetiology of such events.

Using 'emergency', 'crisis' and 'disaster' as conceptual categories will not in itself make the problem go away. The definitions which have been offered for these terms in this chapter are themselves problematic, although they do at least provide a way in which theorists might consider the requirements to facilitate management and response.

Chapter 5

BUSINESS CONTINUITY MANAGEMENT

> There is nothing more difficult to take in hand, more perilous to conduct, or more uncertain of success than to take a lead in the introduction of a new order of things, because the innovation has for enemies all those who have done well under the old conditions and lukewarm defenders in those who may do well under the new.
>
> (Machiavelli, *The Prince*)

'Business continuity management' is a new area of professional activity, but also an area of academic study and research, which aims to facilitate the mitigation of emergencies, crises and disasters in organizations. One theorist argues that, business continuity planning may in fact be defined as: 'thinking the unthinkable or mitigate the unthinkable' (Ginn, 1992).

The most serious risk that can be posed to any organization is survival. This area of increasing concern is referred to as 'business continuity' or 'contingency management'; also sometimes as 'crisis management'. The need for improved business continuity management (BCM) is increasingly accepted as sensible and pragmatic (Rolfe *et al.*, 1998). This has been accompanied by the emergence of a number of practitioner-based associations. For example, the Business Continuity Institute has a large and rapidly growing membership in over 20 countries which are graded in accordance with perceived ability and experience. Further evidence of interest can be found in the growing number and popularity of international conferences and workshops on the subject (BFI, Survive, HO Emergency Planning College). The UK government has also demonstrated interest in promoting BCM through a number of Home Office documents (HMSO, 1997, 1998, 2003) and ministerial attendance at some of the workshops. UK interest in BCM faded temporarily after the year 2000, as many businesses felt that the concerted approach to confronting the millennium computer bug, promoted by Prime Minister Tony Blair, had become a non-event.

However, since then interest in BCM has again increased, following renewed activity by international terrorists and 11 September 2001. The focus of much of the regulatory control has now moved towards bringing about two separate but focused objectives: compliance with regulatory pressure (Cadbury, 1992; Hampel, 1998; Turnbull, 1999), and resilience (HMSO, 2004).*

Business continuity management, or at least a plan for it, is today a requirement for nearly every large organization. The trend in recent years for leaner organizations, outsourcing many of their functions and maintaining low stock levels, has become mainstream teaching in our top management schools. One could argue that the entire thrust of what is taught as operational research (OR) aims to achieve just that. The effect of this is to create organizations where important functions are funnelled through key buildings, processes or technologies. When things work, you have one of the most efficient means of production known to human history. When the system breaks down these organizations can demonstrate a lack of capability to absorb and respond to the crisis.

The pure and speculative divide discussed in Chapter 1 is problematic as far as business continuity is concerned.† This distinction no longer holds for most contemporary organizations. For example, the loss of a building and its contents, while catastrophic, is theoretically replaceable by insurance. The building is, however, less important than the processes that took place within it. The loss of systems and the technical, human and the complex interactions between them are potentially more serious. Buildings do not make or do anything; it is the people and processes contained within them that make a product or service come about.

Many university management and business schools are beginning to recognize the importance of business continuity in their curricula, but coverage is still patchy at best. Where courses are offered, these are normally options, rather than core, and often restricted to very specialized master degrees. This is surprising, as it is hard to imagine a management activity that is not closer to the heart of corporate life. Business continuity

---

* The terms 'resilience' and 'homeland defence' appear to have replaced earlier initiatives on civil contingency planning.

† Pure risks or 'acts of God', such as fires, floods, land movements or storm damage are examples of these. Speculative risks are the business failures that entrepreneurs entered into willingly (see Chapter 1).

planning is about achieving a balance between preparing for situations in which contingency plans will have to be used, while at the same time doing everything conceivable to stop them ever having to be used.

The problem in education is one of compartmentalization. Business continuity is a fundamental aspect of modern corporate management, which should acknowledge that training must include a large number of diverse theoretical disciplines. Hence if one were to construct a discipline of business continuity management, the syllabus might contain at least some of the following:

- General management theory
- Emergency planning
- Risk assessment
- Crisis management
- Simulations and gaming
- Target hardening
- IT management and cybercrime
- Security management
- Health and safety
- Human resource management
- Insurance
- Systems and social networks
- Team and group analysis
- Terrorism
- Situational crime risk
- Organizational psychology
- Legal studies
- Trauma counselling
- Whistle-blowers

This list could certainly continue, but the point is to demonstrate the multidisciplinary nature and range of skills that practitioners might desire. It is certainly not possible to cover all of these issues in sufficient detail within one piece of work.

This chapter will view the development of business continuity management, and review a number of strategies available to identify, assess and minimize known risks. The chapter also considers the role of the emergency services. Organizational risk and security needs to understand how the emergency services operate and communicate, and what restrictions their activities may have on the management of an organization during and after a crisis. This is also significant because many large organizations already use contingency plans which are similar to, or based on, those of the emergency services. This similarity is no accident, as emphasized in earlier chapters; many risk and security staff are ex-police officers enjoying a second career. It is therefore hardly surprising that many emergency plans look very similar. Readers may wish to consider the appropriateness of these plans in the context of non-disciplined, large, corporate organization contexts.

The development of business continuity management

Elliott *et al.* suggest that the evolution of BCM can be divided into three phases: 'technology', 'auditing' and 'value-based' (Elliott *et al.*, 2002).*

In the *first phase* during the 1970s and 1980s the focus was on *technology*. Business continuity planning was about the protection of hardware systems vital to organizational performance. As organizations began to transfer administrative operations from human to computer systems, the impact of computer failure began to take on serious operational significance. A loss of IT systems can have a rapid and catastrophic effect on an organization.

This first phase of BCM has grown considerably in recent years with an increasing prevalence of IT systems in virtually all aspects of organizational life. It is hard to think of an organization where the computer is not vital to successful operation. In this respect BCM is about the prudent management of IT resources in a large corporate system. Triggers are likely to be external physical factors, for example, flood, fire, power failure or terrorist attack. Hence the focus of response for these types of scenario is likely to be on the ability of an organization to arrange alternative sites and sufficiently rich back-up systems to enable it to continue to function after the failure. A number of commercial organizations already offer sophisticated IT back-up system services for these types of eventuality; very large organizations are likely to be able to do this themselves.

The *second phase* of BCM outlined by Elliott *et al.* began during the 1980s and 1990s. This second phase can be characterized as a shift in emphasis to the auditing of organizational systems in order to achieve *compliance* with corporate governance and regulatory pressures. Organizations are now under a greater degree of regulatory control than ever before. The importance of this topic has been mentioned already in relation to security and health and safety. In addition to government regulation, there have been a number of new initiatives requiring compliance originating from within industry itself. For example, prior to the year 2000, many organizations ensured that their IT systems were protected from the millennium bug. While the risk perception of the problem

---

* Elliot *et al.* is perhaps the most authoritative academic work on the subject of business continuity to have been published at the time of writing. Students and practitioners with an interest in business continuity would do well to study this text.

was far in excess of actual threat, organizations that had not had their systems checked could be blacklisted as either suppliers or customers of other organizations.

A growing international trend of tightened corporate governance and control has emerged during the last 20 years for large commercial organizations (Cadbury, 1992; Hampel, 1998; Turnbull, 1999; KonTrag, 1998, in Germany; and Sarbanes-Oxley, 2002, in the USA), amidst some spectacular corporate collapses and disasters, such as Perrier, Enron, Anderson and Barings. Similar initiatives in public service organizations have also been introduced in healthcare, education and transport. The recommendations of Turnbull suggest company directors can face personal liability for business failures. Company auditors, for example, would be expected to require and review compliance statements. It is difficult to assess the impact of these initiatives on corporate governance for individual members of staff although, under British common law, individual staff members prosecuted for failure to exercise due care might wish to use the absence of a corporate plan/procedures as a defence.

Good corporate governance is suddenly no longer an optional extra. In the early 1990s, some 30% of organizations had some form of contingency plan (Hearndon, 1993; Elliott *et al.*, 2002). Ten years later, nearly every large organization operating in the European or US context must comply with a complex 'latticework' of regulatory requirements. Interwoven among these requirements are industry-specific forms of regulation, such as the security industry association regulation and licensing of security guards and standards of practice, for example ISO 9000, BS 7799. Organizations need to comply with more than one set of regulations, which may have inconsistencies in application.

The *third phase* of business continuity management outlined by Elliott *et al.* is described as the '*value-based*' phase. Here the emphasis moves beyond compliance to understanding how the organization works, and improving performance. BCM in this phase is not just about minimizing downside risks, but also recognizing that human and social risks are as important, if not more so.

It is suggested here that the very nature of many organizational systems may represent a constraining factor for crisis management. Most organizations typically consist of a number of separate departments staffed by appropriate experts. Such organizations are often portrayed in diagrams which look like Darwin's theory of evolution inverted. Typically, in such structures communication will take place vertically rather than horizontally. In any case experts will by nature be interested in risks pertinent to their own sphere of interest. The key issue here is in designing '*resilience*' (Home Office, 1997a) into the organizational structure without constraining the purpose for existing.

The organizational structure in which system failure takes place can also contribute to the risk. Tightly coupled systems as described in Chapter 2 (see Perrow, 1984) tend to be rigidly controlled from the centre of operations. Operators in such systems are trained to adhere strictly to prescribed rules and procedures (created, ironically, for safety reasons) but these can act to limit the scope for innovative and flexible responses by operators confronted with risky situations. One key feature found in the successful management of ill-structured crisis situations is the flexibility of working arrangements. Yet this is in stark contrast to the highly structured and inflexible procedures characteristic of most security arrangements (Borodzicz *et al.*, 1993; Borodzicz and Pidgeon, 1996).

In most organizations it is not clear who is responsible for the management of total risk and there is unlikely to be a central department whose task it is to collate all the potential risks. As discussed in Chapter 3, typically, responsibility for both risk and security is a compartmentalized affair, which can impede an organization's ability to recognize, learn from and recover from a crisis. The division of risk analysis means that different parts of the organization become managed as sub-systems in their own right, and little attention is paid to the interaction of these sub-systems. The only risks taken seriously are those threatening the integrity of a sub-system, but these are themselves defined by experts in that sub-system. Such discrete risk analysis is unlikely to take account of the global effects of system failures.

Identifying and assessing known risks

Identifying risk for an organization is a time-consuming task and if not handled well can result in no more than a 'tick box' approach, often heavily criticized by those who are against regulation. Risk identification involves listing and reviewing every type of risk that an organization might conceivably face (this may not actually be possible, but it is still important to try to do this). It is important, at this stage, that both 'pure' and 'speculative' risks are included in the identification and that the process covers all levels of the organizational hierarchy. Experience suggests that some of the most pertinent and difficult to manage risks are often handled at a junior level. When done constructively, there are obvious links here to bringing about a good 'safety' or 'risk culture' within the organization by involving more junior staff in the risk and security problem.

Effects of human behaviour on management strategies should also be considered. Is the organizational structure and culture flexible enough to be able to cope with sudden shifts in business requirements or changing markets? To what extent are risks being rationally appraised? The work on irrationality by psychologists suggests that our judgements about risks are liable to influence by mitigating factors (Otway and Von Winterfeldt, 1982, in Royal Society, 1992). The homeostasis model also suggests that the very process of managing or reducing a particular risk exposure, if not sensitively handled, might simply move the risk somewhere else.

The risk assessment should also encompass a thorough *security survey*. There are a number of security surveys on the market. Generally it is acknowledged that there are three distinct phases to the process (Hearndon and Moore, 1999). First is to identify risks, which include *physical assets*, *personnel*, *information*, potential areas of *liability* and *business interruption*. Often because of the way risk, legal issues, personnel and security are managed separately in organizations, the survey is not coordinated properly.

A survey of physical assets should consider the environment of the organization and how that space might need to be defended. One problem here is the extent to which an organization is still able to function effectively when secure. While the overall effect of security in commercial aviation over recent years has been to increase the security of passengers, the great benefit of air travel (at least for short-haul flights) – speed – seems to have become lost in the security checks. Similarly, the best way to manage the risk and security of a university department, library or hospital might be to not let people in. In terms of the organizational purpose for existing, this would constitute an organizational disaster. Security then, like risk, is about finding a socially acceptable balance.

Another approach is to look at the environment in which security is a potential problem. An environmental approach to crime prevention originated from the work of Oscar Newman (1972, 1976) and Barry Poyner (1983). The idea is based on *crime prevention through environmental design (CPTED)*. CPTED works on the basis of a reduced likelihood of crime through the design of a defensible environment based on an enhanced criminal risk perception. The context to CPTED is a diverse mix of behavioural theory from psychology and the social sciences, physical and urban design, and community organizational theory (Hearndon and Moore, 1999).

CPTED is about understanding the designated use of an area: providing good lighting and the avoidance of high-growing shrubs and trees or other obstructions to surveillance of strategically placed potential crime targets. Good crime analysis and an understanding and control of through traffic is also important. Ideally this is built in at the design phase of a building. It is not always possible to do this when the organization has changed its purpose or when working within the confines of older buildings areas!

Target hardening normally encompasses three issues. First, conducting a *risk assessment* (likelihood vs. impact), then dealing with issues of *physical security* and finally conducting a *security survey*.

Particular attention needs to be given to such obvious target hardening techniques as perimeter barriers (doors, windows, lighting, security glazing, roofs, etc.). Alarms, CCTV and entry access control systems are another issue. Again there is a concern with compliance with rules and regulations about the monitoring of these devices (Button and George, 2000), which can vary from country to country. While the main aim of physical security in this context is to 'deter, delay and detect' (Hearndon and Moore, 1999), it is also important to remember that this may conflict with contingency arrangements for when people may also need to leave urgently! One very good reason for unifying the processes of both security and risk management from a business continuity perspective is to resolve these conflicts centrally.

The risk matrix

Each department or business function would need to assess the 'range', 'type', 'frequency' and 'importance' of activities in which they are involved and assess the associated risks of these. Each risk can then be evaluated in terms of a simple matrix where impact is scored against frequency (Figure 5.1).

In Figure 5.1, risks can be scored individually on a subjective basis. In the case shown the evaluation is medium (value '2') for both frequency and impact, thus scoring 4. Risk high in both frequency and impact, scoring '9', would need to be considered very seriously indeed. For most organizations subject to rules of corporate governance this is already a standard requirement.

Impact

	Low	Medium	High	Totals	Frequency
Low				1	
Medium		X		(2)	
High				3	
Totals	1	(2)	3	4	

Figure 5.1   A simple risk matrix

It is important to recognize, however, that these scores are subjective; hence wherever it is reasonably practical, some type of qualitative understanding should be added showing how the risk is embedded within the organization's critical processes. Would the same risk in another part of the organization be scored differently?

> Risk management has been described as an 'art', because creativity seems to play an important role....The activities that constitute one organisation's risk control efforts may be quite different from the efforts of a similar organisation in another part of the world.
>
> (Williams *et al.*, 1995)

There are a number of advantages to this process. First, it simplifies what at first appears to be a daunting task by breaking risk management down into manageable units. Second, each part of the organization can be involved in the risk management process, and despite the inadequacies of the data produced, a guide is provided to some of the major risks. The positive value in terms of involving more junior staff in this process cannot be discounted. Third (and perhaps the most obvious advantage), is that many large organizations subject to rules of governance and compliance are already obliged to carry out these assessments anyway.*

In Table 5.1, clearly Risks 9, 3, 1 and 4 might merit more careful consideration than the others. In this example the scales for 'impact' and 'likelihood' are graded 1 to 10.

There are also some serious concerns about this methodology. But any analysis that does not give consideration to a risk with either a high impact or likelihood would be a concern. It is also important to consider motives and biases that might influence those carrying out the scoring process. Staff may wish to emphasize the importance of their own function in an organization, play down another process or even try to get rid of a responsibility altogether. Alternatively, if the process is seen as just another

---

* In the UK, many large public organizations – such as the health service, local government and education – are already obliged to carry out risk identification and assessments of the risk matrix type. For example, HEFCE (the Higher Education Funding Council for England and Wales) demands that all universities now conduct a review of risks to be rated by impact versus frequency (HEFCE, 2001). Even where the requirement is not direct, it might be implied through subsequent litigation after a breach of risk or security. This could be in the form of litigation claims, or refusal of insurance.

Table 5.1 Example of risk assessments contrasted

	Likelihood	Impact	Risk score
Risk 1	7	6	42
Risk 2	3	8	24
Risk 3	6	9	54
Risk 4	7	6	42
Risk 5	2	5	10
Risk 6	3	7	21
Risk 7	4	3	12
Risk 8	2	1	2
Risk 9	10	8	80
Risk 10	8	3	24

Source: Reproduced from *Risk Management: A Guide to Good Practice for Higher Education Institutions*. HEFCE, 2001

kind of organizational interference in work, the whole thing might be simply made up – an example of one of the worst problems with compliance. It may not be possible to evaluate the global impact on an organization of a risk when viewed from the perspective of a single process or departmental perspective. There is also a concern about risk myopia. What if a risk is not identified or the organization changes either staff, systems or activities after the assessment has taken place? Clearly, if this process is to work at all, then it needs to be under a constant state of review.

Organizations also have other types of risk data available to them, but are often reluctant to utilize this for litigious reasons. For example, changes to health, safety and employment law have not been mirrored by practice in the workplace. The number of potentially litigious staff claims has increased to the point where the activity of employment poses a number of serious risks in itself. Many of these cases started out as cases of *whistle-blowing*.

Whistle-blowing

'Whistle-blowing' is a new name for an old practice. While not normally a topic associated with security management, whistle-blowing is a subject overdue for serious consideration by risk and security managers. There are a number of alternative terms often used to describe the practice: 'conscientious objector', 'ethical resister', 'mole', 'informer', 'concerned employee', 'rat', 'licensed spy', etc.

Whistle-blowing, traditionally, has been thought of in negative terms; for the perpetrator personally, the experience is usually not a good one. There is little legislation around to protect them and they usually have to pay a very high price in terms of subsequent employability. Often, whistle-blowers find their careers ruined, unable to practise their former work. Some influential voices, however, have begun to suggest that whistle-blowers – rather than being disloyal – deserve praise and should be recognized as good corporate citizens.

So what exactly is whistle-blowing? Vinten defines it thus:

> The unauthorised disclosure of information that an employee reasonably believes is evidence of the contravention of any law, rule or regulation, code of practice, or professional statement, or that involves mismanagement, corruption, abuse of authority, or danger to public or worker health and safety.
>
> (Vinten, 1994: 5)

Whistle-blowing refers to a wide range of activities that are dissimilar from a moral point of view. Students, for example, could be said to be blowing the whistle on fellow students who cheat; employees may make disclosures to directors about misconduct.

Usually this type of whistle-blowing is referred to as *internal* and is made on the understanding that the report will be followed up and a sanction imposed. In contrast, and perhaps more serious, is *external* whistle-blowing. External whistle-blowing occurs usually because the complainant believes that internal complaints either have been or would be a waste of time. It is also potentially more damaging to both accuser and accused.

The career of the whistle-blower has been compared to that of a bee, in that they have only one sting and must therefore use it at the point of maximum damage. Once this has been used then they are at the mercy of their victims' retribution. Studies of whistle-blowers show them to be generally quite conservative in temperament and devoted to their work, and usually in their thirties and forties. Whistle-blowing usually results from either a request to do something illegal or having witnessed an illegal act.

As early as 1989 Glazer and Glazer did a study of whistle-blowing and found that it usually led to career disruption and often personal abuse. Another study of 161 whistle-blowers found similar findings with over 80% experiencing severe retaliation.

In one unfortunate case, Stanley Adams, a former executive of the Swiss pharmaceutical manufacturer Hoffman La Roche, was imprisoned under Swiss law for exposing price-fixing methods to the European Commission. He was subsequently given no support from the EU although he experienced his wife's 'probable' suicide and financial ruin. There was a subsequent film made of the tragedy, called *A Song for Europe*.

> Virtually all of the ethical resisters we studied had long histories of successful employment...they began as firm believers in their organisations, convinced that if they took a grievance to superiors, there would be an appropriate response. This naivety led them into a series of damaging traps. They found that their earlier service and dedication provided them with little protection against charges of undermining organisational morale and effectiveness.
>
> (Glazer and Glazer, 1989)

The UK Public Interest Disclosure Act 1998 aims to encourage organizations to permit employees to raise concerns anonymously and in confidence. Where possible, it is recommended that the whistle-blowing process be operated by a third party. The aim of the 1998 Act is to tackle a culture of silence by providing protection in law for whistle-blowers who follow the Act's guidelines.

Issues covered by the UK whistle-blowing legislation are far-reaching, including public dangers (both potential and real), working conditions and stress, financial malpractice (fraud), breaches of legal obligations (including regulation and codes of professional conduct), environmental damage, security breaches, health and safety, discrimination, pilfering and property theft.

What the Act does for the first time is protect whistle-blowers by wherever possible encouraging employees to raise concerns anonymously and in confidence using a telephone hotline operated by a third party. It is argued by many theorists that, properly handled, whistle-blowing could avert serious disasters and crises for organizations by opening up the informal organization to scrutiny. Frank Heinrich-Jones argued that many serious disasters such as the Zeebrugge ferry disaster, Piper Alpha, the BCCI collapse, and the problems at Bristol Royal Infirmary could all have been prevented had whistle-blowers been heeded (Heinrich-Jones, 1999: 23–24).

Four strategies for managing risk

Having decided what the risks are, the next stage is to choose an appropriate strategy to deal with the risks. Most theorists would argue that there are four key ways to deal with risk.

Risk avoidance

Can you avoid the risk completely? For example, if you have laboratories or danger-ous chemicals, or if the organization's sole purpose is to carry out work of a politically or ethically sensitive nature – e.g. abortions – risk avoidance might not be an option. Similar issues surround transport or medicine. State healthcare is a good example here; despite the obvious risks and litigation, operations and treatment are obliged to continue for the public good.

Risk transfer

If stopping the risk is not a possibility then could the risk be subcontracted or insured? This would mean higher costs to maintain the activity but at least it would be retained. This can be problematic, as it is not possible to subcontract every-thing; some part of the responsibility will have to remain, if only the management of the process. In some circumstances, there may even be legislature that restricts the right to subcontract an activity. Even in almost completely subcontracted organizations – such as the railways in the UK, where different parts of the system are owned and operated by separate organizations – when there is an accident the litigation will bounce around until it finds evidence of negligence and then it will stick.

Even where the risk can be bought out through insurance, this often comes with preconditions for cover which require the organization to put in place a range of target hardening measures. Organizations may also be obliged to consider how they would respond to minimize the effects of a risk failure through contingency planning.

Risk retention

One can decide not to insure against certain activities. This may already be an imposed condition by insurance companies, through a refusal to provide cover. Continuation with activities where insurance has been refused should only take place after careful consideration (Beck's theory from Chapter 2 is pertinent here!).

Organizations should also take steps to identify risks and evaluate them in terms of likelihood and impact on the organization's activities. The decision to retain a risk may come about as a result of consideration through the risk matrix.

Risk reduction

There are two possible approaches here. One is to use *target hardening* techniques to try and reduce the likelihood; the other is to deal with the impact. There is a range of possibilities here, which come at different costs. One should be aware that the amount spent on 'target hardening' or 'mitigation' does not always equate to the level of protection actually obtained. Systems may also be of benefit only when augmented by human systems of security and the use of *project risk management approaches** and *soft system approaches* developed in operational research.

Dealing with unknown risks

The chapter so far has dealt with risks that we are able to identify. While the strategies for dealing with them are not perfect, they are the best that we have got. We need to ask ourselves why organizations fail despite good risk planning. It is suggested here that the area most in need of research and development in risk management is crisis management. A danger in carrying out risk and security assessments is that we may not even be looking at the right organization. Weir argues that all organizations exist only in a *degraded mode*. Constant shifts in organizational purpose and staff, self-interest groups and intra-organization conflicts render any process of risk assessment/identification almost out of date as soon as it is completed. Added to this is the whole invisible culture, 'how things really work here', that provides key movers with the ability to make short cuts and engage in minor rule breaking (Weir, 1996).

All complex and sociotechnical systems tend to operate in a degraded mode. Under normal operating conditions, the actual state of the system will usually

---

* See Chapman and Ward, 2002.

contain improvements, short cuts, error-correcting routines and other elements 'patched' into the system in response to local failures...

(Weir, 1996)

A lot of research has been carried out in the area of emergency management and disaster response. How organizations successfully emerge from a crisis is, however, more controversial.

Organizations are under pressure to respond to crisis situations for two reasons. First, a crisis will affect an organization's ability to trade with potential implications for profit, reputation and survival; the Anderson case was an example of this. Second, a crisis can also rapidly descend into media speculation about organizational dealings and affairs, making it impossible to function normally.

This poses a number of problems to which the answers are far from clear. Who within the organization should be responsible for BCM? How should they be trained? Can such training be evaluated or validated in any effective way? Who can be relied on to carry out the training?

One organization attempting to address these issues is the Business Continuity Institute (BCI), formed in 1994. The long-term aim of the BCI is to bring about professionalism to the business continuity industry through accredited training for its members, based on ten 'disciplines'. Many of these disciplines overlap with some of the issues discussed in this chapter and the next.

The ten disciplines of business continuity management

1. Project initiation and management
2. Risk evaluation and control
3. Business impact analysis
4. Developing business continuity strategies
5. Emergency response and operations
6. Developing and implementing business continuity plans
7. Awareness and training programmes
8. Maintaining and exercising business continuity plans
9. Public relations and crisis coordination
10. Coordination with public authorities

(Sharp, 1999)

An ability to respond to crisis events is, it is argued here, as important as the very risk management measures taken to prevent them. This point cannot be emphasized too strongly! In Chapter 2, a variety of risk management theories were presented. While all of these theories offer a sophisticated analysis of how risk comes about, there is still no complete method of risk management. Frequently, organizations put all their efforts into risk assessment and prevention, under a misguided assumption that risk can be effectively squeezed out of the system. A dangerous trend towards the tick box culture, safety cases and finitely engineered project risk management approaches, while sometimes useful, cannot guarantee 100% protection. Hence a generic ability to respond to crisis events is a pragmatic business need for any organization. This process – sometimes described as 'crisis management', 'contingency planning' or 'business continuity planning' – may also have added peace-time effects. When practised properly, crisis management can enable organizations to take up opportunities. Corporate activity, whether for profit or public service provision, will involve taking risks. As soon as any organization begins to function it is therefore at risk.

There are a number of traditional indicators of an organization's performance and effectiveness in its field of operation. For example, profitability, efficiency, market share, innovation, staff or customer loyalty, quality of product/service and share price are criteria frequently used to evaluate effective operational management.

The ultimate acid test for any management system, whether applied to commercial or social goals, is the ability to control strategic viability within the organization while still maintaining an operational capability. Indicators of good BCM practice for strategic management contexts are more difficult to identify. Risks posed by criminal fraud, strategic systems failure, extreme weather and the effect of those with a grievance against the organization can be equally catastrophic in effect and should also be taken seriously as a threat to strategic viability.

For most organizations, coping with crisis situations will require a new approach to training and management. When a crisis does occur, it is often of a highly unpredictable nature and may overwhelm key decision makers by speed of onset and ill-structure. Stage three of Turner's model in Chapter 2 provides a good context in which to consider the crisis. The problem is that our response to these types of incidents is at best dependent on our definition of what is happening. When interdepartmental and even inter-organizational situations occur, the potential for differing or multiple perceptions are increased (Browning and Shetler, 1992).

One key problem is that those members of an organization with the responsibility for its safe running and operation do not have, in the context of the organization's safety culture, any historical reasons to suspect that these problems are in fact latent incubating system faults. 'Accidents do not occur because people gamble and lose, they occur because people do not believe that the accident that is about to occur is at all possible' (Reason, 1997: 39).

When minor problems do become apparent they may be perceived as normal operational difficulties, rather than system faults which violate the integrity of the system itself. Perhaps the key questions for anyone in the organization brave enough to question the highly structured approach are: what constitutes an extreme situation and how can we recognize the triggers?

The emergency services

One way organizations might approach BCM is by learning from the experience of the emergency services. These organizations have considerable experience and expertise in the area of emergency response almost as a daily activity. The emergency services already have a range of training programmes. It could be argued that many organizations have already imported the emergency services model. Many organizational security or risk employees are frequently ex-police or military personnel, and hence they often bring much cultural baggage with them (Borodzicz, 1997).

Until very recently the emphasis among the emergency service organizations was to produce rigorous and highly detailed plans and command structures for emergency situations. These would be supported by a number of simulation exercises run in desktop and realistic settings. 'Command and control', 'tactical, strategic and operational' or 'gold, silver and bronze' are examples of highly structured command structures based on highly disciplined 'top-down' militaristic modes of operation. Typically such an approach would include extensive use of checklists, pre-drilled response techniques and communication procedures. Borodzicz (1997) found that such a disciplined and preordained response was acknowledged to be essential. However, for ill-structured crisis situations, a very different response style was needed, based on flexibility and negotiation – concepts alien to the emergency services and the military in both staff selection procedures and training. Ill-structured crises are a challenge to any preconceived emergency plan, as the scenario never quite fits the preconceived preparations.

The Civil Contingencies Bill in the UK (HMSO, 2004) represents one of the most radical overhauls of the way government handles national or 'homeland security'. The bill represents a shift away from 'civil defence', largely inherited from the Second World War, to a more unified and government-controlled approach to response.

The bill offers some positive and much needed changes to existing arrangements. Much of the early part of the bill is actually devoted to defining 'emergencies', although the bill still does not distinguish between events from a response perspective as suggested in the last chapter. However, much of the bill uses language reflecting a need to establish flexible approaches to training and preparations. The bill also greatly extends the government's powers to intervene and take control during situations defined as an emergency.

For the emergency services, there is a long tradition of training decision makers to manage events using a variety of well-rehearsed and structured response techniques. While these agencies are generally very good at responding to emergency events, there are acknowledged difficulties in managing crisis events where there is a need to operate outside this framework (Borodzicz, 2000; Lagadec, 1997; Turner, 1994). Typically, this would involve a multi-agency environment where decision makers must make do with incomplete, missing, misleading or overwhelming information.

A number of high-profile UK disasters such as the King's Cross underground fire (Fennell, 1988), the *Marchioness* river boat disaster (Hayes, 1992) and football disasters such as Bradford and Hillsborough (Frosdick and Sidney, 1997) have highlighted the difficulties posed to officers from all three services in responding to both the physical and social dimensions of these incidents. Terrorist outrages of the kind seen more recently are a more serious concern; obviously one overriding interest here is the threat posed to human life. However, attacks (and the threat of attacks) against targets such as financial areas, airports and other transport hubs pose an equally difficult challenge in terms of response. Terrorist threats, when actualized, can even cause social and economic impacts equalling those of natural disasters, such as earthquakes, fires and floods. The Twin Towers outrage in New York, for example, could be compared in physical terms to the energy released by a small nuclear warhead, at least in terms of impact. The rise in concerns about the chemical and biological capability of international terrorists are also a significant social concern.

For the three primary UK emergency services, competency requirements for key decision makers are still very much based on rank rather than proven skill or ability. Such skills might be reinforced through the attendance of in-service training programmes, but little in the way of competency assessment is carried out for officers designated as incident commanders. For the police, this might include attendance on the MODACE (management of disaster and civil emergencies) course; the fire service also runs a similar (brigade management) course. These courses currently operate in a residential format; attendees are presented with a week-long series of lectures. Learning is therefore passive, and it is not even required for participants to attend the entire course. While the content and delivery of these courses is currently under review for both organizations, to date these courses have no assessed element, although at the time of writing this is being considered.

The primary motive for response to crisis in the three principal services can be viewed as three different approaches to the same basic problem – saving lives. While all three services are concerned with the protection and saving of life in major crisis situations, their ways of achieving this are different and over the years (with the introduction of advanced technology) have become so highly sophisticated that most people are largely unaware of what they can now do. The police have skills in the management of people and are able to quickly mount a communications context and sterile area in which other response services can operate. The fire service is expert in the treatment of hazardous phenomena (not just fires), and the rescue of trapped people. The ambulance service – rather than simply providing a transportation medium for the sick, infirm and injured – also now carry paramedics and some quite sophisticated medical diagnostic and life-saving equipment (legally paramedics are the only people, other than doctors, permitted to carry out diagnostic procedures, administer drugs and treatment to patients). Although this system varies slightly from one country to another, particularly with variations in the command structure, overall this division holds.

For the emergency services, simulations and training exercises offer staff the only means to understand and participate in disaster management before a real event occurs. Simulated training exercises can also be used to train organizations which need to work together in order to deal with disasters. Multiservice response exercises are increasingly recognized as of value and importance for the emergency services. This is highlighted in many of the recent official reports produced by both the government and the emergency services themselves (HSE, 1991; HMSO, 1992a; LESLP, 1992).

It would be pertinent to consider some contextual information relating to the hierarchical structure of the response services, and the historic reasons for their present manifestation. It is further worth mentioning that the response arrangements in the UK are regionalized; arrangements, although similar, may vary slightly from area to area.

Primarily the police have a coordinating role in major emergencies. Police staff are equipped with only rudimentary skills in first aid and fire-fighting, but their main role is to facilitate the other agencies by providing them with a sterile area to operate in, and access routes to and from the scene. The police operate a management structure known as 'gold/silver/bronze' for dealing with major incidents. This is in order to coordinate the police presence. Bronze level corresponds to 'officers on the ground', providing a visible police presence. Silver level can be characterized as the frenzied 'control' or 'incident room', set up at the local police station coordinating the local response. In contrast, gold command can be portrayed as a remote police headquarters, where major policy decisions and agreement to strategic resources can be made by very senior officers. The gold commanders should thus be able to take a global overview of the situation; in practice this may also be true for silver.

The best (unrestricted) description of the UK emergency services' command structures and procedures for a major incident can be found in the Home Office publication *Dealing with Disaster*, first published in 1992 and now in a fourth edition (2004). This gives general principles for the operational management of major incidents and defines command as 'the authority for an agency to direct the actions of its own resources (both personnel and equipment)'. The term 'control' is defined as 'the authority to direct strategic and tactical operations in order to complete an assigned function and includes the ability to direct the activities of other agencies engaged in the completion of that function'. The police typically have a coordinating role and responsibility for control of the disaster site, although control of specific functions – e.g. rescue or medical evacuation – may be assigned to one of the other emergency services.

According to the UK Home Office publication *Dealing with Disasters* (Home Office, 1997) the police and fire service definition of a 'major incident' is as follows:

> A major incident is any emergency that requires the implementation of special arrangements by one or more of the emergency services, the NHS or the local authority for:
>
> a. the initial treatment, rescue and transport of a large number of casualties;
> b. the involvement either directly or indirectly of large numbers of people;
> c. the handling of a large number of enquiries likely to be generated both from the public and the news media usually to the police;
> d. the need for the large scale combined resources of two or more of the emergency services;
> e. the mobilisation and organisation of the emergency services and supporting organisations, eg local authority, to cater for the threat of death, serious injury, or homelessness to a large number of people.
>
> (Home Office, 1997: 38)

The police also have an important role to perform in detecting crime and bringing to prosecution those responsible. This can sometimes involve collecting evidence while the response to a crisis is underway. In cases of arson or terrorism, this role takes on particular significance.

Historically for the police, large incidents can be characterized as the management of people's behaviour at large public gatherings. Operationally at such incidents the police need to maintain social order; this means that vital tactical and strategic key decision makers are kept geographically remote from the scene. This remoteness also ensures the preservation of the decision-making response process and prevents it being subsumed by the incident itself.

In contrast, the fire service takes its command structure to the incident itself. Fire service operational performance depends upon being able to respond to the physical nature of an incident's requirements. The organization is highly disciplined and is run along militaristic lines involving inspections and parades where fire officers are expected to turn out smartly. There is a pre-arranged level of seniority, corresponding to the size of the fire service response at the scene of any incident. When an incident requires a greater number of appliances, a more senior officer will automatically be posted to the scene in order to take over command. The fire service has a history of dealing with large fires. In order to minimize the risks to fire service personnel at the scene, and in contrast to the police service, major tactical decisions need to be made as near to the scene of operation as possible. Fire service safety management also requires the establishment of an 'inner cordon' or 'rescue zone', within which humanitarian services, damage control and salvage can be effected. They will also advise the police about wider evacuation issues.

The ambulance service needs to be considered in the context of the National Health Service (NHS); their duty is directly to the patient. As well as providing medical care to the patients themselves they are responsible for bringing other parts of the NHS to the scene of trapped or sick individuals. They need to coordinate with other sections of the NHS regarding resources for dealing with survivors while still maintaining emergency cover for the rest of the area. Ambulance personnel may need to enter, or advise the fire service about the treatment of injured persons within an inner cordon area. The ambulance service will also need to liaise with the police authorities about the identities and numbers of casualties removed, and assist the police with more difficult evacuation areas, for example, hospitals, nursing homes and sheltered accommodation units.

The ambulance service also has an emergency plan. The first role in such a plan is to estimate the number of casualties, and then if necessary to mobilize a surgical team. At large incidents they would also arrange for parking and loading officers to be present, but this can often mean using up valuable trained paramedics who might be more effectively used elsewhere. The ambulance service also operates an automatic backing-up procedure which, similar to the fire service, involves drawing in resources from the surrounding area to replace the local ones deployed.

It is important for security managers to be aware of the extent to which 'taking control' will mean the exclusion of an organization's legitimate staff from gaining access. Even after the emergency services have left, permission for re-entry may be required from local authority structural engineers.

While risk and security professionals do not need to be experts in the management of civil emergencies and disasters, a good understanding of the role of the emergency services is essential. The nature of a crisis event is such that it is unlikely that any organization will be able to respond sufficiently on its own without the specialist services of the police, fire or ambulance. It is also likely that those responsible would need to contact a number of other agencies and service providers, ranging from utilities and structural engineers to caterers and providers of alternative accommodation.

Understanding what these services will and will not do for you in a crisis is therefore key to developing contingency plans. These organizations are by their nature highly disciplined and structured in the way they respond; understanding how to tap into their command and decision-making structures is therefore essential. Local authority emergency planners are another important part of the disaster recovery process, often acting as an information conduit through which a number of agencies can communicate.

Media

One stressor for management teams responding to a crisis is dealing with the media (Seymour and Moore, 2000). Dealing with the media can often be more tricky than the crisis itself. When a major incident occurs the press and broadcast journalists will be at the scene of the event within the first hour – sometimes within minutes – and will often expect to be able to interview senior personnel from the organization. While there may be major incident procedures designed to cope with this, such as staff dedicated to media duties to provide briefings, this will not always satisfy the demands of the media. The need for rapid and accurate information is most acute during a crisis; key decision makers are not alone in this requirement for information. The importance of log-keeping during a crisis is also very important (Regester and Larkin, 1997). When explaining difficult decisions to inquiries after an incident, it is important to be able to show what information was actually available to the decision makers.

Senior staff should be given media training and usually have gained some significant experience dealing with journalists. A crisis or disaster will attract the international media and managing their requirements can provide another difficult demand for key decision makers.

The use of simulations to train key staff in dealing with the media will be looked at again in the next chapter, but there are some simple rules worth bearing in mind for dealing with journalists.

Do when talking to the media

- Take your time
- Think before you answer
- Keep to your own area and level of expertise
- Say if you don't know, cannot or may not answer the question
- Stick to the facts
- Assume that everything is 'on the record'
- Be firm, fair and honest

Do not when talking to the media

- Lie, guess or speculate
- Get upset or angry with the reporter
- Let yourself be stressed by the situation or the reporter
- Use expert language/jargon
- Discuss confidential information
- Use the expression 'no comment'
- Talk about things outside your area of expertise

(Swedish Emergency Management Agency)

It is very important for organizations to consider carefully, and in advance, the designated people who should be put onto these teams. Some members of staff, directors, CEOs, etc., are likely to have to represent the organization in an official capacity at press conferences and the like. These people are going to require two things: training in responding to the media, and accurate information on the day.

The contribution of risk to BCM

In this chapter, it has been argued that education has a vital role to play in business continuity purposes. If the primary form of training is through simulations and games, then the scope for knowledge transference is there. Education has a role to perform in the design, implementation and evaluation of simulations for BCPs. Properly funded research is also vital in order to establish principles of best practice.

It is argued here that a pragmatic context must be developed in which the theoretical approaches to BCM training presented in this chapter are subjected to rigorous research and development.

Bringing about change

Bringing about change in BCM suggests a number of options: self-regulation, government regulation, training exercises and education. Each of these has a part to play.

The reluctance of organizations to cooperate on the Y2K issue (although with hindsight we know it was a non-event!) is an example of the scale of the problem. For most commercial organizations, the knowledge of another organization's problem represents a business opportunity to be capitalized on. This is often perceived as a good reason for keeping your own problems to yourself, an approach not dissimilar to putting one's head in the sand!

Despite some of the political interest mentioned earlier, there is an almost total lack of consensus between academics and practitioners when it comes to choosing experts to run BCM games. For consultants this is a good situation; anyone can call themselves expert. In the current situation, there is probably more literature available on hiring a clairvoyant than finding someone knowledgeable on business continuity planning.

The Kobe earthquake in Japan and recent terrorist bomb outrages against the City of London and Manchester in the UK highlight the diverse nature of risk and the level of media interest. Risks posed by criminal fraud, strategic systems failure, extreme weather and the effect of those with a grievance against an organization can be equally catastrophic in effect and should also be taken seriously as a threat to strategic viability.

This issue of expertise and competence in relation to consultative practice in BCM has yet to be tested in law. Clearly you would not normally call a plumber to build your garden rockery. It is therefore curious that something as vital as the security and viability of a major organization is often placed in the hands of those who have training that is either questionable or non-existent. While being an ex-policeman does not disqualify someone from the skills of BCM, it is not necessarily a qualification in its own right.

Despite the importance of contingency planning, there are a number of dilemmas posed. Implementation requires the use of specialist skills, but experts do not agree on what these are and how training should take place. Specialist training is in any case often either time-consuming or expensive, or both. The rewards of training are often not something overtly visible on a balance sheet or profit and loss account, and in contrast a failure to train is highly visible once the organization has been exposed to crisis. A lack of preparedness can cost damage to property and staff, leading to litigation and even bankruptcy. Insurance in these types of contexts is usually unavailable (in fact, most insurance companies no longer actively sell insurance for disaster but do for 'risk management services'). Legislation is likely to make organizations not only liable for their actions, but also inaction.

For the consumer, BCP represents an overhead of bewildering proportions. Once you bring an outsider into your organization and ask them to envisage your own private hell, are you not technically negligent if you do not act in accordance with their (perhaps) expensive recommendation? Are you not damned if you do but also damned if you do not?

The ultimate test of any crisis simulation will be the extent to which decision making of individuals and collective groups will be influenced so as to behave differently. There is no scientific test which can accurately measure the extent to which conceptual or behavioural change will in fact take place among groups following qualitative simulation training. However, it is argued here that if crisis simulation praxis and validation are to be improved, then a pragmatic context must be developed in which the theoretical findings of BCM training can be subjected to rigorous research and development.

Why simulations are important for BCM

Before moving on to the next chapter, on simulations and games, it is important to consider why these training devices have now become a cornerstone for modern crisis planning.

There are a number of reasons why further research and development might benefit practitioners and theorists. First, while considerable theoretical work has been undertaken on simulations and gaming – for example, the fields of aircraft piloting and business training have benefited from some considerable simulation research – there is, however, virtually no academic work in the area of BCM. This is despite strong commercial and political pressures on and within organizations to run risk-simulation scenarios. It is therefore proposed that further research will contribute to both theoretical and practical knowledge about simulated and actual risk contexts. It might also facilitate a framework within which exercises might be evaluated in terms of effectiveness of training. It is argued here that this can only take place if exercises are subject to some theoretical underpinning.

Second, simulations can be used for multiple purposes. These could be, for example, training, organizational (or part of organizational) performance audit, and learning about the nature of potential hazards. In addition, simulations can be used as a training device for a number of response contexts; it is argued here that the requirements of emergencies, crisis and disasters are distinct in this respect. It is therefore suggested that by learning more about and being able to differentiate between these goals, exercises could be targeted more effectively to operational and safety requirements.

Third, simulation exercises can be a very expensive instrument both to implement and/or plan. It is therefore proposed that in a context of finite training resources, a clear identification of good simulation practice would be of benefit to practitioners in the field. A further benefit from this research might be the development of guidelines which improve the effectiveness of simulation exercises and the development of an approach to simulation analysis within a risk management context.

Fourth, with the increasing levels of litigation following as an aftermath to major incidents, organizations increasingly need to demonstrate to the legal establishment, and to society more generally, that all possible precautions in order to avert and where necessary manage potential hazards have been taken. The role of the judicial process and litigation trends have played a major part in constructing contemporary social models of acceptable risk. A massive legal industry has grown around the legal adjudication of risk issues which the designers of simulation exercises can no longer ignore without liability. One legal criterion is to establish blame, guilt, liability or negligence (Wells, 1995). The 'no-win, no-fee' practice in America has contributed to the generation of a huge, specialized legal industry associated with adjudicating such risk claims. Many American exercise designers introduce their exercises by means of a legal disclaimer.

The commercial implications of such a legal obligation raise serious ethical questions regarding the 'expertness' and 'motivation' for running simulations. If simulations are to be used as a form of 'insurance' against litigation, it is important to establish whether these exercises are appropriately valid. The next chapter will look at crisis simulations and consider how these might be used to augment any programme to control risk and security management.

Chapter 6

USING SIMULATIONS AND GAMES FOR CRISIS MANAGEMENT

The focus of this chapter is on simulations and games. The ubiquity of use of simulations in risk and security contexts is not matched by knowledge and understanding of the attributes and dangers posed by this form of training. Many organizations regularly use simulations to train for crisis events as a response to business continuity and compliance requirements. As learning tools, simulations are extremely effective. Simulations can also affect our emotions greatly both for the good and bad. Less is known, however, about their effectiveness as 'negative learning' tools, particularly when used inappropriately.

In terms of obtaining a level of resilience to crisis, a theoretical context is required in order to validate training. This chapter aims to provide an introduction to that theoretical context. Simulation exercises provide the only experiential means by which to train people in an environment that is as realistic as possible for an as yet unknown crisis. Real crises (fortunately) do not happen frequently enough to allow us to use them as an organizational training environment. In this sense, at least, a crisis simulation is somewhat unique, because effectiveness cannot be gauged against other modes of training. Exercises and simulations also pose specific challenges to trainers and educators in their role as designers, facilitators or evaluators.

> Crises and disasters are complex events taking place within complicated environments and resulting in diverse responses. To represent those conditions adequately extensive preparation has to be undertaken to provide a training situation in which learning, understanding and added competence can result.
>
> (Rolfe, 1998: 14–15)

A number of areas of disciplinary learning could be used to facilitate the usage of crisis simulations suggesting a scope for knowledge transference. For example, there is a considerable theoretical body of knowledge dedicated to simulation design, implementation and evaluation in many other training contexts, which could improve our ability to run crisis simulations. A number of organizations run specialist journals and conferences and promote research into simulation and gaming.* Despite the prolific usage of simulations in risk contexts, there is little knowledge transference taking place (one aim of this book!) from these sources.

What is a simulation?

The word 'simulate' originates from the Latin *simulare*, 'to make like', and its modern meaning implies the use of pretence or imitation in order to create some resemblance or representation of an original source reality. However, usage of the term in the context of those involved in modern simulation exercises is not easily defined. This is due to the multivarious use of simulations in a range of complex and diverse settings, from training for wars and the management of abominations, to children's play and structured learning tasks.

Simulations as a cultural phenomenon almost certainly pre-date any literary records on the subject. It is argued by Petranek that in the development of the 'Self', 'Me', and 'I', simulation plays a critical role (Petranek, 1989, 2000). Learning through the process of simulations could, for humans, represent learning in a most naturalistic way.

The range of training applications for simulations would be impossible to adequately describe here, but the main groupings are briefly referred to.

Primitive/traditional usage

There is a wealth of anthropological evidence to suggest that in many traditional hunter-gatherer societies, the acquisition of certain hunting skills are developed as part of children's play, forming a key part of the training for the future food-finders of such

---

* The main academic journal for simulation and gaming is produced by SAGE. This is also the journal for ISAGA (International Simulation and Gaming Association), who run annual conferences on simulations. A number of countries also have active societies, conferences and regular journals/publications to promote research and an exchange of ideas on this topic. Not all are listed here, but these include: USA, UK, Japan, Germany, Holland, Italy, France.

communities. It can also be argued in this context that the value of simulations for the learning experience is both profound and long-term, due to learning on both conscious and unconscious psychological levels. For example, anthropological studies of some Inuit communities, who until only recently led a traditional life, indicate that without certain forms of ritualized play among the young, necessary physical skills could not be developed sufficiently in time to sustain life in the extreme climatic conditions which these societies inhabit (Brody, 1987).

Role play/educational

Theatrical drama and later on film provide a context for a further prolific use of simulations; this time as an art form where both real and fictitious events are acted out. The contents and effects of drama and the realism portrayed in many modern films are matters of some controversy on moral grounds. With the advent of advanced media technology, and at a time of increasing violent crime levels in society, there is some considerable debate as to how realistic the choice and portrayal of such events should be. There has also been some debate among those employed in the performing arts regarding the extent to which roles should be performed 'off stage'. This is high-lighted in many contemporary schools of drama, such as 'Stanislawski' or 'method acting', where the emphasis is upon the psychological factors which affect the actor or actress. Stanislawski proposed that by living their roles as much as was possible in their ordinary lives, actors could create an experience for the role which would result in a more realistic style of acting (Taylor, 1979).

The value of taking on and performing a role from an educational perspective cannot be valued highly enough. Role play allows participants to operate within two levels of reality, 'the everyday and the imaginative' (Landy, 1991; Collier, 1998). Simulations are increasingly used in classrooms at schools, to facilitate or even replace formal teaching methods. A lot of very interesting experimental work on simulations as learning tools has been carried out within educational contexts. Ironically, compliance and regulation, at least in the UK, has now reached even the classroom. Simulations are particularly suited to educational contexts, because they encourage students to learn in a participative way. This is both more enjoyable than formal methods of teaching and, where role play is used, enables students to learn creatively. The use of inter-active forms of gaming will be discussed again later in the chapter with reference to learning.

Martial arts and fighting

Fighting is another widespread application of simulations, in both early and late human use. In our own society, the range of these applications can be seen to span from tribal war dances and jousting ceremonies, which simulate aspects of battle as a form of entertainment, to modern military manoeuvres simulating the serious features of modern warfare. These war gaming exercises are sometimes carried out on a huge scale.

In the same context, eastern philosophical attitudes to training are espoused in the martial arts of China and Japan; tea ceremonies, skills associated with various specialist food preparations, flower arrangements (*ikebana*) and styles of armed and unarmed combat (*budo*) can also be viewed as simulations. These eastern art forms perform a dual role. They are simulations serving a present purpose, as a form of art (in the Chinese language, the word 'simulation' as translated is used to mean the equivalent of a 'dress rehearsal' in the theatrical sense), but they also train and condition the practitioner for some future and unknown scenario.

Business applications

Another prolific use of simulations has been in the area of business games and training. These types of games are used to train people for a variety of tasks ranging from investment decisions to customer service applications. The format for these types of simulations and games is as diverse as the applications required. BCM is but another addition to these types of games, drawing on both other types of business training applications and war gaming as its roots.

Crisis simulations

While simulations offer a very practical means to train organizations for a crisis, crisis simulations are unique at least in terms of learning value. Effectiveness is difficult to measure against other types of training or even at all! For example, simulators used for quite complex operator training tasks can be contrasted against other learning methodologies, such as flight training simulators. Research conducted by Rolfe (1992, 1998) referred to this as 'positive' and 'negative transfer of training' in his work on flight simulators. The reason why it is possible to do this for such complex tasks is because the response can be structured to precisely meet the requirements. Key to a successful outcome in this context is the speed and skill of response rather than a reinterpretation of the situational requirements. Simulations used in educational environments can also be measured against more formal teaching methodologies. In this context it is possible to measure performance for matched groups in tests or assignments and demonstrate training value.

In contrast, the learning value from a crisis simulation is much more difficult to evaluate. A crisis scenario is a unique event, unlikely to fit with an organization's history, policy or procedures. Definitions of success could range from saving the organization, lives or the environment to seizing opportunities that might not otherwise have been apparent or available. The very fact that one is able to tightly define players' roles, expectations or actions may mean that the exercise is not really providing a crisis management experience at all. A successful response in this context is more difficult to define and hence measuring the effectiveness of such simulations is problematic.

There is also much confusion about how and when simulations should be used in crisis preparations. Simulations come in a number of diverse operational formats. These might include open or closed format simulations (Christopher and Smith, 1987; Leigh, 2003), they may be based on 'magic, trickery and illusion' (Van Ments, 2003) or as some form of 'interactive lecture' (Thiagarajan, 2003). All of these simulation modes could be offered as 'role play' or 'table top' design and may even be run using computer interfaces or even full-scale 'mock-ups'. Decisions about choice of methodology may often be based on financial or time resource expediency, rather than educational or competency requirements.

Simulation theory

One way we might begin to theorize about simulations is to produce some form of taxonomy to encompass all simulations under a unified framework of typologies. However, due to the practice of contemporary simulations spanning an almost limitless range of applications, this is problematic. Modern simulation usage, of one sort or another, enters into nearly every aspect of our lives, from children's games and theatrical performances to complex technological applications such as flight simulators for training aircraft pilots and scientific discovery through experimentation. The range and scope of these applications make any attempt to provide a comprehensive taxonomic frame-work of simulation a difficult theoretical problem (Cecchini and Frisenna, 1987: 60).

A further problem is the effect of the multidisciplinary nature of academic theor-izing about simulations. Simulation use in multivariate contexts has led to a number of terms in order to describe fundamentally similar phenomena. As Taylor suggests:

> Individuals as well as institutions have felt free to draw upon separate semantic sources to suit their convenience and local as well as disciplinary meanings have been established as and when the need arose. So it is that war gaming, social science, computer technology, operational research and game theory have all contributed towards an embarrassingly rich vocabulary.
>
> (Taylor, 1971)

Therefore before we can even begin to categorize simulations, we are faced with a number of linguistic terms to describe what are intrinsically similar phenomena. For example, 'a hot wash-up', 'discussion', 'analysis' and 'debrief' are all terms describing funda-mentally similar features of a simulation exercise.

How we describe and conceive simulations will depend at least in part on who we are, but more fundamentally what we use them for. In other words, the purpose of a simulation will mediate the nature of the discourse that we use to describe it and in this way we can talk to other practitioners in our field. For example, with those involved in multiservice emergency response simulations, we may wish to describe the debrief stage as the 'hot wash-up', which signifies its social and cultural connotations to them.

Certain simulations could, arbitrarily, be grouped together by scenario type – for example, business applications or operator training devices – but these could equally be grouped theoretically as experimental or social models and similarly by purpose, as learning or system audit devices. Attempting any taxonomic classification of simula-tions may appear desirable to achieve a pragmatic approach, but this needs to be balanced against a difference in style and design. It may, therefore, prove more fruitful to consider all simulation activities as defined by a number of common features.

One common feature of simulations is that they *represent* a source reality in order to achieve a particular goal or experience. This could be simply to 'play', by means of make-believe or pretending in children's games, or to entertain as in the case of theatrical productions, but it could also include learning about serious practical skills or finding out about human behaviour by isolating aspects of social interaction under laboratory conditions.

By adopting a representational perspective we could consider 'simulation' as an umbrella term, which contains concepts like rules and strategies, systems, models, games and role play as aspects of it. Representation then is effected by means of abstraction from a source reality. This is achieved by modelling that system on the basis of a selection of conceived features: the essential characteristics, rules and strategies (processes). In this context, the modelled simulation has the qualities of a low-cost error model, in comparison to a real system where errors can be expensive or even disastrous. Participants in a simulated environment are hence able to make errors in relative safety and learn by them. In reality this process may be more of an art than a science. Deciding upon the correct set of features to model may be a somewhat ambiguous and problematic task, particularly with subjective social phenomena.

A second common feature to simulations is that they *simulate* certain aspects of reality at the expense of ignoring others (Abt, 1970). This is due to purely pragmatic reasons. If a simulation were to offer all the aspects of the real situation from which it had been abstracted, then it would no longer be a simulation, but the source reality itself. In this respect, simulation scenarios can be seen to offer an ethical and pragmatic alternative to an unacceptable reality. This reality may be unacceptable for moral and/or ethical reasons (as will be discussed later in this chapter), or on economic or safety grounds. For example, it would be quite unethical to train a pilot for emergency flight procedures in a real jet aircraft full of passengers, or to really commit murder in a classical Greek tragedy for effect. It may also be physically impossible to create the real situation that the simulator wishes to experience, such as a thermonuclear explosion in outer space or travelling at the speed of light.

A third common feature of simulations is that they create dynamic realities by their own production. These realities, created by players in the process of simulation, can be viewed either as a 'representation' of a real-world operating system or, alternatively, as an 'operating reality' which exists in its own right (Crookall and Saunders, 1989: 12). Crookall and Saunders point out that these categories are not mutually exclusive. On the contrary, while a simulation may represent only some small part or aspect of a real source system, to those participating in the simulation, they are ostensibly involved in an 'operating reality'.

These common features relate to contemporary simulation usage, which can be broadly split into two groupings: social role play, and highly structured devices for operator training or system evaluation.

Social role play theorists have considered simulations from the perspective of a 'game'. Here the object is to play out a particular game, as is done, for example, in the SIMSOC scenarios (Gamson, 1966). Role play or 'gaming' analogies have proved particularly useful in the context of business and other social applications which aim to teach social skills, group work or negotiation. These tend to be open-ended and dependent upon the players acting out a reality in the format of a game structure.

Structured approaches to simulation are broadly carried out within an experimental paradigm. Such simulations can be used as a method to examine the validity of a hypothesis or some previously untested assumptions about aspects of system performance, but more commonly are applied to the task of training operators for particular functions, such as pilot training or computer-assisted control room functioning. Some of these simulations can be highly specialized and often very expensive to develop and manufacture; for example, pilot training simulators or ICCARUS (Intelligent Command and Control Acquisition and Review Using Simulation). This type of exercise is often used in conjunction with other types of training to facilitate overall effectiveness. Much of this work on operator training devices has been particularly useful in validating their effectiveness, as will be discussed later in the section on validation. Structured simulation devices often involve computerized interaction with other structured systems. The simulations are usually quite small with very few people involved, frequently only one. They are practised by isolating certain features of a reality in order to observe operator performance by measuring predetermined variables.

With subjective variables (social factors) thus reduced, simulations on this scale also appear to facilitate hypothesis making since the simulation goals will be much simplified – e.g. learning about perceptions, memory or decision making within the context of known outcomes. The work of Kahneman and Tversky and Lola Lopes (discussed in Chapter 1) provides an example of the way in which psychologists have applied this to the study of risky decision making in the laboratory, by contrasting perceived risks with actual risks in order to provide some form of calibrated response. Similarly, approaches to risk using a psychometric methodology measure popular conceptions of risks against those defined by experts. Such an approach aims to discover the cognitive processes or strategies employed by decision makers in a variety of scenarios.

For structured simulations, reality has to be simplified in order to expose the factors considered most important to the simulators' objective. The pay-off for doing this is some form of quantified evaluation. While this approach can at least allow for some form of measurement, the validity of such measurements is somewhat questionable. Shrinking reality to the point where only the bare bones are presented clearly removes something, and it is not easy to measure what this is. The gestalt of the total situation will be different, even though the aim at the outset was to obtain a psychological affinity between what has been presented and reality.

However, both operator trainers and experimental models, in contrast to simulations which involve the representation of social interaction (such as in Gamson's SIMSOC scenarios [Gamson, 1966]), remove social and cultural features. Therefore social and cultural features are at best only crudely represented within experimental models. As is often the case in scientific experimentation generally, the social world is found to represent variables best avoided, if 'clean' results are to be obtained. Structured simulations therefore need to be carried out within strictly controlled environments.

A strict notion of control in simulations has been criticized by a number of theorists involved in an educational context. For example, Boot and Reynolds have argued that psychological approaches to simulations attempt to control players' roles in simulations/ games too tightly. Boot and Reynolds also suggest this stems from a poor understanding of the complexity of social processes involved. They state:

> The impression we gained was that, in the proliferation of these activities, technical skill in their design had advanced far more rapidly than wisdom concerning the complexity of the processes which they involve.
>
> (Boot and Reynolds, 1983: 3)

Boot and Reynolds criticize the trend in experimental simulations towards 'tighter design', with an assumption that this will increase the measurability of learning, arguing, in contrast, that students will be tempted to abdicate their own responsibility for learning (Boot and Reynolds, 1983: 6). In the process of representing reality, another reality is created, as the simulation brings the model to life. Such representations will become secondary, if not peripheral, as actors are increasingly forced to take chances and experience the consequences. In this context the simulation is unlike a theatre performance or psychological experiment where the actors have only roles to interpret within set parameters; the simulation allows for strategies, actors are required to choose between options and interact with other decision makers who may be equally empowered. Hence unlike the theatre players or the subjects in the psychological experiment, the actors in the simulation are constantly negotiating and constructing their reality; they are then confronted with this reality and its implications as they live in a world. As Crookall and Saunders quote from Thomas (1951): 'If men define situations as real, they are real in their consequences.'

Other theorists, also within the context of an educational perspective, have questioned the wisdom of a rigid approach. Bernstein suggests that the unintended consequences of exercises may also constitute essential learning, on the basis of personal learning affecting the participant's overall perspective (Bernstein, 1971). Similarly Goodman argues that removing the social reality from simulations also reduces the capacity for discovery among players who are subsequently reduced to 'animated' forms of problem solving (Goodman, 1971: 42).

Some theorists have argued that strict control is simply not required in certain simulation scenarios. As Hunt suggests, the purpose of participation for players is often in order to gain experience through participation, rather than forecasting outcomes. This is particularly true in the context of business gaming applications (Hunt, 1982).

How real should a simulated reality be? If at four in the afternoon a simulation exercise stops and the participants all go off to drink tea, is it not obvious that it was all an exercise of no consequence to the real world? It would be a mistake to assume the simulation process occurs in some form of social vacuum. The actors involved bring to the situation their own cultural baggage; this may include training, organizational experiences and prejudices, factors which they would also bring with them to a real event. But they also bring with them notions of an exercise and training expectations as perceived in the context of the organization culture. Players may be concerned about performance monitoring or measurement against other participants in some specific way. It could therefore be argued that these concerns may also apply as pertinent to a real event, but then participants would not have had time to consider the issues beforehand.

Simulations in emergency response organizations

The most common means of training for disasters in the UK emergency services has been through simulation and role play exercises. The nature and scope of such exercises can vary greatly depending on the type of incident being simulated and the level of realism desired by exercise planners. Simulation exercises are versatile phenomena, used for a variety of management purposes in the emergency services. The purpose of an exercise may be to expose decision makers to particular types or parts of a crisis scenario as training, or to highlight the difficulties which decision makers face when a variety of organizations suddenly find they have to operate together. Simulations may also be used as a way of testing how an organization performs under stress; in other words, as a form of organizational audit device. In a similar way, simulations can be used to learn about the nature of disasters themselves, as a form of case study. However, most commonly, emergency simulation exercises are run for a combination of these reasons.

Two representational formats for simulations are typically deployed. The exercise may be quite realistic (high-fidelity), using *mock-ups* of disaster incidents for players to directly interact with, or *table top* exercises (sometimes call 'paper-flow', or 'low-fidelity'), which concentrate more on the management functions. Realistic scenarios are of practical value to acquaint players and managers with the scope and limitations of equipment and resources. This type of simulation could, for example, be used to practise dealing with a burning building, requiring fire service personnel to enter and carry out search and rescue techniques using special types of breathing equipment or even to practise putting out the fire itself.

With the low-fidelity format, the scenario is simulated in order to recreate the management atmosphere of an incident by means of interactive message feeds to the players. An example of such an exercise is the simulation of a 'major incident' described by Richard North and David Wilcock. This exercise was a real-time management simulation for dealing with the first 20 minutes of a major incident by serving constables in the police force. The purpose of the exercise was to highlight the practical difficulties of maintaining clear communication and the need for clearly defined and acknowledged responsibilities assigned to various roles. Prior to the exercise (based on a train crash), the physical reality of the scenario was communicated to the players by means of video footage. The exercise then focused on the confusion and chaos occurring between the control room and sergeant, stressing the need for good command and control procedures. The exercise ended as soon as the sergeant notionally reached the simulated scene (North and Wilcock, 1991).

Another example is provided by Moore, who describes a 'community disorder simulation', designed to focus on the management issues of the incident. The exercise was run at the UK Police Training Centre, and was designed to provide experiential training by presenting a series of problematic developments during a crowd control operation. Rather than presenting players with a series of win/lose finales, the exercise focuses on the types of issues raised in the management of serious public disorder situations. Moore suggests that the exercise fulfilled its aims, allowing officers to practise the types of decisions they would encounter in real public disturbance situations. Moore also argues that, owing to the large number of officers required for such incidents, it is practically (and financially) difficult to run such scenarios in a real-life context (Moore, 1985).

Simulation exercises are used in the emergency services for a number of purposes. Frequently, simulations are used as practical learning exercises, to help staff become acquainted with the use of equipment, or management of a particular type of scenario. Such exercises would be used to help individuals develop personal skills specific to certain types of incident (McDonald *et al.*, 1992).

Many 'paper-flow' or 'table top' exercises have been developed to facilitate risk communication. An example is a bush-fire simulation game called *Black Christmas*, which simulates an Australian bush-fire over four days. The exercise is designed for threatened communities. The exercise, using fire fighters, undergraduates and secondary school students, aims to familiarize the players with bush-fire management techniques and the nature and behaviour of bush-fires, considering issues such as radiant heat and evacuation. The bush simulation also considers preventative issues such as good precautionary practice and behaviour during bush-fires (Cunningham and Teather, 1990).

Less frequently, simulation exercises may be used to assess capabilities, or train certain key individuals in an emergency response organization. For example, in the police service, it may be important to know whether certain officers can cope with particular types of crises. However, Tony Moore argues, some 'senior' or 'middle ranking' officers will prove poor 'incident or ground commanders'. He suggests:

> Exercises can be used to assess whether individuals are likely to measure up to the requirements of a particular job or task, thus doing away with the policy of 'trial and error' used by the police so often in the past 'sometimes with quite serious consequences both to the individual and to the officers deployed under their command'.
>
> (Moore, 1988: 125)

The assumption that simulators are being used and hence the right people will be selected raises a slight concern. Simulations do not in themselves train or sort anyone; it is the scenarios, people and debriefs that are most important in bringing about a change effect.

Increasingly, computer interfaces are also being used for simulation training. The use of multimedia and interactive software have enabled planners to develop ever more advanced simulations formats, although these have been restricted to command and control type functions within one particular service. One such system, ICCARUS, has been used with the British fire service.

ICCARUS is an interactive computer-based simulation tool for training fire service commanders. It is claimed by the designers to be 'an "intelligent" simulator which would "exercise" senior officers in command and control problems of large fire management' (ICCARUS Project, 1989).

ICCARUS is designed for use by a single fire officer, who sits at a computer terminal where the simulated incident is managed. Through multimedia technology, the officer is presented with a view of the simulated scenario on a video screen and can respond to the incident by deploying resources using the mouse. The program claims to be interactive in that resources once deployed actually change the nature of the scenario which is presented on the screen. The resources available are limited and once deployed become unavailable for use in managing other aspects of the incident (ICCARUS Project, 1989).

Another example is a computer-based simulation described by Morentz called *Saving Lives: The Emergency Management Game* (1985). Five levels of play permit users to explore the interdependencies among decision makers in an emergency management context. The simulation considers a number of response issues, such as hazard awareness, preparedness/actions, warning responses, event behaviour and recovery behaviour.

In recent times there has been a dramatic growth in expenditure among the emergency services on simulations using high-tech interfaces and modern communication devices (Crego and Harris, 2001) and Vector Command (Vector Command UK, 1999). Typically these types of simulations attempt to create for decision makers an experience as close to reality as possible. They have been extremely useful in terms of improving emergency response to structured situations. Players can go over a scenario using video footage of their own performance in order to reflect on their actions. These simulations also allow decision makers to access the types of information realistically available using pre-recorded information and 'playbacks'.

A number of issues, however, appear to be problematic with the use of computer-based simulations as emergency service training tools. First, it is questionable whether such devices can be described as 'intelligent' or 'expert' systems. For highly structured types of training, such as command and control, a computer system may be able to simulate the phenomena required with some degree of fidelity, as used in Minerva and Vectra. However, for ill-structured crisis situations requiring a degree of inter-agency cooperation, computer systems may be more problematic; designing sufficient flexibility for both game designers and players to simulate a crisis is very difficult.

Second, such highly structured and inflexible training tools may act to increase tensions between response organizations when faced with an incident requiring delicate negotiation in response procedures. It is still simply too complicated to programme a computer to take account of all event and response possibilities for all contexts. The dynamic and changing nature of a crisis is likely to complicate this further.

Third, the use of computer formats may act to reinforce an erroneous belief in highly structured response methods. This is because planners seeking to produce a computer simulation are constricted by a set number of outcomes and responses in order to fit with the practical requirements of machine code. It may not be possible to programme a computer sufficiently to include the complex intricacies of human interactions suggested by the risk communication, systems and safety culture theorists in the last chapter.

Inter-agency crisis training

However, exercises can also be used to train organizations which need to work together in order to deal with new or more complex types of crisis. Multiservice response exercises are increasingly being recognized as of value and importance for the emergency services. This is highlighted in many of the recent official reports produced by both the government and the emergency services themselves (HSE, 1991; HMSO, 1992a, 1992b; LESLP, 1992; New, 1992).

The London Emergency Services Liaison Panel (LESLP) stresses the importance of joint services training exercises as being:

> …the acknowledged means by which plans and procedures may be validated. Of equal importance is the opportunity they provide for the development of liaison arrangements in a less stressful situation.
>
> Exercises should not be treated lightly. The organisations involved expend large amounts of time, effort and resources, and invariably impact on the routine of the local community.
>
> (LESLP, 1992: 37)

There are two reasons why simulations have become an indispensable training tool for the emergency services. First, there are not enough real crisis situations available for the training of decision makers; in any case, it would be preferable to have decision makers trained prior to being deployed in a real scenario. This is also reflected in both Turner and Perrow's arguments, that crisis events may be high in terms of impact but are relatively low-frequency events for any particular organization (Turner, 1978; Perrow, 1984). Second, mounting public pressure for a safer environment is exerted through media attention, public or informal inquiries, pressure groups and legislation. For response organizations, simulation exercises are a means of demonstrating both awareness and readiness to deal with these issues of crisis.

Multiservice training usually takes place in the form of exercises run within each county. Many counties run a variety of exercises each year using role play, paper-flow, computer-based and real-life type simulation exercises. Multiservice exercises may also be run in the context of a particular organization or industry. However, despite the increasing frequency and costs of multiservice simulations taking place, there is a surprising lack of theoretical work available on simulation validation in these contexts.

There are various centres for emergency training excellence in the UK. For example, the fire brigade have a training centre at Moreton-in-Marsh and the police a centre at Bramshill, as well as a Home Office centre at Easingwold, which runs a large range of regular exercise conferences and workshops for dealing with disaster management issues. Each service, however, runs exercises which are primarily geared towards particular organizational goals and these may not necessarily be congruent with the goals of total incident management.*

There is a further dilemma here. Training for a crisis may require a level of flexibility in management and decision-making skills distinct from the problems associated with managing ordinary events (Turner, 1994: 87). Such changes may not be easy to impose on the organizational structure of an existing emergency service that, quite rightly, is proud of its reputation in dealing with normal emergencies. This has, historically at least, formed the greater part of the work of emergency services.

There is also a growing number of private companies and consultants offering training for emergency response. Many consultancies offer courses and guidance in the planning, implementation and analysis of simulations for a whole range of risk scenarios, for example, the training of risk professionals, assessing the effectiveness of organizational systems, as a tool of research, as a consciousness raising exercise, to assess the state of communications, to assess decision making and inter-group relations. While the list presented is by no means exhaustive, it does demonstrate the diversity of contexts in which risk simulations are being applied and their interdisciplinary potential. Despite evidence that most organizations and consultant advisors would now consider some form of simulation exercise to be a desirable part of any hazard prevention plan, what these exercises achieve (or even set out to achieve) is not always clear. It is suggested here that to consider the use of simulations as validating devices in their own right needs careful consideration.

---

* Both the most recent version of *Dealing with Disaster* (HMSO, 2003) and the Civil Contingencies Bill (2004) aim to bring about a more joined-up approach to disaster response. Although there is an expectation in these documents that simulations should be used, little guidance is given on how these should be run.

The private field of training is less well established. There are many new private consultancies which offer business continuity training exercises, the quality of which is difficult to validate. For many of the smaller authorities in the UK, 'buying in' prepared exercises may prove an attractive option, especially if they do not have the human and financial resources necessary to design and implement a full range of training exercises themselves. This problem has been highlighted by the Health and Safety Executive and the Home Office in an information sheet on avoiding the pitfalls of employing a bad consultancy (HMSO, 2003). Before considering how simulations might be validated, it would be pertinent to consider some of the theoretical literature available on simulation and gaming.

Using simulations to train organizations for crisis

The commercial implications of employing experts to run crisis games raise serious ethical questions regarding the 'expertness' and 'motivation' for running simulations. If simulations are to be used as a form of insurance against litigation, it is important to establish whether these exercises are appropriately valid. One buys insurance on the understanding that if an event happens the insurer will actually pay. Why should one not expect the same of the investment in a crisis simulation? A key issue then is assessing the value of a crisis simulation.

This section will look at some of the issues related to the management of such difficult scenarios in relation to simulation training for key decision makers in a BCM context. Exercises will then be considered from four perspectives: selecting an appropriate crisis team, purpose of training, definition and learning.

Selecting the crisis management team

The selection of appropriate personnel for crisis management exercises is essential. Exercises can be used to select the types of people most suited to operating in a crisis team environment. Most managers like to think that they can manage their departments better than anyone else, particularly in a crisis situation. However, this is an unfortunate fallacy. Some managers are indeed naturally good at working on crisis committees and generally have the flexible range of personal skills necessary in order to facilitate crisis management. Others can also be trained to do this. Unfortunately, for some managers, it may be preferable that they concentrate on activities where they are already proven to be operationally effective (Borodzicz and Van Haperen, 2003).

Another issue with staff selection for BCM training is the level of seniority in the organization. The most natural assumption is that because the matters in hand are strategic, the staff appointed to manage should carry rank. In the author's research into emergency service training, this assumption was found to be highly controversial for crisis management (Borodzicz, 1999b). The emergency services were found to concentrate much of their management training at the top, with structured operational training at the bottom! Most organizations, when confronted with a crisis, usually find that it is junior staff who have to initially respond; by the time senior managers become involved, it is often too late for crisis management, and the incident will have become a disaster. A similar situation is also the case in many corporate organizations. It is necessary to train as wide a variety of staff in crisis management as possible. Readiness therefore means demonstrating a capability at all times and at all levels within the organization. It is also worth noting at this point that most holistic staff development programmes neglect this aspect of personnel training.

Selecting a crisis team for an organization will involve having a pool of key people available based on their abilities to perform in crisis teams under simulated conditions. Teams need to be able to operate in the context of a heightened threat perception where decision makers are either overloaded with information, starved of information or both (Staw *et al.*, 1981: 502; 1997: 77)! Another requirement of crisis teams is that they are able to operate creatively and flexibly; teams have a tendency to find this difficult and may resort to rules and regulations rather than free thinking (Lagadec, 1993).

Another concern with crisis teams is measuring team performance. Learning is a difficult enough task to evaluate for individuals. Group dynamics can change quite radically by changing just one person in a team.* Staff change is a continual feature in most organizations. It would be impractical to presume that a team recently trained is going to be there and in the same format when a real crisis occurs. For large organizations there is also a likelihood that tiers of teams might need to operate at different levels of an incident. An example is given below based on a distinction between 'basic' and 'advanced' levels of response (Salas and Cannon-Bowers, 1993; Cannon-Bowers *et al.*,

---

* Some of the best work on teamwork has been produced by Belbin (1981, 1983). Klein (1995) has also developed a training technique and assessment scheme for advanced team decision-making. This is based on assessing team resources, identity, self management and thinking.

1995; Flin, 1996). Different teams might also deal with different aspects of a crisis; for example, one team deals with business continuity while another handles media and a third deals with human resources (Table 6.1).

Screening and filtering processes can at best only be crude ways of selecting people for such skills. There are severe problems associated with identifying desired personality traits, and even more severe problems finding people that match them. The discipline

---

Table 6.1 Characteristics, requirements and key dimensions

Basic team characteristics

Individual task proficiency
Clear concise communication
Collective orientation
Shared goal and mission

Advanced team requirements for enhanced performance

Shared understanding of the task
Shared understanding of other members' responsibilities
Team leadership
Collective efficacy (sense of 'teamness')
Anticipation
Flexibility
Efficient implicit communication (aware of each other's needs)
Monitor own performance

Key dimensions

Adaptability
Shared situational awareness
Performance monitoring and feedback
Leadership/team management
Interpersonal relations
Coordination
Communication
Decision making

Source: J. Cannon-Bowers *et al.* (1995) Defining competencies and establishing team training requirements. In R. Guzzo & E. Salas (eds), Team Effectiveness and Decision-making in Organisations. Jossey-Bass, San Francisco.

of occupational psychology is littered with attempts to do just this. The reasons why some staff might prove unsuitable for crisis management are complex; it is important that careful consideration is given to team selection.

The focus and purpose of training

If the purpose of training is not clear for the exercise designers, then it surely will not be for the players. It is important that some effort is put into clarifying this. Exercises could be used to assess individuals', groups' or whole organizations' capability to respond to a crisis. Exercises can also be used to assess the impact of various types of threat. While there are potentially many reasons to run an exercise, if players do not understand the purpose they may fail to engage with the training or even ruin the simulation. It is also important, as with any other learning function, to help players achieve the purpose of the exercise.

Where exercises are being used to create the experience of crisis, prior to even beginning to script an exercise designers need to identify the key processes and management systems that are vital to the continuity of the organization. This might seem a straightforward task, although the skills needed to do this are hard to define. Most organizational systems have evolved over a period of time, and would typically contain a number of sub-systems added in order to enable vital processes to withstand a variety of predetermined operational hazards. The organization may have been subjected to a quite detailed quantified risk assessment procedure for this very purpose.

An understanding of what is meant by 'emergency', 'crisis' and 'disaster' is argued to be of critical importance in a business continuity context. Specialist training for a crisis is particularly difficult and can be very expensive. The rewards of such training may become apparent only if and when a real incident occurs.

Turner, commenting on the research carried out by a European consortium team, argues that a 'clarity of goals' is an essential feature of good simulation design (Turner, 1996: 33). Understanding the difference between 'emergency', 'crisis' and 'disaster', it is argued here, will facilitate the development of a more focused and meaningful training programme for key decision makers. It is argued here that developing an awareness of these terms among those being trained may also encourage a more realistic response.

The role of the exercise designer in a BCM context is to look for ways that the system might operate in a context unlikely to be envisaged by someone who knows it intricately from the inside. There is something sinister about the mental process required for this task, akin to that of a clever bank robber or terrorist planning their next major job. The bank robber will know that the bank has gone to some considerable effort to make the cash secure; impressive safes, time-locks, security guards, etc. would form obvious defences. The bank robber has to devise a scenario which involves either bypassing these defences or putting them out of action altogether. This could be by stealing the money through a complicated computer fraud, or more likely by using someone on the inside to help them fool the bank into thinking that security systems are operating when they have in fact been shut down for the duration of the robbery. Similarly, the terrorist with political demands knows that the emergency services will respond in a particular way to bomb threats; they might therefore frustrate the response staff by placing strategically placed secondary devices, for example, on evacuation routes.

Exercise designers who want to test an organization's response to crisis need to bring about a crisis of confidence for those who manage the vital systems. They need not only an understanding of the way the organization perceives and manages its known hazards; they also need an ability to deconstruct the system in a way which might prove culturally difficult to those who work within the organization.

The marginal position of the consultant or academic researcher is ideal for this, utilizing their ability to quickly grasp the fundamental principles of operation for the organization while still maintaining a cultural distance. However, there is often an ethical issue to be addressed here, relating to the cash-nexus relationship between consultants (which some theorists compare to 'clinicians') and the organizations they work for:

> We might say that the client of the ethnographer is humankind, whereas that of the clinician is a particular organization, which in itself might be a boil on humanity's face. In other words, ethnographers, if they so wish, are free to declare the existence of a particular organization as a problem in itself, whereas clinicians, like doctors, must improve the performance of their clients.
>
> (Czarniawka-Joerges, 1992: 165)

Consultants may be reluctant to make management teams or individuals look or feel inadequate in a simulated context, particularly if continued employment might depend on them. It is therefore important that those who lead the organization are sufficiently committed to be prepared to take a few bruises in the training.

Definition – what is the nature of the risk?

What is the message to be made clear to the target group? In order to focus on an exercise, we would need to be able to define more closely the nature of the risk that is being simulated. Exercise planners should be aware of and make distinctions between event quality as a guide for planning teams to think about in scenario design. The material in Chapter 4 is of particular relevance here. For example, players who thought they were dealing with an operational emergency but were actually confronted with a crisis scenario based on strategic viability might have a negative exercise experience, despite following their own procedures rigidly and efficiently.

However, the problem may lie in imposing the response procedures too rigidly, failing to be flexible and not considering the cross-agency nature of the overall response. There is a congruence between what is suggested here and the recent work of a number of authors, for example, Turner's (1994) arguments for greater flexibility in response.

In this case a failure to deal with a scenario might be blamed on poor exercise design or the actions of the other players and/or agencies involved. Learning in this context could become inappropriate, as false assumptions about appropriate response become internalized. This could also be compared to the concept of negative learning highlighted by Rolfe (1992). It is argued that discussing event quality with players as part of the debrief process may bring about a more meaningful experience.

The learning component – what skills should players acquire?

Why do players need to learn? If it is not clear to players why they are involved in an exercise, then players are likely to invent their own reasons or simply go through the social motions of involvement. Players need to understand the relevance of their participation if this is to be a significant learning experience in crisis response. A context of rigid command structures may serve the needs of simulated emergency response, but it may be a ball and chain for decision makers in crisis. Players need to establish the significance of declaration, communication and negotiation; this can be facilitated by playing roles different to those in the normal domain of expertise. It is argued that players need to attend crisis simulations not to re-establish what they already know, but to learn about something new; in other words, how to manage other people's crises as well as their own: 'A crisis plan is needed to prepare all sorts of persons to know what to do in the event of a crisis' (Millar and Heath, 2004: 6). Physical participation in an exercise is not the same thing as active learning. The popular saying, 'You can take a horse to water but you cannot make it drink' could apply here. There is a growing literature on 'organizational' and 'safety culture' which suggests employees respond to various hazardous stimuli in accordance with informal rules as sanctioned by the organization. It is suggested here that, for employees, simulation training is also subject to the same constraints of organizational or safety culture. Further, that sustained simulation training for a small group of employees within an organization may result in bringing about a 'simulation culture'.

To avoid this, crisis exercises need to be designed so players are unable to cope with the scenario presented unless established procedures are radically altered or deviated from. The players themselves should be highly involved in bringing this about on a mutual basis. This should be built into the design, briefing and debriefing of crisis exercises.

This argument, it is acknowledged, gives key decision makers and trainers in organizations a difficult legal dilemma. Failure to respond in an orthodox manner may invite considerable controversy regarding the 'reasonableness' with which agencies have acted, particularly if there is much litigation. Conversely, if a successful outcome is brought about, unorthodox procedures may bring about considerable popular praise. The increasing popularity of television programmes based around the theme of managing difficult incidents highlights this point. A useful by-product of this media attention is a number of new scenario types for use in crisis simulations.

Simulations as learning tools

To investigate the usefulness of simulation exercises for crisis management training, some understanding of the learning process is crucial. The literature suggests a variety of different and sometimes contradictory models. Some of these are briefly reviewed here.*

Learning is defined as 'to get knowledge of (a subject) or skill in (an art, etc.) by study, experience, or teaching' by the *Oxford English Dictionary*. Three key areas of

---

* For a more detailed view of learning in relation to simulations see Borodzicz and Von Haperen (2002: 140–142).

learning theory have been influential with simulation theorists. First of these is Piaget's *theory of cognitive development* (Piaget, 1972; Gredler, 1992; Stern, 1997). Piaget argues that learning takes place each time we experience a new perception. This will make us question our existing views and reorganize them. The collection and organization of our thoughts he describes as 'schemas'. When we experience new perceptions, there is a reordering as new information is 'assimilated' into our schemas. Piaget argued that this process leads to what he described as 'higher levels of thinking' (Piaget, 1972). Piaget's theory would appear to apply to simulation training contexts. By providing players in a crisis simulation with a variety of crisis 'experiences', players might be able to form schemas for coping with the scenarios.

The cognitive development model has been referred to by a number of theorists in simulation contexts. Tsuchiya and Tsuchiya (1999), for example, define learning in a similar manner to Piaget. Learning occurs either when there is a match between 'design for action' and the 'intended outcome', or when a mismatch between intentions and outcomes is identified and corrected to generate a match (Tsuchiya and Tsuchiya, 1999: 53; Borodzicz and Van Haperen, 2002).

A second theoretical model, developed by Lewin (1936), considers the importance of *learning in the group context*. Again this is of importance to those involved in simulating group decision making. Whether groups of decision makers are able to collectively learn from a crisis training exercise is of critical importance. The group forms the social context of Lewin's theory, because it is within the social environment that inter-action and hence learning is taking place. Learning for Lewin is a process of mutual interpretation and feedback between different learners gradually leading to hypothesis generation (Gredler, 1992). Hence the processes of discussion and feedback during the simulation and the debrief might represent very important opportunities for learning.

Klabbers has developed Lewin's model to suggest that 'the learner is a person interested in participation in certain kinds of activities'. Learning, then, can be defined as an 'improved participation in interactive systems' (Green, 1997, quoted in Klabbers, 1999: 25). Klabbers (1999: 26–27) argues that simulation designers could balance acquisition and interaction, offering learners an opportunity to learn through practice, discourse, communication, interaction and improved participation in interactive systems.

It is often argued that learning in a crisis context occurs along three dimensions: personal, interpersonal and institutional (Serrie, 1992; O'Connel, 1997: 32; Lagadec, 1997: 27; Stern, 1997: 70; Borodzicz and Van Haperen, 2002). However, the basic learning unit in modern organizations has increasingly become that of a group or team (Senge, 1990, quoted in Stern, 1997: 70). Therefore, these models need to be contrasted with concepts of learning that are of particular significance to learning in a simulation context. This will contribute to building an understanding of group- or team-oriented learning, and acts as the foundation for further improvements to crisis training.

The third model presented here is Kolb's *experiential learning model*. This theory of learning is the most interesting from a simulation perspective. Kolb would argue that learning takes place as a reflective process after an experience (Figure 6.1). This is particularly interesting for simulation training as it suggests that learning is an active, if not interactive, reflective process. One theorist, Blockley, interested in risk and hazard engineering, has developed Schon's concept of the reflective practitioner in a risk context for engineers (Schon, 1983; Blockley, 1992, 1997). He argued that we should be doing all we can to encourage decision makers to learn from reflective practice.

A number of theorists have argued that learning does not take place on its own. It is important to recognize that simulations are not self-teaching and that good debriefing is required to reflect on purpose and actions (Gillespie, 1973; Petranek, 2000). From a simulation perspective, experience-based learning is particularly useful in two ways. It enables trainees to acquire knowledge, competence and skills, but also to craft their own mental model, to try it out and observe and evaluate the results (Thompson and Dass, 2000: 29).

If we are to synthesize (albeit crudely) Piaget, Lewin and Kolb's approaches to learning, then it would be important to understand the prior knowledge of learners, their social and operational context and the degree to which they are able to reflect on previous experience and training to develop new mental models. Simulations then, theoretically at least, should represent an ideal environment in which to facilitate such learning. But it would be wrong to see these as the only tool.

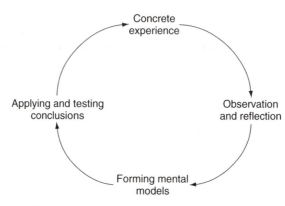

Figure 6.1 Experiential learning model

Source: Reproduced from D. Kolb, *Experiential Learning* (1984). Reprinted by permission of Pearson Education Inc., Upper Saddle River, NJ

Debriefing

Debriefing is one of the most important and most overlooked areas in crisis simulations. Often, debriefing is an optional add-on or winding up of the day. In contrast, many theorists have emphasized the importance of the debriefing process in simulations.

For Crookall and Saunders, the connecting bridge between 'abstraction' and 'presentation' is to be found in the debriefing process. In debriefing, the reality of the simulated representation and the reality of the real world confront each other.

> Debriefing allows parallels to be drawn between simulation realities and 'real' realities; it allows realities to be examined in a new, more 'realistic' light. Participants are then able to export the learning and insights gained from their experience in the simulation exercise to their other 'real' (non-simulation) world.
>
> (Crookall and Saunders, 1989: 18)

So for Crookall and Saunders, simulation is fundamentally a learning exercise, where participants create a dynamic simulated reality for themselves and then subsequently learn from being involved in that experience.

However, what is learnt from a simulation exercise and what was originally intended to be taught may not be congruent for a number of reasons. While it is important at the early stages in designing an exercise to carefully consider the reasons for having an exercise, players may become misguided or unclear about the purpose of the exercise (this is also true for the authors of simulations). Players may believe there is a hidden agenda operating for the exercise planners or may display a negative attitude to the exercise which they believe is an attempt to bring about some unwanted organizational change. Players may simply feel the exercise is a waste of their time. These problems could be due to the exercise planners' motivations (purposes) for running the exercise, poor planning or implementation.

Some theorists have been critical of a *laissez-faire* approach to debriefings, arguing that planners often rely on their personal experience and communication skills to get them through the debriefing process rather than planning this as an integral part of the simulation. This is often facilitated by an approach to exercise design, where planners see the performance of their simulations as 'an art' in itself, often leaving too little time for the debriefing at the end. Coote and McMahon have argued that certain key features need to be outlined in the design of any debriefing process to help avoid these pitfalls. Of importance is whether the game is designed to impart learning directly through participation or over a longer period, after 'psychological consolidation'. Coote and McMahon also recommend that planners should consider whether it is desirable to have a debriefing process as an inherent part of the game. This would reduce players' dependence on the game controllers to facilitate formal learning at the end (Coote and McMahon, 1988).

Pearson and Smith have also advocated the importance of the debriefing process, arguing that it needs to be considered in relation to both the exercise briefing and play. They suggest that players may be so involved in the experience of a simulation that they are unable to step back and reflect on it. They argue, therefore, that the debriefing process is of importance in allowing such reflection to take place (Pearson and Smith, 1986).

Horner has suggested that simulation exercises themselves may have limited value. He argues that the debriefing, in contrast, is of major significance. Horner highlights two main reasons for the importance of debriefings:

a) identifications of failings and short-comings allows individuals to learn from their mistakes and thus extend their range of experience:

b) monitoring the course of events allows modifications to be made to improve procedures; and may suggest new procedures and the appropriate form of contingency plans.

(Horner, 1976: 10)

However, this positive view of the debrief process needs to be considered against the findings of some theorists. In emergency response exercises, players may sometimes misconceive a simulation as a test of their personal abilities, when the purpose was in fact quite different. This can have disastrous effects on the running of the exercise, particularly if the players treat the exercise in the spirit of a competition and the outcome is not good. Debriefs in these circumstances can lead to a process of bitter recriminations where players attribute their poor performance to the unrealistic nature of the exercise scenario, materials used or exercise design faults. Learning in these circumstances may be severely limited and the opposite effect may result, with players' erroneous conceptions about crisis management being reinforced!

Simulation training for crisis poses a tacit acceptance that the unthinkable may happen. This acceptance can facilitate a shift in attitude among responsible decision makers that training for crisis scenarios will require a shift in thinking away from highly structured contingencies for emergencies and predictable disaster plans. Crisis in a training context offers the opportunity to deal with something new, a challenge to existing operating procedures and understandings. Crisis simulations also offer those who design and implement them a similar opportunity. The learning process found in this research was, for the author at least, a profound one and is offered in support of this.

Validation

There are a number of ways in which risk simulations could be validated. These need to both take account of simulation theory from other contexts, and also provide a greater awareness of the plurality of risk. One way we might wish to validate the effectiveness of simulations is in terms of a value-for-money model. For example, we might wish to put a notional cost on a human life, then calculate the number of lives potentially saved by a simulation exercise. This would at least provide a direct cost-benefit ratio (a measured 'transfer of training') similar to the method used for validating aircraft simulators for pilot training (Rolfe, 1992, 1998).

It is also suggested that because of the number of variables involved in business continuity management, a cost-benefit analysis would be simply too crude. There are too many variables to measure precisely whether a positive or indeed a negative transfer of training has come about from exercise implementation. Validation is therefore required at some qualitative level.

Repeating the exercise after an appropriate period of time might be more a test of participants' memories than ability to manage, but it would provide an opportunity for learning on the basis of reflection and hindsight, important for both Kolb and Piaget's theories. Such an approach can also be appropriate to highly structured operator training tasks. Validating performance on group tasks (congruent with Lewin's theory) is more difficult, as group social dynamics are problematic to evaluate. There would still be a problem in collecting enough reliable qualitative data about decision makers who undertake the training and comparing this with a control group after a time period.

The debrief session can be fundamentally important in validation. The debrief enables players to contrast outcomes with a number of potential response strategies.

Lagadec (1995) suggests that the problems found in the debriefing process may in fact illustrate symptoms of a serious organizational shortcoming:

> Yet the very difficulty encountered in launching this debriefing process is highly revealing: it is a clear sign that the organisation is still very poorly prepared to face crises, and consequently that it is highly vulnerable.
>
> (Lagadec, 1995)

The problem is that our response to any crisis incident is at best dependent upon our definition of what is happening. Disagreements between experts about the cause and remedies of these tragedies can frequently be heard in public and governmental inquiries. Training for a crisis can itself create a crisis for the response organizations, as suggested by Lagadec. If this is correct, then the training crisis created is for many organizations a very necessary one.

Simulations can be resource-intensive to produce and it might therefore be pragmatic to assess their validity in terms of achieving their purpose. An important issue to consider at the beginning of any simulation planning process is 'purpose', for it is this criterion which will be used to measure validity. So, for example, theatre productions can be appraised in terms of their ability to entertain us or appeal to our emotions in a variety of ways; for example, by frightening or making us laugh. Experiments can be designed with the purpose of validating or violating a hypothesis and flight simulators have the purpose of training pilots more safely, cheaply and quickly.

Validating or measuring the effectiveness of a simulation will depend on two criteria. First, the ability to define the stated purpose for which the exercise has been created. Second, the ability to actually measure the extent to which that purpose has been achieved. Both identifying purpose and measuring achievement can in practice be highly problematic; this is because the real purpose of many simulations is not always easy to identify, for either players or designers. The purpose may also have changed in the course of the planning process, or the simulation may have multiple purposes. While these issues are problematic in a variety of simulation contexts, validation may prove a particularly acute problem in the case of simulations designed to train decision makers for effective emergency management. The subjective and dynamic nature of crisis response makes it hard to measure in a scientific way.

It is worth considering some of the theoretical work done by psychologists in the area of simulation validation. One approach to this has been developed through the analysis of what has been called 'transfer of training' to participants during simulation exercises.

In 1903, Thorndike argued that a positive transfer could occur, if there were specific elements in the training task the same as in the original. Hence ideally there would be 'identical elements' in both the simulation and real situation (Thorndike, 1903). Thorndike's theory was developed by Osgood, within a stimulus response model. He argued that a relationship exists between the representation of the stimulus in the simulation scenario and the desired response in the actual situation. Three possible outcomes are possible in this model. First, the greatest transfer will occur when the stimulus and response are most similar in both real and simulated situations. Second, if there is no relationship between the real and simulated contexts, then no transfer will occur. Third, if there is sufficient similarity between stimuli, but an antagonism between responses, then a negative transfer will occur (Osgood, 1949).

While both Thorndike and Osgood's theories suggest that there should be a relationship between the original and simulated tasks, the importance of the stimulus–response model is that it suggests a transfer can occur without the totality of the original task being presented, so long as the stimuli and response are similar. This allows simulations to be used in order to train people for a variety of tasks without them having to be in the entire reality which it is desired to prepare them for.

Rolfe has highlighted some considerable work on the measurement of transfer by using a classical experimental design. Rolfe's approach measures the level of transfer by using two matched groups, a control and experimental group, both of which have received no prior training. An essential characteristic of measurement is a comparison between on-the-job training and training received on the simulator device. This is gauged for both types of training as a measurement called 'performance to criterion'. The percentage difference between the two groups' performance to criterion can then be analysed in order to establish the extent to which the simulation device has provided a positive or negative transfer of criterion skills (Rolfe, 1992: 251–255).

Rolfe illustrates this valuation method with reference to three examples from an aviation perspective. The first of these he cites from Valverde (see Valverde, 1973), who describes the transfer of training concept in a paper called 'The proof of the pudding'. This paper exemplified the positive transfer of skills in two matched groups of students who were trained in flying. The control group received a traditional training programme in the cockpit of an aircraft, while the experimental group also received assistance in certain aspects of their learning programme from a flight training simulator. The total training costs for the two groups were then calculated to an average per trained pilot for the two groups. It was found that this came to less than half for the simulator-assisted group of pilots.

Rolfe's second example of positive transfer is from a comparison between the operational kill rates of US airforce and navy pilots. The US navy's now famous 'Top Gun' school of training employed engagement and combat simulators in fighter pilot training. Over a comparable period, US navy pilots were able to increase their kill rate by a factor of five compared to a static rate achieved through traditional training methods (Rolfe, 1992: 256–257).

However, Rolfe also cites in his third example an incidence of what he describes as 'backward or negative transfer' occurring. He cites this from a paper by Ragland *et al.* (1964). Backward transfer happens when some previously unknown phenomenon occurs in an operational reality and this is subsequently modelled and incorporated to an existing training simulator. He illustrates this with the phenomenon first discovered in the 1960s, 'high-altitude clear-air turbulence'. It was found that some fully trained American airline pilots in commercial jet aircraft were rapidly losing control of their aircraft and descending some 25 000 ft. By analysing the black box recorders from these planes, the precise effects of the phenomenon on aircraft handling could be modelled into a sophisticated simulator for training. On the first run of the simulator, the pilots were unable to cope with the effects of the simulated phenomenon; however, once made aware of the experience they learned to handle the aircraft safely (Rolfe, 1992: 257).

This type of validation procedure is effective so long as the desired training is highly structured and from definable units. Transfer of training is now extensively applied to operator training in technical tasks such as flight simulation (Frisby, 1947; Valverde, 1973; Hunter *et al.*, 1977; Ayres *et al.*, 1984; Thompson, 1989). However, this model could equally be applied to other highly structured areas of technical training, such as modern routine surgery techniques or the management of mechanized process systems. So long as the simulator contains definable stimuli and responses in common with the source reality, a positive or negative transfer can be measured.

In less structured simulations, such as multiservice crisis response exercises, a different approach to exercise validation is required. One reason for this is because the types of simulations Rolfe refers to in his examples concern the training of individuals. Whether this type of validation technique can be applied to group management tasks is questionable.

Another approach to validation is argued by Sheridan and Hennessy (1984). They suggest a 'high-' and 'low-' fidelity distinction be made when considering the validity of simulations. High-fidelity simulations are detailed and realistic recreations of the real, offering a rich source of data for analysis. The concern in a high-fidelity simulation is to encourage the actors, as much as possible, to behave and react in the same manner as they would in their real-life contexts and this is facilitated by giving the simulation the appearance (at least externally) of an operational reality. The success of the simulation for high-level fidelity can thus be measured in terms of its success as a tool for the transference of learning from reality to representation. This would (as is the case with real-life data) require a sensitive methodological approach in order to collect and present data successfully to players. In terms of crisis management this is very difficult to do.

A low-fidelity simulation is referential to some part or aspect of its represented reality. In this respect it need not be as sophisticated in design as the high-level type, since it only represents some aspect of the reality. Although a low-level simulation would be reliant upon a particular model of reality, this model could be adapted to the perceived purpose of the simulation. However, deciding which aspects of the reality are pertinent to model is contentious and may require a great deal of skill on the part of the designer.

The distinction between high- and low-fidelity models could be applied to 'realistic' and 'table top' emergency response exercises. The former aims to produce high-fidelity scenarios, giving the appearance to players and observers of an operational reality; this would use a realistic physical scenario or one which is represented in some detail through interactive computer interface. The latter, in contrast, is based on a referential scenario, symbolically presented to players in the form of small models, pictures, verbal and written inputs.

While it may be possible in the context of some highly structured technical tasks to create high-fidelity models, the problems of producing high levels of fidelity in many more socio-technical contexts is more difficult. Schuffel argues:

> Psychological fidelity is more ill-defined. It is usually taken to refer to the extent to which the simulator produces behaviour that is the same as that required in the real situation: perfect psychological fidelity would be found in a simulator that yielded a hundred percent transfer of learning to the real situation.
>
> (Schuffel, 1984)

The evaluation of these low-fidelity simulations is a difficult process. Due to the complex types of social, cultural and psychological phenomena associated with these simulations, evaluation is problematic, being reliant on some qualitative indicators of performance. Simulation design and implementation for these types of applications is something of an art form, with parameters of interest restricted to particular and personalized concerns.

In contrast, another psychological approach to simulation validity is suggested by Stammers. He argues that there are two types of extreme conditions which could be considered as benchmarks for measuring the validity of a simulations: 'face validity', which refers to the general appearance of reality as purveyed to the actor involved; and 'functional validity', the way the equipment provided matches that used in reality (Stammers, 1983). For Stammers, a simulation is a model used in a learning context to achieve a particular goal, and he states: 'Any situation that departs from the real world task demands and exerts some control over the learning progress of the trainee can be termed a simulation' (Stammers, 1983: 229).

In order to accept Stammers' argument, all supervised learning tasks could be described as simulations, and this is not particularly useful for validation purposes. For example, if we teach children to add up using apples and oranges, this would constitute a simulation for Stammers, but it is not clear how this is helpful for the validation of simulations.

Social role play-type simulations, such as business games and crisis management exercises, would appear to fit into the category of low-level simulations. They are certainly low in fidelity due to the number of social factors involved in their operation. For example, the purpose of an exercise may be unclear or even mistrusted by players. For planners, it may be hard to define the aims of the exercise or they may even have multiple or even unconscious aims. It is impossible to know the precise extent to which a player's future behaviour will alter as a result of the simulation experience. Indicators such as protocols and questionnaires are at best subjective, if not crude, methodological barometers, because players may not be able to articulate the results adequately or the questionnaires simply may not ask the relevant questions.

Simulations can be both time-consuming and expensive to produce. In the author's research experience, it is not uncommon for major county exercises among the emergency services to be budgeted in millions rather than thousands of pounds, particularly in the case of expensive computerized simulations such as Minerva and Hydra used by the police (Crego and Harris, 2001) and Vector Command (Vector Command UK, 1999).

Of concern here is the extent to which such training proves to be of subsequent value. In an increasingly litigious and regulated society, the need for organizations to demonstrate a capability for decision making under crisis is an important management requirement.

An interesting seven-point framework for validating business games has been developed by Loveluck. Although Loveluck's work is based on a career of designing, implementing and analysing business games, it is argued that this model could be adapted and applied quite effectively to crisis training exercises. Loveluck argues that low-fidelity simulations – typically, those being advocated here – should ideally display a number of features and that these will be an indication of their effectiveness (Loveluck, 1994). These are briefly discussed below in relation to crisis exercises.

First, simulations should display an external simplicity masking internal complexity. This is often a problematic issue. When designing simulation games for organizations, designers tend to produce complex game designs. In practice, however, complex games are difficult to administer, and may even prove poor learning vehicles for the players. In contrast, a simpler game tends to provide players with a clearer understanding of the issues involved by being focused on the management of a limited number of goals.

Clearly an effective crisis simulation would need to recreate the experience of crisis for the players. Simulations should, therefore, aim at reproducing the fundamental elements of the crisis as closely as possible so that participants can experience elements of the crisis management process that they will have to live through when a real crisis occurs.

A distinction should be made here between physical and psychological fidelity. The former is often perceived to be more effective as a learning environment – this may even be true for emergency exercises – but for crisis situations it is the latter which provides the best learning environment. Gredler has argued (1992: 80–81) that effective crisis management simulations encourage participants to perceive the scenario as a threat, with time limitations for effective data gathering. Simulations should produce similar reactions and feelings in participants as experienced in real-life crisis events, e.g. tension, uncertainty, time pressure, sense of inadequate information and frustration (Gredler, 1992: 82).

Second, Loveluck argues that games should have some theoretical underpinning. Simulations should be designed with some clear purpose. If it is difficult for the planner(s) to define the purpose of an exercise, it will probably be even more so for the players who have far less time to be acquainted with it and probably only a limited aspect of it at that. It should perhaps be part of a game's design that purpose be an integral feature of the debriefing. It is argued that an innovative use of game design and layout is therefore essential to reinforce learning. Thiagarajan (1994, 2003) argues that people don't learn from actual experiences; instead they learn from reflecting on the experience. Debriefing helps participants to reflect on their simulation experience and to learn transferable skills and concepts (Thiagarajan, 1994). Thiagarajan has reflected and developed this point further in his more recent work. He now argues that the only reason for running a simulation is so that an exercise can be debriefed (Thiagarajan, 2003).

The potential for learning from crisis simulations may be most effective when the exercises are beginning to fail. It is only when the procedures or crisis management team appear to be in trouble that they are able to think through a recovery strategy. All too often, learning in this context is replaced with blame for either the exercise designer or the actions of other players. It is therefore very important for designers and facilitators to be aware of and actively intervene at these points.

It is stressed that the characteristics of crisis significantly differ from those of emergencies or disasters. Hence, this difference should be translated into the simulation design, and the simulated crisis should be a radical challenge to the organizational system. Debriefing in this context is likely to be a difficult, if not painful, experience as many assumptions are exposed and challenged.

Third, games should contain 'an element of surprise'. If players have not been surprised, then this is probably an indication that they have not learnt very much from the experience or that they did not need training. The surprise itself could form the basis for learning, for example, by discovering misconceptions in the beliefs of others through role reversal. Most commonly, the surprise would be effected through changes to established work roles or organizational systems. In the case of simulations designed to evaluate systems, the surprise might be for the planners rather than the players. Crisis management training is about moving away from well-choreographed and ritualized drills to highly destabilizing shocks to the fundamental organizational systems. There should be no easy-to-apply formulae of response patterns.

Fourth, the social structure of a group of players may conflict too strongly with the desired power structure in the game. Players who normally hold senior ranking positions may feel uncomfortable having to perform at a low level in the simulation. They may feel embarrassed at having to perform, perhaps poorly, in front of their subordinates. They may similarly be concerned that their subordinates may perform their normal role better. There is also an issue of power to consider. Managers may wish to take part in games as players and it may require some skill to run the game so that they do not make fools of themselves in front of their contemporaries. Subordinate employees are used to hearing the outcome of management decision processes. They may be somewhat surprised and even raise questions of validity when they see how the decision-making process takes place. Designers and facilitators need to be aware of the emotional impact of crisis games, particularly between the gamer, player and setting, since this can lead to severe friction or even open hostility towards the training.

The unintended consequence of giving team feedback without respect to the relationship between individual and team performance is that incorrect behaviours may even be reinforced. Flin (1996: 79) has observed that incident commanders and command structures feedback should be critical but constructive and designed to identify strengths as well as training needs.

Fifth, in management training, 'verisimilitude' is valued more highly than realism. Loveluck argues that, in a business management context, trainers will often place too much emphasis on the need for realism, possibly at the expense of running a good simulation. This point is of particular importance for the emergency services. The trend in recent years for both the police and the ambulance service is to try to produce high-fidelity simulation environments using computer interfaces. It is suggested here that a crisis exercise, where used as an effective learning tool, should have good psychological fidelity. Physical fidelity, while adding to the ambience of training, adds little or nothing to the crisis training value.

The objective for consultants may be to keep the business of their clients. This may cause a sales/ethics dilemma. Clients may not like the product, particularly if the training process itself brings about a crisis. Loveluck notes (1994) that clients tend to require intricate and highly elaborate designs that are often intended to demonstrate the complexity of either their managerial function or their organization. In practice, complex simulations are difficult to administer and may even prove poor learning vehicles. Loveluck argues that in a business management context, trainers may place too much emphasis on the need for realism, possibly at the expense of running a good simulation; therefore 'verisimilitude should be valued more highly than realism' (Loveluck, 1994). The trend towards highly intricate and realistic computer-aided simulations, such as Minerva and Vector, may be a case in point. These tools do provide highly realistic theatres for running simulations, but the quality of the exercises run on them will still be limited to those of the game designers and facilitators. The training value is in the exercise, not the props used to aid delivery. These computer simulations have great potential in terms of the repeated running of exercises which, once perfected, can be rolled out to large numbers of people in the organization.

Sixth, there is a difference between running and merely administering a game. Running games is a skill that can be learnt by some but not all. This is quite distinct from the umpiring approach used in large military gaming contexts. It is therefore, necessary to train those running games, and ensure that they are capable. Similarly, the designers of games need to be aware that they may not be the best people to run them, despite their expertise in game design. Loveluck argues that the expertise required for the design of a simulation is different from that required for steering and sensing the social dynamics of a group. This point takes on significance in the context of an earlier one about learning in crisis training exercises. One of the best ways to learn about crisis management is through the preparation, administration and debriefing of a game.

The planning stages, at least, would force designers to think of ways in which the system might be vulnerable. Both plans and response teams need to be tested regularly, and learning should take place. One strategy for doing this is to rotate the roles of exercise writers, directors, players and facilitators; this provides players with a variety of viewpoints or what anthropologists might call a 'thick description' of crisis response (Geertz, 1973).

Seventh, games are culture-sensitive. Moving a game from one social context to another can be problematic, since the running of games requires certain personal sensitivities and skills. The cultural context within which social interaction takes place may substantially change during games. Such things as the use of appropriate humour can dramatically alter how players respond.

Organizations with strong training cultures may have extreme difficulties adjusting to the open-ended nature of crisis management. The need to establish correct actions/procedures similar to those required for emergency response may blind players to the opportunities for unorthodox flexible treatments required in crisis. Crisis simulations could facilitate productive changes to organizational culture by allowing players to identify, manage and even profit from crisis situations. It is, however, very important that this should cut across both hierarchical structures and departmental barriers.

The morality of simulations

There are a number of ethical issues associated with control and implementation of simulation exercises. Boot and Reynolds, who have used simulations in an educational context, point out that for any learning exercise there is the confrontation of role relationships existing between tutor and student. They also suggest that simulations should be viewed in the context of the socio-political issues which underpin them (Boot and Reynolds, 1983: 3).

There are circumstances where simulations raise moral and ethical questions which create considerable controversy. In psychology, disputes about the acceptable limits of experimentation have led to guidelines being produced by the British and American psychological societies. An extreme but not isolated example of this is the now famous Milgram experiment to test obedience to authority. Subjects were asked to inflict what they thought were electric shocks to an associate, under the impression that this was in some way part of a word memory task. In reality no associate existed; the groans and screams which subjects could hear when the shocks were applied were in fact from tape recordings of actors. The undisclosed true purpose of the experiment was to find out how far subjects would go in administering the shocks under the persuasiveness of laboratory-simulated authority. All the subjects expressed concern when asked to administer lethal doses of electricity to their associate but, under firm instructions from the experimenter, the majority of subjects complied with the experimenter's request to do so (Milgram, 1974). Many of the subjects involved in this experiment were subsequently concerned to find that they had the capacity to commit such an atrocity upon another human being.

British Psychological Society Guideline number 4.3 states: 'Deception is unacceptable if the participants mind when the deception is revealed' (BPS Ethical Guidelines, 1988). A game/role play analogy may be quite useful in the simulation of business environments, where the greatest misfortune may be the bankruptcy of some individual or organization, but this analogy may seem less ethical in the context of some crisis simulations, where the subject may be so serious as to include deaths and permanent physical disfigurements.

The extent to which simulations can be considered in the context of games is somewhat problematic. While there are clear notions of 'gaming' implied by the metaphoric use of this term in the literature, such as winning and losing, this is often hard to reconcile with the awesome severity of the realities which simulations are based on. Trying to make cross-cultural comparisons is also problematic; even taking a simulation from one organization and using it in another in the same culture may prove difficult.

How are we to assess the morality of emergency simulations? Many are never recorded or written up in any formal sense. Often those who may have been violated are never able to bring this to attention. Simulations can have the same devastating psychological effects found to result from real incidents, such as post-disaster stress syndrome. This is a subject that requires more research.

Players may be sought out on an apparently voluntary basis, but if the simulation needs to remain a mystery in order to work, as is highlighted in Loveluck's requirement for 'an element of surprise', the players will never really know the precise nature of their voluntary involvement. How voluntary is voluntary? Players will inevitably be reliant on a certain degree of trust in the moral high standards of the planners and those that recruit them. Historically, white coats and other such labels congruent with the term 'expert' have proved questionable as arbitrary indicators of ethics.

Simulations which cause undue stress and other symptomatic effects on players can lead to serious consequences. Exercise planners may place undue stress on players in a number of ways. They may simply require players to do something impossible, and then make them feel inadequate as a result of their poor response. A poignant example of this is given in an independent evaluation of the ICCARUS exercise by Dr Valerie Hay who discusses the training of one fire officer:

> Commenting upon his own performance with ICCARUS – he noted 'that if you put younger officers in front of it and they lost it as I did, it's almost a suicide note on the mat'.

(ICCARUS Project, 1989)

This remark would appear to relate to Loveluck's fourth proposition that the potential emotional impact of games must be carefully considered. Players who have or are suffering from post-traumatic stress syndrome may have a recurrence of the symptoms when faced with a simulation which is too realistic. Some planners may simply go too far to produce a realistic exercise. A code of ethics may be desirable, but may also pose a constraining feature to exercise innovation and design. The issue of social acceptability in crisis management simulations has yet to be addressed.

What constitutes an acceptable exercise is clearly to some extent subjective. Simulations are likely to affect individuals in a multiplicity of ways which are not easy to predict. Particular attention needs to be focused on ethical and moral issues in emergency exercises. The subject simulated is likely to be distressing and a perceived feeling of inadequacy may not facilitate what is already a difficult job.

Culture, gender, ethnic origin and status for players and facilitators will inevitably affect exercise outcome to some extent. Culture (more specifically organizational) will define how rules and scenarios are interpreted, analysed and responded to. For emergency service organizations with strict hierarchical structures and strong organizational cultures, games are likely to be taken very seriously indeed, with the potential for a number of unforeseen consequences – for example, players may engage in a game of damaging organizational rivalry. It is therefore important that both exercise designers and facilitators can to some extent be seen to be separate from the normal organizational management structures and, for the duration of the exercise at least, empowered with sufficient authority to be treated seriously.

Chapter 7

THE MANAGEMENT OF RISK, CRISIS AND SECURITY

Risk

Risk, crisis and security are not new problems nor will they be easily solved for humans. Approaches to these themes date back to some of the earliest recorded writings to be found in the world. To presume that with the benefit of science and technology we could somehow make the problems of risk go away is just plainly naive. The use of science and technology has caused many of these problems in the first place. Risk and security remain basic human needs for any ordered society; our understanding of failure, however, has changed radically.

For cultural theorists, it is our reluctance to believe in deities that has brought about this change (Douglas, 1994; Lupton, 2004), or our arrival in modernity (Beck, 1992; Giddens, 1991; Green, 1997). Belief in a higher being allows us to put failure into the context of a grander scheme of things. While the author does not personally advocate a belief in deities, they are expedient in avoiding having to understand why disasters happen. Science, technology and perhaps even modernity may in time come to be seen as alternative religions, or at least belief systems in their own right. For some authors they already are; the anthropologist Bruno Latour has questioned the entire basis for an argument of postmodernism (Latour, 1993).

> I can now conclude this essay by tackling the most difficult question: the question of the non-modern world that we are entering, I maintain, without ever having left it.
>
> (Latour, 1993: 130)

If we have truly arrived in a 'postmodern society', then why do things still go so wrong and so catastrophically? This question is a valid one and should be put to all those who claim that a risk irrationality is due to a misunderstanding of science.

Major risk failures are no longer seen as acts of God, but the direct result of human error (Reason, 1990), irrationality (Lopes, 1987; Kahneman and Tversky, 1979), cultural misunderstandings (Pidgeon, 1992), failed communication (Irwin, 1995; Drottz-Sjöberg, 2003), systemic failure (Turner, 1978; Perrow, 1984) or just a plain homeostatic need to keep enough risk in our lives (Wilde, 1994; Adams, 1995). Taking on these theories collectively, it is unlikely that we could ever successfully manage risk.

A good analogy for the management of risk might be weather forecasting, particularly if you live in northwest Europe where there is an abundance of weather! While it is possible to train to be an expert in weather prediction, the prognosis is still only slightly better than half that the prediction will be right. If our weather forecasts were to be given in terms of impact versus likelihood for particular weather phenomena, would this make them more reliable? The answer is probably not. The very term 'management' is perhaps the wrong term to use altogether; maybe it would be more honest to call this area of study 'risk mismanagement'.

Security

Security management suffers from a more extreme version of the same problem, if someone or a group is determined to bring about a security failure, whether for personal gain, opportunism or political/religious reasons. The likelihood of their success is very high indeed, unless we are prepared to turn our dwellings, work and leisure places into modern-day fortresses. The only way we can make an organization or process totally risk-free is to shut it down! Clearly for many areas of activity, such as health, education and transport, this is not a socially or politically acceptable option. Acceptable security risk, in the absence of any academic consensus, must for the time being remain in the hands of courts and politicians.

The current heightened state of domestic and international security has brought about some irrationality in the way that security risk is viewed. Risks of a chemical, biological and radiological nature from extremist groups – while it must be admitted they are high-impact events – for most organizations occur at a very low frequency indeed. Other types of risks, emanating from human security and systems failure, are far more common and likely to nibble away at us. The status and training of security employees is a real concern; a number of very well-meaning theorists have argued that the process of security requires regulation and control (George and Button, 2000).

The question of how we define security, however, and what should be included in that definition is and remains contentious (Borodzicz, 1996a; Manunta, 1998b). It is argued here that a debate about the nature of modern security in relation to both risk and organizational studies is urgently required. Of concern is the demarcation line between risk and security; who deals with insurance and business continuity or who designs training exercises. Many of the responsibilities that could be assigned to either role are frankly ambiguous.

Crisis

There is now emerging a significant political, social and legal requirement for key decision makers to be trained to a degree of competency in crisis management. While it is a requirement of regulatory authorities for organizations to consider contingency arrangements and training for major crisis situations, little in the way of established orthodoxy exists to suggest how organizations should train for such contingencies.

Civil emergency planning, as we have come to know it, is in a state of transition. How we, as a society, expect the leaders of our organizations – even countries – to respond to major crisis events is one of the most topical debates of our time. Attempts to legislate and regulate organizational activity in relation to risk and security, one might argue, represent a significant crisis risk in their own right.

Crisis response has taken on a new significance in the context of terrorism. Terrorists want to create a crisis for governments. They do this by studying the response plans and designing scenarios that will test them and show them wanting. The need for a disciplined approach to crisis response needs to be dangerously balanced against flexibility.

In Chapter 2, various conceptual approaches to risk were considered. Risk was described from a number of theoretical positions. Of these, a number appeared to be of central theoretical importance for the management of crisis; in particular, safety culture, systemic approaches, risk communication and homeostasis. This debate is useful in highlighting the relationship between politics, economics and safety. The management and prevention of risk is a laudable aim, but this must be viewed within an understanding that good risk prevention will never guarantee 100% protection from hazards. It is therefore of equal importance that contingencies are taken seriously.

The theoretical risk perspectives presented in Chapter 2 appear exclusive in application; in fact it is argued here that they may be of complementary use in understanding crisis management. For example, the minor operational problems associated with stage two of Turner's model are, from a systems perspective, symptoms of an incubational fault or, for Perrow, too much 'complexity'. From a safety culture viewpoint, the failure to perceive threats to a system's viability represents a poor safety culture. From a risk communication perspective, failure is evidence of a competing expert diagnosis (multiple realities). Psychologists would argue that our own irrationality is the problem. From a risk homeostasis perspective, the only reason something is going wrong is because our attention is on something else! If risk failure is inherent in every organizational system, then in the absence of a 'magic wand' to make the problem go away it might be prudent to make some preparation for the eventuality of crisis.

Any team unfortunate enough to have to respond to a major crisis event will become the focus of the media. Accidents and the response to them have become an area of intense media attention. The social perception of disasters has changed from one of resigned fate to a failure of increased and perhaps unreasonable management expectations.

What is suggested here is that contingency plans for crisis should include a flexible or generic operational element.

Why we need competent crisis managers

There has been too little research into the competencies required of crisis management teams (Smith, 2000, 2004). The need to train for the response to crisis situations has focused attention on the competency and training of incident commanders in a variety of organizational contexts. For the police, fire and ambulance services, there is a long-established tradition of training commanders who are competent to undertake operational decisions in an emergency. Ill-structured crisis situations, however, pose more serious concerns. Crisis situations over recent decades have at times caused the questioning of the role of response organizations. The UK has also experienced terrorism over the past 30 years, particularly in Northern Ireland but also on the mainland. More recent and growing concerns about the threat of international terrorism, particularly since 11 September 2001, have increased the need for flexible contingency plans which might need to broaden inter-agency cooperation to include military as well as a variety of government and voluntary agencies. Central to such plans is the need to train key decision makers to be both competent and accountable for their response.

Agencies ranging from the prison, health and education services to safety-critical industries, such as the utilities and transport providers, may find themselves managing situations which can rapidly transform into multi-agency crisis events, requiring sensitive handling, often in the full glare of the media.

Managing uncertainty is not a new problem, although the context in which uncertainty takes place has become more complex. Contemporary society has developed many sophisticated systems for preventing and managing risks. There is now a considerable and fairly sophisticated body of academic research and literature on the subject of risk management. There is also a range of university and professional courses and training programmes. Despite this plethora of information, we seem to live in a more dangerous world than ever before. Contemporary society with rapid communication and transport systems has brought about an increased expectation of safety on the part of society. Professor Douglas argues that people are no longer prepared to accept disasters as 'acts of God', instead perceiving them as management failures (Douglas, 1994). The role of social and technical complexity in modern management systems has also been commented on (Turner and Pidgeon, 1997; Perrow, 1984).

Much of the current focus appears to be based on a combination of regulating as much risk as possible out of the system and dealing with the rest through insurance and contingency plans. More recently, a number of theorists have argued that despite improvements in both of these areas, crisis events still pose a serious threat and more attention should be given to preparing for such events (Lagadec, 1997; Turner, 1994; Borodzicz and Van Haperen, 2002).

Why crisis training poses a dilemma

Current approaches to training among the emergency services in the UK are extremely competent. However, our experience in dealing with crisis events often suggests that the very rules, procedures and techniques used to bring about excellence in emergency situations may actually contribute to a failure in crisis. The skills required for emergency and crisis response are both distinct and different (Rosenthal, 1996; Borodzicz, 1997).

For a group of decision makers trained to a high standard in structured emergency response, an unorthodox or flexible approach may be perceived as analogous to a paradigm shift or, put more simply, rule breaking. In the author's own research (Borodzicz, 1997, 1999a), it was found that in every single case of a successfully managed crisis event, the positive outcome could be directly linked to creative or 'flexible' rule breaking by key decision makers in the response. Hence, there is a need to develop an organizational culture capable of identifying, managing and even profiting from crisis situations. This should cut across both hierarchical structures and departmental barriers.

Despite this amorphous context to crisis management, trainers still tend to favour highly structured (militaristic) simulation models, argued here to be totally inappropriate for crisis training (Borodzicz and Van Haperen, 2002, 2003). The reason for favouring such models is that many trainers were themselves selected and trained in this way, either in the emergency services or the military. A second reason is that these types of simulation are more easily evaluated in terms of measuring performance to a pre-designated criterion. While it may be possible to compare good and bad decisions with hindsight, as is the case of much of the literature on disaster management, it is much more difficult to gauge decisions in terms of right or wrong at the time of a crisis.

Simulations of crisis events, if effective, should be modelled on events that are 'ill-structured' (Turner, 1978) and complex. This would, therefore, require facilitators and players to interactively create a solution as part of the game scenario in an unstructured and flexible manner. This adds a second challenge to game designers who as part of the facilitating experience are required to engage in a learning process themselves. Players need to learn how to work together and respond to the crisis. Game designers, in contrast, would need not only to construct the crisis for players, but also to ensure the players find a solution while obtaining a positive learning experience. Some of the concerns about reliance on overly structured and militaristic models in game design are indicative of the misunderstanding and failure to model crisis accurately by trainers. It is argued here that qualitative skills, such as flexibility, negotiation and the ability to communicate effectively, may be key to facilitating crisis management. Whether these skills have been exercised in a simulation, let alone learnt, is much more difficult to evaluate.

Learning for facilitators and designers is often a much more intense experience than that received by the players themselves (Borodzicz, 1997, 1999a; Borodzicz and Van Haperen, 2002, 2003). This creates another dilemma in terms of using simulations to demonstrate competency to respond to crisis events. Performing one's role in a crisis simulation may actually be indicative of a player's ability to conform to an 'in-service' organizational culture rather than deal with a real crisis. Most academics involved in teaching will be familiar with the distinction between students who can pass exams well, as opposed to those who demonstrate practical life and work skills. Professor Flin has argued that the need for flexible and creative thinking among those responding to crises can constitute a significant additional source of 'stress and mental demand' (Flin, 1996). It is argued here that this may be of equal if not greater significance for those designing games.

Martial arts and crisis simulations

A useful but somewhat surprising analogy to crisis simulation could be made for martial arts practice. These eastern fighting forms perform a dual role. They are simulations serving a real function, as a form of art (as we have noted, in the Chinese language, the word 'simulation', as translated, is used to mean the equivalent of a formal 'dress rehearsal' in the theatrical sense), but they also train and condition the practitioner for some future and unknown scenario.

Typical of martial arts training is the use of a variety of techniques with a high degree of proficiency and skill. However, to attain the status of a master, the student would need to demonstrate an ability to adapt or apply these techniques in the context of a simulated but unstructured fight situation. In *budo*, the emphasis is upon training the practitioner to respond almost unconsciously to a series of pre-planned events. The practitioner of *budo* is relentlessly trained in many hundreds of combinations of techniques; however, when called upon to respond to an attack in self-defence, the appropriate technique must be chosen and executed without even momentary hesitation if the martial art is to be effectively used (Ratti and Westbrook, 1970). For example, in responding to a direct punch, the martial artist might be trained to use a variety of blocks, avoidance stances and counters.

The psychological demeanour encouraged by the practice of martial arts is now commonly recognized as being of potential value in the training of certain elite military groups who may be faced with unexpected and unpredictable scenarios.

There is an analogy here to what Uriel Rosenthal has described as first- and second-order techniques in crisis response. First-order techniques are emergency responses that can be drilled into players by relentless training and testing until performance achieves a criterion standard. Second-order techniques are to be found at a higher level. Here the responders have to blend or adapt a repertoire of available techniques in a creative way in order to deal with a crisis situation that could not have been foreseen. In this case, the practitioner would not know in advance what type of attack would be forthcoming – response would, therefore, require the practitioner to adapt one or more techniques.

The psychological demeanour encouraged by the practice of martial arts is now commonly recognized as being of potential value in the training of certain elite military groups who might have to deal with highly ill-structured and difficult scenarios. Despite the acknowledged value that this type of training may have, there is still surprisingly little scientific analysis about how or why martial arts training works. It is argued here, from the author's own experience, that one of the key skills martial artists gain from practice is the ability to respond in a flexible yet calm way. An analogy here might be the application of rules without rules. It is pertinent to acknowledge that, in martial arts training, teaching is also considered to be personal training for the instructor in its own right. The role of exercise designer and facilitator is often given to an outside consultant. This is a shame as they are likely to have learnt more than anyone else in the training experience. Consultants are also unlikely to be around when the crisis occurs. The old saying, 'If you want to learn something, do the course; if you want to really understand it, then teach the course yourself' holds true here.

While a business continuity plan is essential, that plan needs to be tested regularly and this should be focused so that learning can take place. Those acting as exercise directors, players and facilitators need to be rotated in order that learning is taking place at more than one level.

Simulations have the potential to provide a powerful tool for experiential training and assessing competency skills in incident commanders. However, serious ethical and methodological concerns need to be addressed and overcome if simulations are to be properly used in this context. As in any other form of education and assessment, learning outcomes should be clearly identified and linked to the assessment procedure. However, unlike other forms of education and training, these are more difficult to define for crisis management. There is also a danger that simulation may be seen as a complete training and assessment system in its own right. The role play experience is an important one, but without other forms of training it may not achieve the desired result.

There is a danger that by allowing teams to be flexible and even to experiment in their response, the old blame culture could be brought back. Experiment, by its very nature, suggests that occasionally even the best of us can get it wrong. Flexibility thus allows us to learn from both our strengths and fallibility. Generic plans are only of use if they can be flexible enough to adapt to operational needs. From the author's experience of observing exercises among the British emergency services, flexibility appears to be the missing ingredient (Borodzicz, 2004).

Impact mitigation for crisis requires some careful thought. The only option here is to start to imagine the unthinkable! Dealing with a crisis is problematic. These are typically low-frequency high-impact events.

> At the worldwide level, dependency on plan detail is key but as we must plan to respond to the unthinkable, this may be less critical than having the right people with the right skills and the authority to act.
>
> (Graham, 2001)

Resources and information for responding are likely to be insufficient and out of the hands of those who normally run the organization. Crisis management in contrast is a non subcontractible responsibility for management. People who run small businesses are only too aware of this. The need to develop an organizational culture capable of identifying, managing and even profiting from crisis situations is important. This should cut across both hierarchical structures and departmental barriers.

Referring to Chernobyl:

> The civil defence response started badly. When the duty officer was alerted, he was not told the correct code word and dismissed the alert as a joke. However the informal communication networks had functioned and most heads of civil organisation (fire brigades, schools, institutes and workshops) had assembled.
>
> (Heath, 1998)

Much can be done to ameliorate risks through insurance, better health and safety management, proactive risk assessments and monitoring, improved safety or security culture. However, the risk of a crisis always remains a very real possibility. Ironically, the better we become at managing risks, the more complex and difficult to handle are the organizational failures that slip through the net. The nature of organizations has changed considerably in recent years; new forms of organizational structure and communication have radically altered the way we work. The way we approach risk, crisis and security needs to adapt to this changing world.

Good risk and security management, ultimately, is simply about good management. Any training or educational course that claims to train and develop managers without teaching risk is failing to prepare students for the real world.

Please take care. It is very dangerous out there!

APPENDIX: FOUR VERY DIFFERENT CASE STUDIES

Case study 1 – 11 September 2001

It is likely that 11 September 2001 is a day that will be etched into our memories for generations to come. The political ramifications of this act of terrorism can be argued to have changed the world. The attacks have been condemned by virtually every democratic government in the world, and formed the basis for an international war on terror, which continues at the time of writing. While it is hard to imagine how the terrorists involved thought this attack would help their campaign, it is certainly beyond the scope of this case study to answer such a question.

Terrorism and the associated risks posed have certainly caused governments throughout the world to review their response arrangements. Prevention is not always going to be possible, particularly when people are so devoted to their cause that they are prepared to kill themselves in order to achieve their aim of killing others.

The time span for responding to the crisis phase of a terrorism outrage is usually very short or non-existent. Decision makers attempting to respond both strategically and operationally, at least in the early phase of a response, are frequently unable to perceive the scale or nature of the total unfolding event. The response agencies in New York believed they were responding to one, then two, towering infernos; with the benefit of hindsight, we now know that they were dealing with the two largest unplanned building collapses in modern history. More than 300 fire fighters responding to the twin towers were killed in trying to rescue people from the burning buildings. Most were killed when the buildings unexpectedly collapsed during the rescue operation.

In all, more than 3000 people died in this tragic event; more than throughout the entire 30-year campaign by the IRA. The effects of the two buildings collapsing after being struck by the passenger jets could be compared, at least in terms of energy released, to a medium-size nuclear bomb. The sheer audaciousness and scale of the attacks took those with responsibility for response by total surprise.

Similarly, those responding to the immediate and disastrous effects of the building fires did their best to apply their previous training in search and rescue to the task in hand. The speed and efficiency of the response – for many of the agencies, but particularly the fire service – simply increased the death toll when the buildings collapsed.

Common to both this case study and the one on King's Cross were early decisions to try to evacuate, which tragically increased the death toll. At King's Cross, many of those killed would have survived if they had not been evacuated from their trains. In New York, the rescuers themselves formed a sizable number of the deceased. Both events, while on different scales, raise questions about how we should plan and train for evacuations. Another similarity between these case studies is the reported orderliness in which the public conducted the evacuation. Although nearly everybody must have known that this was not a drill, many survivors reported on the good-natured behaviour of those leaving the buildings.

The attack

Four flights took off that morning fully laden with passengers and fuel. Perhaps even the terrorists on board each flight could not imagine the hell that was about to ensue. The terrorists took control of each of the flights shortly after take-off. Two flights were flown at full speed into each of the twin towers in New York, a third hit the Pentagon building in Washington and the fourth crashed in Pennsylvania. The death toll is presumed to be in excess of 3000 people.

Start of the four attacks

07.55 Flight 11 (American Airlines) takes off from Boston, destination Los Angeles. By 08.47 the plane crashes into the north tower of the World Trade Center, killing all on board.

08.05 Flight 93 (United Airlines) takes off from Newark, destination San Francisco. It crashes at 10.06 near Shanksville, Pennsylvania.

08.10 Flight 77 (American Airlines) takes off from Washington, destination Los Angeles. At 09.45 the plane crashes into the Pentagon building.

08.15 Flight 175 (United Airlines) takes off from Boston, destination Los Angeles. By 09.03 Flight 175 had crashed into the south tower of the World Trade Center.

A lot of what took place in those flights will never be known in the public arena. The pilots were killed and hijackers with rudimentary flying skills aimed the planes at their targets with deadly effect. What is perhaps so frightening about the whole event is the simplicity of the method used to take control of the planes. The hijackers had only three requirements to carry out the attack. First, they were armed with no more than 'box cutters', a simple tool legally available at DIY stores throughout the world. Second, they needed some flying experience; this was obtained at a local flying school in the USA. The third requirement was an ability to read timetables and buy plane tickets. All three of these requirements are still available to just about anyone. Prevention, therefore, is almost totally reliant on screening all the people who get access to planes.

Analysis of response

The four attacks pose a number of serious questions in terms of managing the new threat. First is to question the length of time that the planes were allowed to continue flying until they had reached their target. Because the attacks were the first of their kind, it is clear that any decision to shoot down the planes (if even considered) would have, politically at least, been a very difficult decision indeed. For the first two planes the timescale of 52 and 48 minutes allowed little time for any discussion on this. In any case it was probably assumed that the hijackers would make some sort of political 'demands', as had become standard practice for nearly every previous hijacking.

There was, and perhaps could have been, no emergency plan devised to try and cope with a specific attack of this kind. While the planes were in the air for some considerable time in this context, it might have been unreasonable to intercept the flights without understanding the hijackers' intentions. Most hijackings end one way or the other on an airport runway; these were quite different. Any response by the US government which might have led to bringing down civilian plane or planes would have been ethically and morally unthinkable.

The third and fourth planes do raise issues about the continued lack of intervention. It must have become clear by then what the intentions of the hijackers were. It is pertinent to question the standard procedures of those responsible for the personal safety of the US President (the President was moved to his jet, Air Force One, and was rapidly airborne). Any decision to shoot down the planes would surely have required a decision at this level. Having the President moved at a time when he had to respond to the most significant event in his presidency may have actually hampered the logic of the discussion process.

The second question relates to the response by the New York Fire Department, whose staff attempted, and so valiantly, to rescue people from the twin towers. Within nine minutes of the first attack, the first fire fighting units were on the scene. After 13 minutes, 19 response units were at the scene. The fire service was now alerted and response units were mobilized from all five boroughs.

Large numbers of horrified office workers fleeing the terrorist attacks witnessed the determination of the fire fighters attempting to advance into the building. The comment of one of the escapees from the first World Trade Center tower, Louis Lesce, who passed a fireman on the 86th floor while on the way down typifies the selfless bravery:

> He was going to a place where I was damn well trying to get out of. I looked at him thinking, 'What are you doing this for?' He looked at me like he knew very well. 'This is my job.'

Entire companies were lost. The previous worst record for loss of life was when the Fire Department lost 12 firemen in 1966.

The violent energy that was unleashed by the weight of the buildings coming down and the devastation was on a scale not witnessed before in any major incident. It is inconceivable that any fire service handbook would have covered such an eventuality. Many people killed in the towers were members of the fire service themselves. It is interesting to speculate whether another fire service could have responded differently. In all, 343 fire fighters were either reported missing or identified among the dead. Would the command and control methodology used in the UK have brought about a different result? London's more compact geography would have meant that more fire fighters would have been able to attend. London's population is also more densely concentrated than New York's, particularly if one considers the Greater London area. It is likely that the London Fire Brigade would have responded in the same way. An initial response would almost certainly have concentrated first on getting people out, and second on fighting the fire. The question of the building collapsing is clearly an issue today, but only because of our hindsight knowledge.

Case study 2 – Business continuity training at a bank

The author wishes to thank Perpetuity Press for allowing publication of the following paper from their journal, *Risk Management: An International Journal* (2003) 5(1): 33–50*.

---

* Perpetuity Press publish *Risk Management: An International Journal* and can be contacted at PO Box 376, Leicester LE2 1UP, UK, email info@perpetuitypress.com, phone +44 (0) 116 221 7778.

Learning and training: a reflective account of crisis management in a major UK bank

Dr Edward P. Borodzicz[1] and Kees Van Haperen[2]

[1] School of Management, University of Southampton. [2] Hi-Q Systems Ltd

Abstract

The authors were invited as part of a group of consultants to prepare and run a series of simulations for a major international UK bank. The purpose of the training was to test management response structures against systemic violations. Simulated crisis scenarios are frequently cited as effective tools for organizational learning.

In a crisis context, organizational learning takes place along three dimensions, individual, team and organizational. It was found that design and implementation of simulation tools were critical to how the organization confronted the crisis. The issue is raised that simulation exercises may concentrate learning outcomes for exercise designers, facilitators and observers. In contrast, learning outcomes for players and the organization may be more difficult to define. Although it was found at the organizational level that the Bank had been able to improve the framework for crisis management, at the level of those doing the job, training outcomes remained questionable.

The paper reports on observational data material collected during the training and presents initial findings. It is investigated whether simulation exercises provide a useful training method for corporate crisis management. Based on the assumption that performance could be used as an indicator of learning, learning outcomes are analysed for individual, team and organizational levels by comparing and contrasting performance of players between exercises for a number of key crisis management skills. Additionally, the role or influence of the quality of the training framework itself – e.g. scenario realism, instruction techniques, etc. – is analysed and it is investigated whether this facilitated organizational learning.

Introduction

Organizations are frequently finding the need to respond to situations of corporate crisis. The types of situations that can bring about corporate crisis are varied. For example, terrorist and extremist group outrages, complex and sometimes tragic systemic malfunctions or product contamination and the mishandling of the media are only limited examples of the types of scenario that can lead to corporate crisis.

This paper reports on research into the effectiveness of business continuity simulations at a major international UK bank ('the Bank') over three years. Like other financial institutions, the Bank suffered major losses when the Irish Republican Army (IRA) shifted attention to the financial heart of the UK mainland. It experienced disparate problems when a series of bombings took place that are better known as the St Mary Axe Bomb in 1992, the Bishopsgate Bomb in 1993, the Docklands Bomb in 1996, and the Manchester Bomb in 1996. Although all of these events caused serious disruptions to business operations, the Bishopsgate and Manchester Bombs are seen to have been of special significance in establishing a business continuity and disaster recovery policy.

The Bank decided to plan several simulation exercises which were initially designed to assess the suitability of existing management structures and to provide significant decision makers with experiential learning during simulated crisis situations. The Bank had been concerned following the series of terrorist outrages and was reviewing its ability to respond to a serious violation of its systems. Simulations offered the only means to test the functioning of the Bank without seriously disrupting that functioning.

Although the primary aim of the exercises was to 'securitize' the commercial operation of the Bank through crisis situations, the exercises also raised some interesting theoretical issues associated with the application of this methodology as a training device. First, decision making among groups is recognized as problematic. There has been a considerable literature devoted to group functioning and dynamics (Belbin, 1981, 1993) but this has not been applied to crisis management contexts other than by Janis's applications in the 'Groupthink' phenomenon (Janis, 1989). This is of particular concern as organizations operating under conditions of stress are likely to significantly alter the way they operate (La Porte and Consolini, 1991).

This paper will first discuss some generic features of training in an organizational context and highlight the importance of defining training objectives appropriate for organizational learning. This will be followed by an explanation of the Bank's efforts from an historical perspective and will discuss the evolution of the framework for crisis management prior to, during and after each of the exercises. Throughout, the paper reports on the performance of the Bank's crisis management teams for each of the exercises. Subsequently, the findings are analysed and it is assessed whether the simulation exercises enabled organizational learning at individual, team and organizational levels.

Training

Lagadec argues that the thought process during critical moments cannot be validly developed unless the people and systems involved have been prepared in depth (Lagadec, 1993: xiii). In relation to effective corporate crisis management or business continuity planning this would mean that people need to be aware of their responsibilities and prepared to understand and work with the plan (Meyers, 1993: 117). The actual capability to respond to a situation, however, exceeds the plan and hence preparedness should include training and exercising to enhance the ability to manage a crisis.

It is often argued that a relationship exists between plans (i.e. contingency or crisis management), training programmes, resource allocation and simulation exercises (Paton, 1999: 129; Peterson and Perry, 1999: 243). Comfort (1988; Paton, 1999: 129) argues that if this relationship is not acknowledged, plan effectiveness will be diminished when put into practice. It can also be argued that exercises serve as both an extension and reinforcement of training, and as a test of planning adequacy (Hildreth, 1989: 40–41; Wilson, 1989: 254–256; Belardo *et al.*, 1983: 588–606; all quoted in Peterson and Perry, 1999: 245).

An effective crisis management and business continuity training plan will need to resort to many different, complementary methodologies. Moreover, for training to be effective it should at least be based on a detailed analysis of the crisis response roles (Paton, 1999: 131; Paton, 1997; Paton and Smith, 1998). Different people need to be trained to different competence levels and need to acquire different skills. Rolfe (1998: 9–15) has pointed out that training at the level of those that write the plans, and hence at the level of knowing what to do, is very different from training for those that need to do it. This statement can be explained through Bloom's taxonomy, in which different levels of cognitive development are identified (Table A1).

With regard to Bloom's cognitive levels, Rolfe's 'knowing what to do' would represent the lower two levels of knowledge and comprehension, while 'knowing how to do' would at least represent the third cognitive level of application. Bloom *et al.* (1984: 18) further argue that the organization of different levels of cognitive development from simple to complex is based on the idea that a particular simple behaviour may become integrated with other equally simple behaviours to form a more complex behaviour.

Hamblin (1974, quoted in Bramley, 1990: 94) argues that learning should, as far as possible, be evaluated in terms of predefined objectives. According to Hamblin (1974),

Table A1   Cognitive levels

Knowledge	The ability to recall specific and isolable bits of information, including knowledge of terminology, specific facts, conventions, trends and sequences, etc.
Comprehension	The ability to understand a literal message, i.e. translation, interpretation and extrapolation.
Application	This ability follows on from the previous level and represents the ability to correctly apply abstractions in appropriate situations; for instance, as solutions to problems.
Analysis	This level refers to the ability to break down material into its constituent parts, i.e. as analysis of elements, relationships and organizational principles.
Synthesis	Production of unique communication, a plan or proposed set of operations, or derivation of a set of abstract relations.
Evaluation	Judgements in terms of internal evidence or external criteria.

Source: Reproduced from B.S. Bloom (ed.) *Taxonomy of Educational Objectives*. Published by Allyn and Bacon, Boston, MA. Copyright © 1984 by Pearson Education. Reprinted by permission of the publisher.

training could lead to five different stages (Figure A1). Objectives should define which of these levels needs to be achieved through the training activity. Bramley (1990: 94) states that 'trainers should specify in what ways they are hoping that the trainees will react'. Bloom *et al.* (1984: 26) have also highlighted the importance of objectives and state that they should be explicit formulations of the ways in which the learners are expected to be changed by the learning process, i.e. in their thinking, feelings and actions. In a corporate context, as is argued by Bramley (1990: 95), ' the expected changes in job behaviour should be linked with changes in effectiveness of the organisation'.

It is noted that, according to Bloom *et al.* (1984: 27), the learning or training objectives must be related to the psychology of learning, because this would enable trainers to determine the appropriate placement of objectives in the learning sequence. It would also assist in discovering the learning conditions under which it is possible to attain objectives, and it provides a way of determining the appropriate interrelationships among objectives (Bloom *et al.*, 1984: 27).

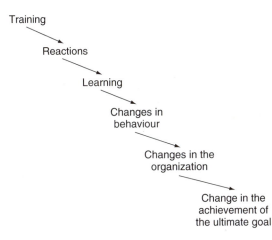

Training
Reactions
Learning
Changes in behaviour
Changes in the organization
Change in the achievement of the ultimate goal

Figure A1   Hamblin's five stages

Source: Reproduced from A.C. Hamblin, *Evaluation and Control of Training.* McGraw-Hill, London, 1974

Research methodology [exercise observation, evaluation and debrief]

The main aim of the research was to investigate whether through the use of simulation exercises organizational learning could be achieved. It can be argued that research into the usefulness of simulation exercises should focus on several dimensions. First, it should address learning, i.e. investigate whether individuals and teams demonstrate an improvement of skills and competencies during a simulation and in subsequent simulations, and whether the organization becomes more capable. Second, it should investigate whether the scenario design and facilitation created an adequate learning environment. These two dimensions required that first individual and team performance were evaluated and analysed, after which a larger organizational picture could be formed through deduction of findings. This then needed to be followed by validation of the simulation exercises for their use as a training tool.

Two of the Bank's crisis management groups were recorded throughout the exercises and the initial debriefings, with exception of a debriefing session for one group after the first exercise. The authors were present during both exercises as consultants, and observation notes made of the groups could be included in the analysis. The combination of fieldwork and recordings may be beneficial since observations generated through fieldwork may provide an important resource in deciding how to focus the collection of recorded materials (Heath and Luff, 1998: 309). Although at the time of the exercise the observation notes were made for a different purpose, they proved useful and helped to focus the research.

The videos were first analysed for each team individually, and observational data was gathered on teamworking, leadership, communication, information flow, information presentation and decision making. Subsequently, both groups were analysed simultaneously for a specific selection of incidents; special emphasis was put on inter-group communications. Through comparison of the data from the individual analysis a more complete picture could be created per exercise and this enabled analysis at an organisational level. A third level of analysis took place by comparing and contrasting data for each of the exercises. It is argued that detection of some degree of improvement achieved over a longer period of time may indicate additional learning. Internal publications of the Bank and reports from a consultancy organization were used to investigate and analyse the Bank's planning efforts and progress, especially in relation to the training programme.

The Bank, a historical perspective to crisis management and the simulation exercises

The experience of the Bishopsgate Bomb had already highlighted the need for furthering contingency arrangements and much was undertaken to develop plans. However, the Manchester Bomb highlighted that several organizational issues were experienced that impeded a successful, group-wide approach and that more effort was required to bring all parties concerned on board. Four fundamentals would be crucial to successful business continuity, and getting them right would both minimize the impact on the business and speed recovery (the Bank, 1996c: 1).

These comprise a corporate climate of empowerment in which those best qualified to get on with the job are trusted to do so without the constant need to seek authority; and local ownership of local plans and simplicity in overall group approach combined with a flexible management framework which differentiates between the tactical and the strategic.

Strong professional teamwork is needed between all concerned. This teamwork needs to be forged in normal day-to-day business and exploited to the full when disaster strikes. Highly competent and dedicated people should be supported by resilient up-to-date information systems. Harnessing these talents in a crisis requires continual cooperative effort during normal business operations. It would be true to say that there are units in the group which, in some disaster scenarios, would have to work closely together, but who today barely know of each other's existence. This does not auger well for rapid teamworking in a crisis (the Bank, 1996c: 1).

Shortly after these issues had been brought to the fore, the Bank's senior management decided that exercising could form an effective and efficient method for tackling some of the concerns. It was decided that a simulation exercise, Exercise Consul, in two stages was to be planned for senior managers. These two stages are further referred to as two separate exercises: Consul-1 and Consul-2.

The two exercises were carried out at the London offices of the Bank and were low-fidelity, using paper injects and verbal inputs as the main source of stimulation. Questionnaires were used before and after the exercises to assess changes in players' perceptions of personal and team roles as a direct result of participation in the exercise. Initial debriefs were held for all participants shortly after the exercise and took the form of a question-and-answer session, while observers highlighted significant findings and some of the major issues. Both scenarios were of such gravity that they justified the activation of a crisis management organization within the Bank's headquarters.

The scenario incidents or injects were designed to trigger one of three types of response in the participants. First, to trigger action, which could range from an immediate response, consultation among crisis managers, information gathering, and communication to other stakeholders, etc. Second, to add realism through raising awareness of the crisis situation, which would not require immediate (re-)action; instead it added to the degree of crisis realism. Third, to create workload and 'fog of war'; requiring participants to allocate them a low priority, deal with them at a more quiet time or ignore them.

The structure that the Bank had defined for managing the restoration of business operations in units that have suffered a major disaster resembled the gold/silver/bronze concept of the emergency services. This meant that crisis management and disaster recovery were executed at strategic, tactical and operational levels. The Bank's philosophy was that the nature of the disaster and the impact on the business would define the scale of activation for the response structure (Figures A2 and A3; the Bank, 1995, 1996a, 1996b, 1998).

The exact scale and nature of the situation will also determine the degree of central-ization of command and control; for a situation of minor severity, the recovery operation may best be orchestrated at the local level, i.e. by the disaster recovery team (DRT). However, it is explicitly stated that, notwithstanding any delegation, events which may cause major disruption, e.g. the Manchester Bomb, would require centralized direction on recovery priorities by the Incident Control Group (ICG) and the bank control group (BCG) (the Bank, 1995, 1996a, 1996b, 1998). It is somewhat surprising though, that the same example is used in an internal memorandum to the chief executive to argue

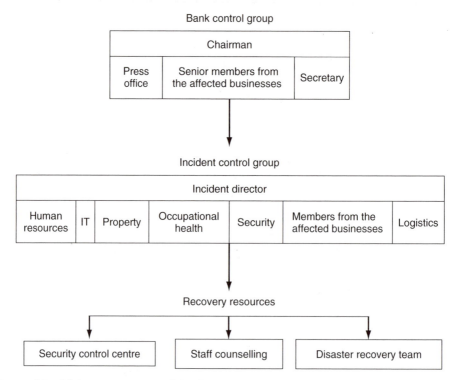

Figure A2 Main components of the Bank's disaster management structure, 1996
Source: The Bank, 1996a: 1

against the activation of a BCG. It is stated that 'many incidents, including the bomb in Manchester, do not reach this threshold of severity and do not require a BCG' (the Bank, 1996c: 1).

The BCG is the name given to the process coordinated by a nominated senior executive by which the executive directors and other major stakeholders are briefed on events (the Bank, 1998: 2). The BCG reports to the executive director of group operations and has been given authority by the executive director committee (EDCO). Corporate affairs, e.g. major corporate reputational issues, are also within the remit of the BCG. It is stated that the BCG will make strategic decisions aimed at restoring normal business operations and include principle decisions to protect Bank interests, 'resolution of major inter-Business priorities during the recovery process', and 'preservation of the reputation of the Bank through high level internal and external communications' (the Bank, 1998: 2).

Because the BCG is not established to manage the tactics of the recovery operation, the ICG has been established under direct leadership of the director (D-ICG). D-ICG will take command of the incident, decide priorities, provide necessary resources to

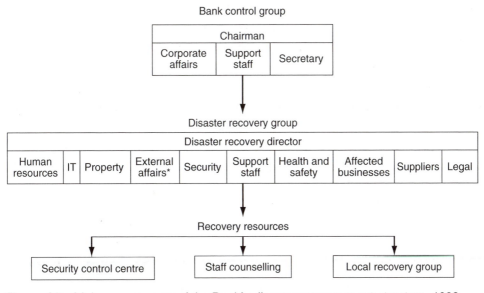

Figure A3   Main components of the Bank's disaster management structure, 1998
*Other than major reputational issues
Source: The Bank, 1998: 1

minimize the impact on the Bank and ensure recovery operations, which give primacy to staff safety and thereafter financial loss (the Bank, 1998: 3). Membership of the ICG will be drawn from key recovery functions and those businesses affected by the incident (Figure A2).

In addition to the BCG, ICG and DRT(s), the Bank has a permanent security cell. This security cell performs a crucial information-gathering and dissemination role, at least during the initial stages of an incident.

Consul-1

The four fundamentals mentioned earlier were, for Consul-1, translated into exercise objectives which aimed at identifying and/or assessing the following:

- The extent of any necessary change to the crisis management structure.
- The effectiveness of existing plans and subsequent issues of command, control and communications in the simulated environment.
- The adequacy of contingency trigger mechanisms.
- Any training requirements (the Bank, 1997a: 2).

The BCG consisted of seven senior representatives who were to look after the strategic interests of the Bank. The group also had two administrative assistants for various support roles. The team had several phones positioned on separate tables, mobile phones, and fax for communication, while a tape recorder was used to simulate radio broadcasts. The ICG, which consisted of 13 people, operated in another building out of a conference room adjacent to the director's office and was similarly equipped, while a whiteboard was used to display significant information. Scenario injects were communicated by the directing staff or a trusted agent* directly with the BCG and ICG.

In general, each group demonstrated good teamworking. The small size of the BCG helped to achieve this easily. The ICG consisted of a larger number of people, which on occasions inhibited teamwork. Various people worked as individual specialists while smaller subgroups were formed to deal with specific issues, such as 'people' and 'property'. To achieve teamworking, strong leadership was exercised by the D-ICG. He ensured that the group had a shared picture, and group discussion and guidance enabled it to work towards common goals.

In contrast, leadership from the chair of the BCG was lacking, but the BCG team itself seemed nevertheless confident and persevered. It can be argued that team attributes such as size and composition might not have required strong leadership. However, decision making appeared to be lacking and, arguably, might have improved if through leadership the group had been steered towards achieving clear objectives. The observational data reveals that some members struggled with basic procedures, which was confirmed by the questionnaires that highlighted various levels of preparedness and that roles and responsibilities were not always apparent.

Communication took place frequently within each of the groups. The BCG members shared information among them, exchanged views and often worked towards achieving group consensus. Within the ICG, the size of the team influenced the level of communication that could take place within the team as a whole. Arguably the formation of subgroups could have affected team communication; the subgroups were observed to share information regularly and worked towards establishing a common picture. Through team discussion between individual members and subgroups more formal ways of communication were created. This combination of informal and formal team communication seemed highly effective and enabled risks to be identified and assessed adequately.

---

* A trusted agent is a member of the Bank representing a specific specialization or business area, who was familiar with the scenario and was to interact realistically with the players.

Communication between the two groups was lacking and often caused BCG members to focus on issues that were dealt with by the ICG. There was also a lack of external communication from the BCG to other agencies. Although the Bank's board members had been informed almost at the outset of the situation, media communication was lacking. As a consequence initial media messages reported the Bank's efforts in a negative context. t'Hart (1993: 41) warns of this phenomenon and explains that authorities often lose control and are overtaken by events; experience shows that 'in most cases mass media are much quicker and more powerful in terms of generating images of the situation for mass consumption'.

Both teams appeared to struggle with the available information. There were no mechanisms in place for accurately logging and displaying information and actions. Although whiteboards were available the apparent lack of an information policy caused certain useful information to get lost while other information that was displayed appeared to have no useful purpose. Furthermore, the participants failed to keep track of received information and actions taken.

For most of the exercise, the BCG and its chair were absorbed by the flow of incidents and failed to detect the situation adequately. It is suggested that the lack of a plan of action, possibly related to the uncertainty of roles and responsibilities, could, albeit in part, be blamed. However, the question why significant issues were not recognized remains unanswered. It is suggested that in part this may be explained by the 'groupthink' phenomenon, or collective foolishness, that occurs as a consequence of the preservation of group harmony and when amiability overrides the group's ability to critically assess decision problems, process strategic information and intelligently choose a course of action (Rosenthal *et al.*, 1989: 21).

The D-ICG, in contrast, had given clear guidelines along which the members were working. They were pursuing the build-up of a picture of the situation, while internal communication led to a consensus, enabling effective decision making. However, only a small number of decisions were made and the group was predominantly occupied with creating an accurate and complete picture of the situation. It could be argued that these activities – i.e. detection – form the first, crucial stage of the decision-making process. Without correct recognition that the situation is a crisis and without some knowledge of the extent, decision alternatives cannot be explored.

Consul-2

As a direct result of Consul-1, senior management of the Bank decided to review the strategic and tactical crisis management arrangements. Consul-1 had revealed that the inter-group communication between BCG and ICG was poor. Often, the BCG members focused on issues that were dealt with by the ICG. It was decided that the organization needed restructuring and that clarity of the roles and responsibilities of each of the two main groups was required.

Stronger emphasis was put on the strategic function of the BCG and its role as interface with the Bank's board and with the media. It was decided to minimize the composition of the BCG to one senior manager assisted by support staff and media experts. After Consul-1 it was also recognized that the 'real' management of a 'disaster' is performed by the incident control group. However, for that group to function effectively it would require additional specialist expertise in the team. Furthermore, it was also felt that the group's name 'ICG' did not accurately reflect its role and was therefore subsequently changed to disaster recovery group (DRG). To prevent confusion with the local disaster recovery teams, these were renamed local recovery groups (LRGs) to send information of importance directly to the BCG.

To resolve communication and information-processing problems, log and action sheets were introduced and a support team was formed to assist the D-DRG by filtering and recording telephone calls, recording and progressing actions, and the reasons for them (the Bank, 1998: 4; STASYS, 1998a: 6, 8, 12). In addition, this team was required to send information of importance directly to the BCG.

In principle, the support team does not have the authority to make decisions. Instead, a senior support team member, called a 'reader' or 'allocator', assesses the information and prioritizes it for actioning by the D-DRG or a DRG team member. Figure A4 shows the communication and information within the new structure, while Figure A5 illustrates the information flows from a DST perspective.

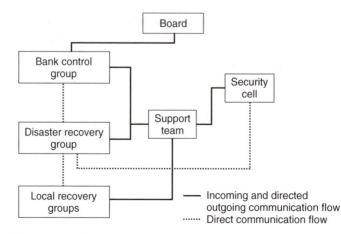

Figure A4   Communication and information flow, revised structure, 1998

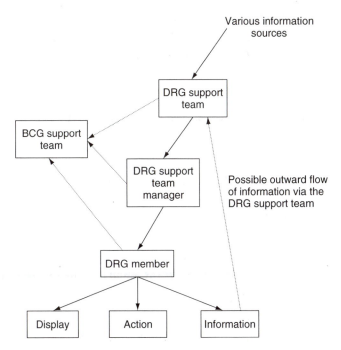

Figure A5   DST information flow

Consul-2 was aimed at testing the amended structure and a slightly different approach was applied to the exercise by using call-out procedures. The chairs of the BCG and D-DRG were the first to be notified, and were given the responsibility for activation of the further structure. In addition, the support team was active at the start of the exercise, while a more realistic information flow was created through the use of the Bank's security cell.

For exercise Consul-2, the following objectives had been defined:

- To examine the revised crisis management structure.
- To test procedures.
- To increase the awareness (the Bank, 1997b: 5).

It is noted that during Consul-2 the training of individual participants was considered a secondary objective.

This time the various groups gathered in close proximity to each other. The DRG operated from the same location as during Consul-1, while the DST was located in an adjacent office. The BCG was situated nearby and initially consisted of the chair and two assistants but was augmented with two media experts after approximately two hours.

Because of the restructuring of the crisis management organization, strategic decision making had now become vested in a single person. A clear divide between BCG and DRG was apparent, which enabled the C-BCG not only to make strategic decisions but also to provide supervision and guidance to the D-DRG. The latter, in contrast, became overwhelmed during the first hours of the scenario. Inter-group communication appeared extremely successful and at various occasions the C-BCG and D-DRG met face-to-face. A joint strategy was devised and the groups operated in consonance, each looking after different issues. It was apparent that the main aim of the BCG was to provide top-cover for issues that could not be resolved by the DRG, to resolve conflicts, especially with regards to allocation of priorities for business recovery, and to make financial decisions.

Injects that were received and logged by the DST were offered to the director at various times. During the initial stages of the exercise these incidents were not actioned because of the absence of DRG team members during the call-out period. Nevertheless, the D-DRG did not use the junior members of staff that were present. Although tasked with information processing, prioritization and presentation, under the circumstances they were the best resource available. However, on several occasions an alternative approach to decision making surfaced when the DST 'allocator' started to prioritize the injects. Those that were deemed to require an urgent response were brought to the attention of the D-DRG, with decision alternatives and a suggested approach. The fact that these injects were actioned may suggest that the way in which information is presented to decision makers is of greater significance than the availability of information. t'Hart *et al.* (1993: 32) argue that when the degree of time pressure is high, structures that appear to enable rapid responses are adopted.

In general, the DRG performance was considerably less effective. For most of the exercise a shared picture did not exist and despite guidance notes several members were unaware of their specific roles and responsibilities. Communication was lacking which might, albeit in part, explain the failure to create a clear picture of the situation. Although with the introduction of log and action sheets a level of bureaucracy had been introduced, of which the effect was noticeable at times, it remained uncertain how significant the impact on the response had been. Methods of displaying information had improved although still relevant information was missing and incorrect information was displayed.

Exercise design and learning

The precise nature of the *exercise scenarios* remains confidential. This is because the ideas could be used against any bank and the authors would not wish to see this threat realized. Both exercises were based on scenarios created to produce a serious crisis for the organization. By serious crisis we mean that fundamental operational systems would be compromised to the extent that the bank would be exposed as a viable entity.

It is often said that crisis simulations require a scenario with a high level of realism. It could be argued that for players to become prepared for crisis management, they must have a feel for what it is to operate under crisis conditions (Gredler, 1992). This would imply that the artificial situation must induce these feelings and trigger reactions accordingly. It is uncertain whether the exercise scenarios achieved this objective. Although some individuals appeared lost – which seems an appropriate crisis emotion – it is questionable whether this was always an intended consequence of the scenario. Factors such as preparedness, competence and skills, but also the pressure to operate in the eye of superiors, seem to play a significant role as well. On the other hand, learning for individuals who experience such reactions may also be seriously affected, which confirms Stern's (1997) argument that a dichotomy exists between crises and learning.

It is further questioned whether the way in which the scenario was administered supports an appropriate learning environment. The exercises were designed following the military tradition in that they commenced at a certain time and lasted several hours but were never paused. Arguably, if participants are not offered any support, they may become frustrated, time is wasted and mistakes may go unnoticed (Stretch, 2000: 38). Moreover, according to Stretch, because it should be expected that players make mistakes, how this failure will be anticipated will be critical to the learning process. It is therefore suggested that steeper learning curves might have been achieved if players had been given the opportunity to reflect on their performance during the exercises, which would also have enabled them to trial their new insights.

An assessment of whether *learning* has taken place should firstly focus on the achievement of exercise objectives. Although organizational learning takes place at personal, team and organizational levels (Senge, 1990; Stern, 1997), both exercises were primarily focused on team and organizational learning; hence for the individual learning perspective assessing whether objectives were achieved is somewhat problematic. Yet, according to Joldersma (2000: 80), it is players' acting and thinking that influences learning at the organizational level.

The questionnaires reveal that most individuals considered the simulation exercises a useful learning experience. It would nevertheless be too simplistic to base any conclusion on these findings alone. At several occasions individual members appeared lost; during initial debriefs these observations were confirmed. It could therefore be questioned whether such conditions still provide a useful learning environment, especially since it was found that instruction techniques were not used to put individuals on the right track.

In an experiential learning environment individuals do not merely learn from their experience, instead they learn by reflecting on their actions (Thiagaran, 1994; Gredler, 1992), which makes learning more personally meaningful, holistic and lasting (Andrusyszyn and Davie, 1995: 3, quoted in Stretch, 2000: 39). Neither the debriefings nor the evaluation reports paid sufficient attention to this. It is questioned whether the Bank's culture inhibited individuals to be specifically addressed. The pre-exercise briefing stated that individuals would not be singled out during the debriefing. Although this may be perceived as a measure to comfort exercise players, at the same time it highlights a potential shortcoming of the training.

Opportunities for team learning

The temporary nature of crisis management teams makes learning at this level an extremely complicated issue. Although the individuals' experience is based on working as a team, the value of learning is uncertain. While the exercises have provided opportunities for individuals to operate as a team, some may never be confronted with a real crisis, while others may need to work with people never met before. Arguably this observation is significant in that it would imply specific training requirements. However, fulfilling them would be difficult because with the number of staff with designated crisis management roles exceeding 100, training in a variety of team combinations would simply not be cost-effective.

Second, although the exercises provided good opportunities for advanced team decision making* the apparent lack of reflection on performance may affect the learned experience. Furthermore, the exercise observations revealed four different forms of leadership; however, it is difficult to draw any conclusions from this. Belbin (1981: 52–53) found that no difference in team performance could be observed between

---

* For a definition of advanced team decision making see Salas and Cannon-Bowers (1993) and Klein (1995).

teams with a strong and those with a poor leader. Although it is acknowledged that a relationship between leadership and team performance exists, it is suggested that the combination of the type of leader and the type of team seems a more determinate factor for performance (Belbin, 1981: 61).

Opportunities for organizational learning

The findings illustrate that not only did each individual exercise provide opportunities for organizational learning, but also the sequence of exercises highlighted that lessons were implemented to improve the crisis management arrangements. The exercise objectives of Consul-2 explicitly addressed the validation of the arrangements that were put in place after Consul-1. Each exercise offered those responsible for planning for business continuity and crisis management the opportunity to validate the Bank's structure and plans. The post-exercise reports (the Bank, 1997a, 1997b) display a dominant emphasis on the organizational learning aspects and focus in detail on how the structure could be optimized and plans made more effective.

Summarizing the above findings, then, it could be concluded that learning at individual and team levels was poor, in contrast to learning at organizational levels. The exercises provided good opportunities for consultants and those responsible for planning crisis management to evaluate and validate the arrangements and to amend them where necessary. In part this difference in learning can be explained with Bloom's taxonomy of learning. Hermann (1997: 243) points that those that administer simulations are also learners and are like participant observers who 'both monitor what is going on to enhance the experience for participants and observe the process for new theoretical insight'. This would imply that throughout an exercise knowledge is acquired at different levels because the base knowledge of participants differs from that of observers. Following Bloom *et al.* (1984), if objectives aim at enabling participants to acquire knowledge and abilities at the application level, observers, in contrast, may already possess the ability to apply. Hence, their learning would take place at higher cognitive levels, i.e. analysis, synthesis and evaluation.

These dissimilar learning experiences have implications for training and it could be questioned whether individual and organizational learning objectives can be supported simultaneously; for instance, the exercises did not provide individual participants clarity in their roles and responsibilities. But after each exercise consultants and bank staff were in a position to implement organizational lessons learned and improve the organization's preparedness.

Although the analysis of the exercise data highlighted that certain lessons learned were not addressed, the Bank appeared well aware that more effort would be required to address all deficiencies. A short period after Consul-2, the Bank commissioned a consultancy agency to investigate certain aspects of the crisis management arrangements in more detail (STASYS, 1998a). Furthermore, a study was conducted into how individuals and teams could be trained to become more competent in conducting crisis management (STASYS, 1998b).

Concluding remarks

During an interview with a staff member* responsible for the planning of business continuity and crisis management it was clarified that after the Consul exercises, priorities at the Bank had shifted from a generic preparedness to a more specific Y2K preparedness. Subsequently, a successful takeover bid dominated the organization's activities. Consequently, the Bank was never in the position to implement the lessons learned from the exercises and act upon the two reports. Interestingly, when implementing a training programme for Y2K-preparedness, the Bank decided – in sharp contrast with their previous approach – not to use external consultants. Instead the Bank's preparedness had reached a level of maturity that no longer required outside expert support, although it welcomed the continued interest of this research.

In an interview with the head of security,[†] it was stated that three factors were conducive to the organization's successful learning. First, trust and confidence placed by the management and board of the organization in those responsible for crisis management. Second, careful selection of individuals responsible for crisis management. Third, an organizational culture and a structure that enabled effective crisis management to take place. It was further stated that the above factors found their roots in the organization's real-world experiences of managing crises and disasters.

This paper has reported on the use of simulation exercises by a major UK bank. The authors found that simulation exercises provide a useful methodology for the training of corporate crisis management. Analysis of unpublished documents, questionnaires and observational data revealed that the validation of simulation exercises is more complicated. Subsequently analysing whether learning has taken place at individual and

---

* An interview with a staff member was conducted on 5 June 2000.
[†] An interview with the head of security was conducted on 12 November 1999.

group levels remains problematic. The exercise scenario did achieve limited individual and team learning; however, there was sufficient evidence of learning at an organizational level. The Bank, albeit initially through the support of an external consultancy, was able to improve its arrangements for crisis management and used simulation exercises to validate them. In fact, it could be concluded that they achieved the aim of establishing a higher level of preparedness. Finally, the perception of those responsible for planning crisis management arrangements improved to such an extent that they felt the Bank was ready to engage in further training without external support.

Case study 3 – The King's Cross underground fire

The case study is based on an original report produced for the European Union STEP Contract No. STEP – CT90–0094 (1993). The author wishes to acknowledge assistance given by the following people in preparing the report: Professor Nick Pidgeon, Professor Barry Turner and Professor David Blockley.

Introduction

On the evening of 18 November 1987 a small fire on the Piccadilly Line escalator at King's Cross underground station was allowed to burn, and resulted in a dangerous flashover which ultimately claimed 31 lives and caused a large number of people to be injured. By any account this was a major disaster for British transport history and it resulted in a formal investigation being carried out by the Department of Transport under the direction of Desmond Fennell OBE, QC. The data for this chapter is based on the findings and proceedings of that inquiry; in particular, how these relate to the first hour of an incident.

The King's Cross underground fire represented an already well-researched case study of events. The inquiry had produced a published and hence publicly available report (Fennell, 1988). In addition, the transcripts and much of the other data used by the inquiry was available at the Public Records Office in Kew, Surrey. The transcripts comprised 300 box files of data, each relating to different aspects of the public inquiry. As well as a transcription of interviews carried out with selected witnesses and consultant experts, copies of letters and reports from all the key agencies involved were included. Contained in the Public Records Office data were a number of other reports specially compiled for the inquiry by academic and other consultant advisors assisting with the inquiry process. The Public Records Office data was vast in comparison with the final published report.

My underlying methodology used in this case study was an ethnographic treatment of secondary data, where both the findings of the inquiry and the inquiry process itself will be 'problematically considered as data'.[*] Although it is appreciated that objectivity in any form of social inquiry is beyond the scope of current research techniques, as far as possible the official inquiry process has been treated in this study as 'strange'[†] so that both its data and presumptions could be critically considered within their social and cultural context. Most fundamentally, this case study would allow me to get as near as was practically possible to a real disaster. By enabling me to base my enquiry on actor and observer accounts as well as the testimony of consulted experts, I attempted to gain as 'thick' a description of the events on that evening as was possible. By beginning my enquiries with a construction of events produced by the Fennell Inquiry, my aim was to deconstruct that account by using data available to it.

Clearly my ability to treat data as strange might be compromised by my own personal familiarity with the case. I already had a general knowledge of the incident from media reports of the time and having been a frequent London Transport (LT) user for some 17 years. Hence it is all but impossible for me to interpret the data outside the context of my own personal experiences. However, my experience with the principal response services and those who work in the LT organization was, in comparison, minor. Some experience as a passenger does have ethnographic advantages, by allowing me (in Geertzian terms) to gain as 'thick' a description as is practically possible. For Geertz, 'thick description' was the cornerstone of social anthropology (Kuper and Kuper, 1985). A simplistic account would be to say that it is not simply a matter of copious

---

[*] 'Problematically considered as data' – this refers to the ethnographic practice of treating everything as data, even when at first glance it may appear quite straightforward and mundane. I would argue that in the case of the Fennell Inquiry what was taken for granted includes a social process, with its own frame of reference and objectives. All are crucial to an understanding of why certain data were selected by the inquiry from the wider body of data available to it.

[†] The notion of ethnography as an anti-theorist movement or sceptical attitude began to emerge in a whole series of social studies aimed at phenomena where the quantitative researcher would prove ineffective. A good example of these can be found in what is known today as the 'Chicago School'. Also, for an exhaustive account of the treatment of data as 'strange' phenomena, see Harold Garfinkel's famous Breaching experiment (Garfinkel, 1972).

data collection, although clearly the more data collected the better, but it is equally important to evaluate data in the context of its meaning and relevance to the actors involved. Geertz (1973) himself felt that only a native could really discern such 'meanings'. I would in this sense constitute a native passenger.

The context of this study was the development and testing of a modelling technique which could be used to compare crises. It was also hoped that the modelling technique would facilitate analysis for dynamically structured processual phenomena typical of disasters and risk-associated scenarios by sequentially plotting events against time. Incidents such as the King's Cross fire are shrouded in legal and political controversy. This makes the normal enquiry methods of the human sciences especially difficult to use after such an event has taken place. The choice of King's Cross as a major tragedy to be analysed was based initially on modelling criteria (Fennell's report contained a chronological section detailing the events on that tragic evening and this would facilitate the modelling exercise).

I also felt that this modelling technique might prove useful for analysing incidents where a long period of time had elapsed. By also using qualitative techniques, in this case an ethnographic methodology, some validation of the modelled data could subsequently be attempted. Neither the findings of an inquiry nor its context can be looked at independently; each provides social meaning and significance to the other. Therefore, while the modelling process concentrates on Fennell's outline of events, this is accompanied by an analysis of the transcripts of the inquiry in order to provide contextualizing data necessary for ethnographic analysis.

Modelling

My research at King's Cross began with the modelling of one section of the published Fennell Report, the chronology of events. The modelling work was carried out using a commercially available computer package designed for drawing flowcharts, called 'Magna Charter'. Using Magna Charter, a sequential time event chart was constructed. Time is displayed in the chart as the vertical axis, while persons and the fire are displayed as the horizontal axis (see www.wiley.com/go/borodzicz). Events are displayed at any given time by looking horizontally across the chart for each time segment involved. The functions of the symbol set used are displayed in the key shown in the chart. There is also a brief description within each symbol in the chart giving further details of the nature or type of event being portrayed. It may be helpful to consider the chart as analogous to a network map, like the famous one published by the London Underground, where significant events are represented in a chronological order but not necessarily in the exact timescale in which they occur.

During the initial process of chart construction, I purposely refrained from reading other sections of the published Department of Transport investigation report, other than the chronological summary section entitled, 'Timetable and Outline of Events on the Night'. My aim at this stage was to produce, using this modelling technique, as far as possible a graphic presentation of the events on that tragic evening as constructed by the Fennell Inquiry. My secondary interest was to simultaneously remain independent of the results and recommendations contained within that report. I felt that the failure to remain independent at this stage might otherwise influence my interpretations within the same frame of reference as that of the formal inquiry. In other words, I wished to construct a simple and graphic description of events with the chart, which could facilitate an analysis of Fennell's findings.

In order to test the reliability of the flow charting method, the modelling was initially carried out by myself and one other person, both independently using the same summary chronology from the Fennell Report. However, after comparing our initial models for congruence, it was decided that one model would suffice as both of these appeared to represent a reliable representation of the data.* Once model reliability had been established, I continued to construct the chart on my own to just beyond the point of flashover.

Constructing the chart was a demanding task. Each sentence in the chronology section was in turn considered for an appropriate symbol, for example, action, decision or communication. This was then drawn under the correct column to represent the person who was involved, and in the appropriate row to represent the chronological point at which the occurrence happened. The symbols were gradually networked together to the other symbols by means of connecting lines. The basis for this networking was that a symbol was either a precursor to another or that it was a result of another symbol. A small amount of text could be placed within each symbol to indicate the nature of the decision or action taking place.

---

* Given the same well-structured data set, there is no reason why two researchers using the same modelling technique should not arrive at the same model. However, this is not an indication of methodological validity, rather a reflection of the physical process of modelling. Validity, I would argue, is dependent upon an analysis of the context of data and its relevant meanings to the actors involved.

While this system did allow for some small amounts of flexibility in modelling style, basically the form that the chart took would be only as dependable as the data on which it was based. The chart tells the same story, but in a pictorial form. The chart also appeared to offer a step-by-step understanding of how events unfolded, at least according to the Fennell Inquiry's construction.

Initial results of the modelling analysis

Once satisfied that the constructed model (see www.wiley.com/go/borodzicz) represented a reliable representation of the data on which it was based, a first analysis of the model appeared to suggest five significant groups or clusters of phenomena taking place within the chart. Briefly I shall consider each of these in turn before looking at some of the more general issues raised by the use of this technique.

1. *The fire itself*   The fire had taken place while the station was very busy and although initially quite small, it had been allowed to incubate to a dangerous flashover point. It is difficult to ascertain precisely when the fire had started or when it was no longer locally manageable. It does, however, appear that initially the fire was still so small that it was hard to find by LT staff looking for it.

2. *Passengers*   LT staff were first made aware of the fire at 19.29 by a report to the ticket office from a passenger, Mr Squires, and subsequently in a similar manner by a further passenger, Mr Benstead, who also informed other LT staff three minutes after the initial notification. It was not until later that another passenger, Mr Kamoun, managed to raise attention to himself and some nearby police officers, by shouting warnings to other passengers and pressing the 'STOP' alarm on the escalator. Other than this, passengers did not appear in the model other than in a completely passive role. The extent to which passengers were aware of the fire, and how this affected their subsequent behaviour, is also not shown in the chart, other than one further notification of the fire to the booking clerk at 19.32 on which there appears to have been no further action taken. It is interesting to consider why the only passenger action which was taken seriously and responded to was the unorthodox one (shouting and creating a commotion); the other two passengers who raised the alarm in the normal manner by reporting the fire to LT staff were simply ignored.

3. *LT's response*   The key feature of LT's response which emerges from the model is an apparent inability or refusal to accept the notifications from the public that something

was wrong. One important factor was clear: a local solution to the fire may have been possible and LT staff were in the best possible position to effect if not facilitate this. Another pertinent factor was the apparent inability of LT staff to find the fire owing to some misunderstanding about its location. Even when the fire was located by LT staff at 19.38 and unsuccessfully tackled with a CO_2 extinguisher, there was still no attempt made to use the water fogging equipment.

Perhaps the most intriguing aspect of London Transport staff behaviour from the chart is the contrast between the extraordinary amount of apparent activity and the total lack of effective response which resulted from it. For example, senior management in other parts of London seemed to be aware of the fire prior to local LT management at King's Cross station. Yet low-grade LT staff at King's Cross appeared to be working closely under police supervision and unknown to their own management at King's Cross. I could only speculate at this stage the extent to which this may have been a direct result of police behaviour at the scene.

4. *The police response to the situation* The police actions can be summarized as threefold. First, they attempted to ascertain the nature of the situation; second, they made efforts to call for an appropriate emergency service; and third, they took control of the movement of people. The first two aspects of this police response were unproblematic in that they quickly ascertained what was going on and called for the fire service as efficiently as the then technology allowed (going to the surface to use their radio to alert the fire service). However, as soon as the fire was acknowledged by the police they assumed responsibility for the movement of people, giving out instructions to LT staff to block escalators and move passengers up from the platform to the surface. This was done by using the alternative Victoria Line escalator and via the ticket hall to the surface. The result of this action was tragic. A decision at 19.39 to evacuate the station by moving passengers in an upward direction, and shutting the Bostwick gates (connecting the London Underground [LU] with the two British Rail stations) resulted in a concentration of evacuating passengers passing through the ticket hall. From the timetable of events it is not possible to identify which police officers closed the Bostwick gates, or who saw them do this:

> 19: 41 – One of the sets of Bostwick gates at the stairs leading to the perimeter subway from the tube lines ticket hall was closed by an unidentified police officer or officers.

> (Fennell, 1988: 51)

Both of these decisions appear to have been taken by police officers independently and on their own initiative, without reference to either LT staff or management advice.

5. *The fire service response*   The response time for the fire service, once alerted, was 10 minutes, but time was not on their side as the flashover was about to begin when they arrived. Perhaps the most significant of the fire service actions was to immediately attempt to move passengers in a downwards direction, away from where the fire was actually moving. This was in stark contrast to and a complete reversal of the police evacuation attempts, which focused on moving people upwards. It would be of interest to know what factors were influencing this decision.*

At this stage the chart appeared to be offering some empirical data. This was facilitated by lines of action within the chart which appeared to represent service specific responses. By using coloured pens, action lines could be highlighted from the chart. Lines of action could be identified for various aspects of the incident management – e.g. the evacuation or the alert – but they could also be indicative of *value*. Lines of action and assumptions of value are, however, problematic and highly contextualize one's representation of the event. What may appear to be a line of action may in fact be a line of inaction. Consider, for example, the cluster of activity taking place between LT staff between 19.39 and 19.42 (see chart at www.wiley.com/go/borodzicz). Clearly a lot of communication and interaction was taking place, but could this be described as some positive action?

The LT staff response to the fire appears from the chart to be quite inadequate. Their behaviour as portrayed in the chart should, however, be contrasted with two features: how they had reacted to previous fire emergencies and training, and how, if at all, they were trained to deal with this type of situation. The key issue raised here for LT staff is the level to which their behaviour on this occasion can be seen to correlate to either experience or training.

This would be dependent on the perceived purpose of one action to be different from that of another. For example, it was clear in one sense that a line of action was

---

* It is suggested here that the fire service were perceiving the threat to human life in a different way to the police service. For the police service, the evacuation zone constituted anywhere below ground. In contrast, for the fire service, the evacuation zone would constitute only that of the underground system which was above the fire.

set in motion by passenger Kamoun's behaviour, the calling of the Fire Brigade. Yet this may also be interpreted as a choice by PCs Bebbington and Kerbey not to attempt to effect a local solution to the fire; in other words, this was a line of inaction in that respect. The extent to which this may be due to a 'mindset' on the part of the police officers involved cannot be discounted. Clearly, if the police in this instance considered their role to be one of people control and movement rather than fire control, then this would explain their motives and actions at the time.

This can be further highlighted by considering the discovery from the model that the police action to evacuate passengers upwards had been in contrast to that of the fire service, who on arrival immediately started to evacuate passengers in a downwards direction (Fennell, 1988: 52). Various reasons may account for this, urgency probably being the main one, but the chart does not indicate what communications, if any, were going on between these two services at the time. Having clearly identified an underground hazard, the police action to move passengers in an upwards direction to the surface was in this context a logical one and congruent with training. This does, however, suggest that the police perceived their role, at that stage, to be one of people managers. However, when this is juxtaposed with the behaviour of fires, for which the Fire Brigade are of course trained, one can see why their reaction was to try to keep passengers below ground, or at least below the fire level.

It is perhaps, in the light of this sort of confusion, more helpful to simply consider the model in terms of actions and not to attempt to speculate whether they are positive or negative until we are clear what terms of reference we are using to make such a distinction.* It may prove more useful to consider actions in terms of 'goal orientation'. In other words, by deciding which goals we are trying to explore it is easier to see which tasks we can and cannot see in the flow chart. In this sense the models may prove to be very useful once one has decided what particular goal or process one wishes to follow through, e.g. evacuating passengers. One can then decide how effective

---

* It is worth pointing out that at this stage of the research process, as far as possible actions are to be simply recognized without applying value judgements about their goals and efficacy. Clifford Geertz offers an insight into the distinction between biological action and social meaning. He does this with the analogy of distinction between a twitch and a wink. Both of these, he argues, represent biological or factual action, yet it is only by means of a full understanding of the social situation that they can be distinguished.

a certain person or group was in bringing this about. The fundamental point is that there are likely to be multiple goals which are pertinent at any one time and establishing these goals is only one part of the problem. We also have to recognize that goals are liable to change during the incident.

The chart appeared as an objective reality. The modelling process had left me feeling highly interactive and involved with the chronology data. As each symbol was drawn and labelled, I was constantly left considering and reconsidering which other symbols on the chart this would be related to. Most fundamentally, I became concerned about a number of 'what if' questions; for example, what if the police had tried to put out the fire instead of moving people: would there still have been a disaster?

The experience of drawing the chart had a profound blinkering effect on me. The graphic portrayal that I produced gave me the feeling that this presentation of events was the 'truth', since it had after all been produced from a chronology which was itself the result of a highly sophisticated investigation process. This involved many experts at great expense from various fields, as well as a judicial process which had the opportunity to cross-examine actor and observer accounts. The chart itself also suggested a reality, based on its chronological appearance.

I had perhaps begun to believe that the representation of events in the chart was a form of core truth, and it was only one's specific interest which affected interpretation. The chart seemed to suggest that by careful and patient scrutiny, one could deduce the points at which faults lay by simply identifying them.

I had also become aware of large amounts of empty space in the chart. People were clearly doing something all of the time they were present at the incident, even if this was considered unimportant to the conclusion of the Fennell investigation. I began to consider the practicalities of representing this kind of data more aptly in a three-dimensional model, or presenting it in the form of a relational database. But this would have been an immense task, and assigning data to specific categories would have been problematic. In effect, what would be required would be a third axis to the diagram where the pattern of social interactions could be plotted simultaneously against dynamic processual events. This would in effect require a third dimension to be constructed in the chart, but even if we had the technological expertise to do this, the quality and detail of data which would be required would surpass the level of data available from the Fennell Report chronology section.

It might prove very difficult to get access to, and further data from, the people who had been involved in the incident. Some of the people portrayed in the chart had died in the fire and others, owing to outstanding litigation, might be reluctant to discuss the events without at least the same legal constraints that had prevailed at the inquiry.

However, I had some other concerns regarding the chart. For example, what were the non-specialized (passengers) doing? Were the passengers being given the opportunity to help themselves? The actions of passengers have clearly been all but ignored in the chart, yet they too may be crucial to the unfolding and manifestation of events (Canter, 1987: 15–30). Similarly, how would this information be modelled, described and analysed within my graphic representation?

At this stage I was in danger of reading too much into the model of representation which itself may be undermined by the subjectivity of the data on which it is based. This is an inherent problem for the human scientist working with secondary data sources. In this case the data was collected by a judicial system whose main interests were to find the cause of the fire and if those involved had behaved in accordance with procedures which were already laid down. This point appeared particularly important. If procedures had been followed then this would suggest that the procedures might be to blame. The nature of any response behaviour needs to be contextualized within each individual's frame of reference for appropriate social behaviour. This will to a certain extent be defined by their group, which has its own informal rules, procedures and beliefs, or what Pidgeon might call a safety culture (Pidgeon, 1991).

Two further issues presented by the chart were a representation of events as unidirectional in flow, and time being presented as an even continuum. The data selected from the Fennell chronology purports to tell a story of the tragic events on that night, which are represented in the chart. In this case, the story suggests a change in situation from one of a very small fire to a fatal flashover in an exceedingly short time period. The chart appears to further legitimize this by adding the dimension of time as an objective calibration to these events. While not wishing to become involved at this point in a major relativistic debate about the properties of time flow, it would be prudent to point out that there has long been a distinction in the way time has been described by natural and social scientists.

For natural scientists, time is unidirectional and its rate of flow is consistent. In contrast, for social scientists, time-flow perception may vary according to personal experience. Time may be perceived for the natural world as unilinear clock time; for the social world this concept may be included but is by no means an exclusive measure of explanation. Unilinear time for the social scientist is merely another way of looking, and this must be kept in the perspective of many rival theories on the concept of time. This 'natural' versus 'social' contrast was identified in Sorokin and Merton's 1937 paper:

> Astronomical time is uniform, homogenous; it is purely quantitative, shorn of qualitative variations. Can we so characterise social time? Obviously not – there are holidays, days devoted to the observance of particular civil functions, 'lucky' and 'unlucky' days, market days, etc.
>
> (Sorokin and Merton, 1937)

The chart appears to slice through time, recording the crisis 'objectively' as a series of minute-by-minute snapshots of the event, as if time could 'naturally' be divided up like the face of a clock. However, the social context in which humans experience the passing of time is not universally experienced in a uniform manner. Rather, the passing of time is for individuals mediated by various contextualizing factors, such as boredom, positive or negative personal construal of events and the experience of pain or comfort.

It therefore seemed natural at this stage to follow up the initial analysis of the chart with a detailed study of the transcripts of the inquiry which were and still are held at the United Kingdom Public Records Office in Kew, London. I felt that the modelled chart should be contrasted with this more detailed data source for comparability. I also felt that there was a need to gain a more empathic feel for the data by reading some of the transcripts of interviews. I hoped this would shed some light on the actions and decisions of some of the individuals modelled, by providing both more detail and contextual information.

I was also concerned that there might be some process to the inquiry procedure itself. There is a growing literature on the history, functioning and scope of public inquiries in general which suggests that they have come to serve particular social purposes (Wraith and Lamb, 1971). In addition, there is a concern for the legal constraints within which public inquiries operate (Wynne, 1981; O'Riordan *et al.*, 1987). Public inquiries collect evidence in a way which is clearly at a variance with the method used by human scientists. Further, and as suggested in Chapter 1, public inquiries have multiple aims, such as public catharsis, apportioning blame and learning. I was concerned to understand the ways in which these different aims might influence the inquiry's construction of reality.

The transcripts

The transcripts included consultant reports on various factors of railway operation, coroner's reports on the bodies of the victims and correspondence between LU and the fire service following previous incidents on the underground system.

The inquiry also appeared to present and select data in a particular way. Consultant 'experts' of all types were requested to submit evidence which was organized and segregated along the traditional disciplinary lines of perceived expertise. For example, a study of the social factors relating to the incident were contained in a report prepared for the inquiry by the psychologist David Canter (1987). Other reports presented data from a number of perspectives, for example, engineering, train design, building structure, behaviour of fires, etc. Reconciling these very different reports, each using their own specialized argot, would have been difficult. These groups themselves submitted reports which were the results of smaller inquiries. The impression thus gained is of clearly defined areas of enquiry being competently and comprehensively covered and brought together. For example, one quite copious section of the transcripts is devoted to the design and suitability of underground train carriages for buffet facilities, arguably of questionable importance to the inquiry. Large glossaries of terminology can also be found which provide definitions of the terms used, and also translations of all the glossary terms into the French language. For example: '"Fire" – A process of combustion characterised by heat or smoke or flame or any combination of these' (Her Majesty's Public Records Office, Kew. Core bundle MT 141 110).

Perhaps the most gruesome and for me personally distressing of these exhaustive reports was the personal nature of the pathologist's description of the bodies. The use of terms such as 'slim young woman' or 'circumcised young man', in conjunction with detailed descriptions of how victim's bodies had been tragically burned and disfigured in the fire, brought home to me in a more personal way the graphic horror of the events.

However, what is quite worrying is the extent to which this type of what I shall call here 'expert exhaustive enquiring' may, on the one hand, produce the type of emotional and cathartic information that a horrified public may demand, such as blame, recommendations and heroes, yet at the same time miss some of the valuable but subtle socio-technical dynamics which facilitated incubation of the incident. By separating the social and technical aspects of the incident as isolated entities, the inquiry was creating a number of realities which it could then adjudicate upon. Clearly, those accounts which appear to be based on fact (technical appraisals) could be contrasted with the subjective accounts (descriptive social features). The temptation to then fit the subjective factors to the factual ones must be a point of speculation.

Consider, for example, the first section of the chart displaying three passengers notifying staff of the fire (see chart at www.wiley.com/go/borodzicz). One needs to contrast the data represented in Fennell's Report with the entire data that was available to the inquiry and consider why only three notifications from the public were considered most worthy of summarizing. According to the official chronology, there were three notifications of a fire; the first by passenger Squire at 19.29, a second by actions of passenger Kamoun at 19.30, and a third by passenger Benstead at 19.32.

It is interesting to consider why the Fennell Inquiry decided to select these three notifications and not some of the following which were available to it from the transcripts. In Chronology bundle 111 it states that between 4 October and 19.25 on 18 October there were 54 substantiated reports to LU about the escalator in question, each by one or more people. These reports described 'heat', 'scorching smells', 'burning smells', 'sparking', 'children playing with matches', 'squeaking and screaming noises' and 'black smoke marks on the ceiling above the escalator'. (It might be interesting to note the applicability of these to the public inquiry's own definition of 'fire'.) These 54 notifications were themselves selected from a total of 363 reports, which the Fennell Inquiry felt could not all be substantiated.

Clearly, had these notifications been included in the inquiry summary, the chart (and its subsequent analysis) would have looked quite different. The point of funda-mental importance here is the basis of the selection process for data to be included in the inquiry report. On what basis were the 360 reports from other members of the public during the preceding 14 days considered to be of less importance? The only criterion that appears to have been applied is whether the warnings were immediately followed by a tragic fire.

A second feature which becomes apparent when reflecting on the chart, and with the benefit of hindsight, is the response of the London Transport staff to notifications of fire. What is originally described as 'a relatively uncoordinated response' from LT staff is actually quite the opposite. There was a conscientious passing of information from one member of staff to another – the problem appeared to be the defective safety culture within which they were employed.* LU staff appeared to be putting out fires

_____

* Congruent with the analysis presented here, Fennell comments that when reviewing the performance of the London Underground staff it should be borne in mind that 'the outbreak of fire was not regarded as something unusual; indeed it was regarded by senior management as inevitable in a system of this age. This attitude was no doubt increased by the insistence of London Underground that a fire should never be referred to as a fire but by the euphemism "smouldering"' (Fennell, 1988: 61).

far too frequently. In other words, a task which should be an emergency operation for staff was actually being performed as a matter of routine work. The safety culture of London Transport staff did not consider fire as a legitimate hazard.

If we are to base our impression on only the three incidents from 363 which Fennell chose, the process of interacting with members of the public reporting fires might well give the impression of concern or at least urgency. However, in view of the number of fire-related incidents which LT staff had to regularly deal with, these actions become more explicable as 'normal' rather than emergency behaviour. It is hence hardly surprising that the LT staff at the scene chose not to inform the station management of this occurrence and probably on many other occasions.

In further considering the appropriateness of LT staff behaviour it might initially be worth considering the LT instructions to staff about fires which are as follows:

IN CASE OF FIRE

If you discover a fire or one is reported to you:

1. Sound the alarm, by operating the nearest call point, notify the nearest fire warden.
2. Attack the fire, if possible, with the appliances provided but without taking personal risks.

If these instructions are to be taken at face value, then the first instruction was clearly ignored by LT staff. Despite a considerable number of suspected and real fires resulting in 54 substantiated warnings, 14 days passed before a passenger pressed the 'STOP' alarm. It is difficult to conceive how the first instruction could be effected with such urgency given the frequency of reported fires taking place in such a busy station. How would LT staff be able to distinguish between the relative urgency of each suspected fire, with so many incidents occurring? The question here is whether LT staff should be put in a situation where they are constantly called upon to distinguish between potential lethal and other types or fire, or 'smoulderings'.

Again, if we look at some of the transcripts we can see why LT staff might be reluctant to have acted otherwise. In a section entitled 'General Principles of Operational Command and Control at Incidents', by the London Fire and Civil Defence Authority, there is a letter from the fire service to LT (CB233) saying that following the experiences of previous fires (Oxford Circus), the fire service should be called even on suspicion of a fire and that there should be no reliance on a two-tier system of hazard management which LT were at that time adopting. The reply from LT (CB2339), signed by a Mr JT Cope, stated that LT staff were quite professional and the two-tier system was fundamentally sound, and there was therefore little likelihood of any confusion.

There was also a dilemma between sending for help and obtaining a local solution; the LT staff and the police dealt with this in different ways. LT staff opted for a solution established through informal practice, while the police opted to send for help. With the benefit of hindsight, it is clear that had these actions been the other way round, the events on that day might have been less tragic. Further, had the fire service been alerted to more of the previous suspected or real fires on that escalator, then it is likely that an internal enquiry might have taken place and the tragic fire could have been avoided.

The portrayal of Leading Railman Brickell as depicted in the chart is another example of the selectivity of Fennell's Inquiry when dealing with social data. Brickell observed the commotion with passenger Kamoun at 19.30 and then, with no explanation for a six-minute gap, reappears in the model at 19.36 descending escalator No. 5 and noticing a small fire on escalator No. 4. At the same time a police officer instructs him to send passengers up the Victoria Line escalator. The impression given here is one of a man who did little and only then because the police told him to do so.

In contrast to this, when the transcripts of his interview for the inquiry are read, it is clear that Leading Railman Brickell worked exceedingly well under difficult circumstances. To illustrate this argument further, I have constructed a second chart using the transcripts of an interview with Mr Brickell for the inquiry as my source data, and this can be used as a pictorial demonstration of the following description (see alternative chart at www.wiley.com/go/borodzicz).

At 17.15 (16 minutes before the original model starts) he had put out a small fire on the Victoria Line escalator, this type of small fire being so routine that he had not even bothered to inform the inspector. When he returned a few seconds later to start collecting tickets, he was notified by another passenger of a problem of 'smoke and smouldering on the bottom of escalator No. 4'. Brickell then stopped collecting tickets and went to investigate. He looked down the three escalators but was unable to see anything owing to the number of passengers using them, but he was able to smell smoke. Mr Brickell then descended to the bottom of the Piccadilly Line escalator where he found that the escalator had already been switched off and, due to the clearing of people, he could look up and see there was a small fire* about two-thirds of the way

---

* The fire appeared as though it was the size of a cigarette lighter flame. However, in fact it was much larger than this. The flame which was visible was only the tip of a much larger one which was burning in the recess of the escalator.

up. Immediately, Brickell started to block off this escalator without instruction from any police officer. Further, he did not use the water fire extinguisher due to the danger from electricity, and he consulted a police officer who decided not to attempt to put out the fire for the same reason. Hence, for Mr Brickell (who was not the most athletic man due to his long-standing ill-health) all was done which could be done; it was simply a case of waiting for the Fire Brigade. He then caught a train out of the station to go home, completely unaware of the terrible events above him, which he would only learn about later that night while at home watching the evening news on television.

Discussion

In order to effectively portray a multitude of organizational processes which are suggested by the response to this crisis and subsequent major disaster, several methodological problems would need to be overcome. A new level of both data quality and technology needs to be available to the modeller. The diagram is like a piece of text, and it should be analysed in the same way as text is treated – looking critically at what has been left out, and considering reflexively whose viewpoint or story is being told. The chart portrays only one representation of reality where there would appear to be others.

The point suggested here is not that the chronology section of the report consciously sets out to misrepresent the truth or reality, or that there was some sort of hidden agenda operating in the inquiry. Rather, that in an event of this scale there are many different accounts of what happened and these are not necessarily compatible with each other. Differing perceptions of the passing of time would, using such a chart, exacerbate these differences. This is further complicated by the different backgrounds and world views of the groups of actors involved, each of which reports events in terms of what they perceived to be the crucial factors. The Fennell Inquiry clearly had to eliminate these differences in accounts in order to produce the summary report, and this required a process of active discrimination against certain data in favour of others. Where such discriminations are to be made by an official inquiry process, it would appear that these are made in favour of expert accounts and at the expense of lay accounts.

It would not be fair to say that the inquiry completely ignored the issue of non-specialist decision makers, since a prominent psychologist, as suggested earlier, Professor David Canter from Surrey University, was employed to research the behavioural and psychological aspects of the fire at King's Cross. Professor Canter also questioned the extent to which passenger behaviour and decision making needs to be at least considered in such enquiries. He points out that the King's Cross underground station is a complex set of passageways and escalators, and that many passengers were highly skilled in travelling through them. Many passengers walked straight into smoke and continued along well-practised routes, stopping only because they were blocked or they were overcome by the fire. Another issue raised by Professor Canter is the number of fatalities which occurred as a direct result of police unloading trains and evacuating these passengers up through the station. Clearly, if they had been left on the trains, some of these people might still be alive today.

As well as considering the issue of passenger behaviour, Professor Canter questioned the interactions of passengers with 'expert decision makers', in particular how they responded to instructions from police and LT staff. Unfortunately, little of Canter's work on passengers appears in the summary report on King's Cross, and even the work he was able to do was carried out under less than optimal research conditions. He states:

> It was not considered appropriate for Professor Canter to interview the witnesses directly. This has meant that reliance has had to be placed on statements made available and the transcripts of the proceeding of the enquiry. In many cases this procedure leads to the evidence taking a form which is not optimal from the point of view of valid psychological data.

> (David Canter, 1987: King's Cross Inquiry Transcripts Box No. 112)

The issue of obtaining accurate and reliable accounts of phenomena is for the human sciences an old problem, not least for the field of disaster research. Barry Turner's book, *Man-Made Disasters*, devotes much attention to the use of 'accounts' for the post-hoc analysis of events:

> First-hand accounts of disasters are of little direct use for our purposes, for, from Pliny onwards, they are accounts of devastating or disruptive events from the point of view of victims or near victims; whilst they may provide much useful information about human emotions and reactions in moments of severe stress, they generally provide little detailed or accurate information about the origins and nature of the event which is producing the stress.

> (Turner, 1978: 8)

Turner quite aptly develops this argument further by referring to what he calls the 'genre' within which different interest groups will report events. He cites journalists as one such interest group displaying a particular approach to the production of accounts of events, by means of contrasting particular stories and reports with other information and events. Medicine is cited as 'another professional group with an occupational interest in disaster as are engineers with a "genre" for identifying system failures in physical terms' (Turner, 1978). In the case of the King's Cross inquiry's summary report, we may need to question the 'genre' of any particular account of the event. We should acknowledge that public inquiries will represent the views of many professional interest groups.

Other factors which might influence the selection of data are the way evidence is presented and the credibility of the presenter. As risk communication theorists might argue, experts (including members of the emergency services) would be familiar with presenting arguments which substantiate their versions of reality; they frequently make such presentations to courts, public bodies and other legal establishments. The credibility of expert accounts would be established through legal precedent and their peer group. Police, in particular, can be regarded as 'professional witnesses' in this context. In contrast, lay accounts such as that of Mr Brickell would lack such presentational qualities (this is quite apparent from reading the transcript of his interview at the inquiry), and when competing with non-congruent expert conceptions would be likely to receive a more sceptical hearing.

In terms of the response to the incident once the emergency services were alerted, two issues are of concern. First, what is the frame of reference (or safety culture) of the emergency service involved? Second is the question of power or primacy. I am assuming here that the frame of reference for the Fire Brigade is to treat the phenomenon, in this case a fire; for the police the issue is to manage people; and for the ambulance service to treat the symptoms (the injured). For the London Underground staff, however, the frame of reference is not so clear; yet this may prove to be the key to fully understanding their behaviour in this incident.

The issue of power is also not made explicit in the model, yet it is implicit in the manifestation of scenarios such as King's Cross. Perhaps we should be flow-charting the power structure, and question who ultimately takes charge of the incident. Who owns the power, is it context led and who is accountable? There may be a perfectly adequate emergency plan, but we must question how this relates to another emergency plan, i.e. if you do not arrive first, as was the case with the Fire Brigade at King's Cross, you may have to inherit another service's emergency plan.

Conclusions

The first section of empirical work would appear to suggest a number of preliminary conclusions. First, there are inherent problems associated with producing any one conception or model of a disaster. The charts produced represent a faithful representation of the chronology section data in the Fennell Inquiry and the account given by Leading Railman Brickell. The chart does not show, however, how data has been collected or what selection process has been used to distinguish between competing accounts. The chart also gives no indication of how different data would be presented or interpreted by the actors involved. The illusion of apparent chronological objectivity suggested by the chart is questionable in this respect, because it may mask the social and psychological processes going on in the crisis. The second chart produced, based on Leading Railman Brickell's conflicting account of events to the inquiry, demonstrates the danger of this apparent objectivity.

For example, the issue of looking at both lay and expert conceptions of risk as suggested by risk communication theorists is simply not considered in the chart. Lay folk are often the blank spaces on our diagram of expert accounts (the second chart based on Mr Brickell's account of events is a good example of this). Expert accounts will systematically discriminate (albeit unconsciously) against lay folk by not considering their actions to be important. Yet the behaviour of non-experts will have made a significant impact in terms of the outcome of the incident, in casualties at least. This may be due to our unconscious desire to emulate previous studies and produce recommendations to improve the actions of the expert decision maker, without reference to the way these decisions will have been perceived or interpreted by lay folk who will do so with reference to their own agenda.

The second and related issue is that of multiple realities. Charts are useful analytic tools, but take little account of 'multiple realities', at least as presented here.* There would appear to have been many realities operating simultaneously at King's Cross. While these realities may not be compatible with each other, they are each valid accounts of events for those who have constructed them. This view of the situation at King's Cross is congruent with a view held by many risk communication theorists, that expert accounts are liable to disagree (Wynne, 1989, 1992; Irwin, 1989; Browning and Shetler, 1992).

---

* For a full account of 'multiple realities', see Browning and Shetler's work on the concept, described in Chapter 1.

Social life is both too subtle and too complex to be reduced to such simplistic analysis. We need to be able to understand the relative meanings and symbolic understandings which are attached to any process by those involved. This must be done through some validating technique which can distinguish between mere biological action and social significance. This requires the deployment of a qualitative methodology as a prerequisite for understanding the background context of the representations to be analysed. The ethnographic methodology has been used in order to treat the apparently obvious and mundane (in this case expert conceptions) as strange and problematic. Using this methodology, competing accounts from lay persons involved can be given equal weighting.

Third, the apparent inability to declare the danger, and despite repeated warnings, on the part of London Underground staff clearly had tragic consequences. Fires were commonplace for them, so much so that actual working conditions had come to include the extinguishing of fires as routine practice. Their failure to declare is congruent with the concept of an organizational safety culture (Pidgeon, 1991), suggesting that fire was not perceived by LT staff as a legitimate threat.

Hence, how were London Underground staff at King's Cross to know that on that occasion they were involved in a much larger event, which would subsequently prove to be overwhelming for their capabilities? Despite some 363 notifications from the public over the previous 14 days about problems with this particular escalator, London Underground staff's failure to declare the situation needs to be considered in the context of their organizational hierarchy and safety culture. In this context they had no history of such an incident. Pre-defined categories will play a mediating role in the nature of any response and, for London Underground staff, fires meant a routine mode of response. For staff to have responded differently would have required them to break with their own, if somewhat informal, operating procedures.

A fourth issue emerging from the study of King's Cross is that the incident appears to be ill-structured (Turner, 1978: 52). This is because despite an apparently correct emergency response by the police attending, the effect of the crisis was exacerbated. The police, once aware of the fire, took the correct action in accordance with their training and *Weltanschauung* (world view). Police evidence to the inquiry suggests they thought they were taking right and proper action under the circumstances by mounting a full evacuation of the threatened area in question, the station. This evacuation was by all accounts quickly effected by moving people upwards and out of the station. However, the tragic result of this evacuation was to increase the deaths and injuries from the fire by guiding people through the flashover. In a surface geographical context, this police action would have been successful. Only through communication with the specialists in underground fire behaviour could the police have realized the danger at the time.

Case study 4 – City University's recovery from fire

The author wishes to thank Sara Gentle for permission to publish her case study, taken from her MSc dissertation, 'Crisis management in a higher education institution: an evaluation of the issues, requirements and regulatory environment, and recommendations for a crisis management team', 2002, Southampton University.

The information about this case study is taken from the City University's publication *Project Phoenix: A Case Study of City University's Recovery from Fire* (Rhind *et al.*, 2001), which was published to share experiences gained from the event with other institutions.

On 21 May 2001, City University, London, experienced that which we all fear most – a major fire. It occurred in a Grade II listed building, the largest building on campus and, if this was not testing enough, the incident occurred at the height of the examination period, further increasing disruption to staff and students alike.

Estimates for the cost of restitution and temporary measures exceed £10m, the majority being attributable to the costs of finding temporary accommodation. A large part of the affected building was out of service for approximately two years. In addition to the fire damage, considerable smoke and water damage extended the clean-up process. At the height of the blaze, 13 fire appliances and a helicopter were on site to try to bring it under control.

Events of the fire

The alarm was raised by a security officer who was alerted by a fire alarm. On investigation, he found smoke pouring from an open letter box and attempted to bring the blaze under control with the help of fire tenders, while awaiting the Fire Brigade.

Within an hour of the blaze being discovered, the head of security had contacted senior staff who began arriving less than 45 minutes after the discovery. The University's press officer also arrived to coordinate press interviews and brief university spokespeople.

At the time of the blaze an examination was in progress within the building. A total of 250 people had to be evacuated and the examination halted.

In total, around 100 staff lost their workspace and some also lost working materials. Teaching areas and administration offices were also damaged or destroyed. The

Computing Department and School of Social and Human Sciences were largely destroyed and the Music Department partially flooded. In all 3000 square metres were lost.

University location

The fire occurred at a location on the campus only 500 metres away from the local fire station. Less fortunate was the location's proximity to newspaper offices and television stations, producing even greater media interest in the story than would normally have been expected.

Bad timing

In addition to the examination period being at its height, it was also a 'slow' news period and the media therefore showed even more interest in the story than they would have done ordinarily. Their coverage had to be carefully managed as it was affecting business continuity at the university; potential students believed that the university was closed so a large advertising campaign was raised to spread the 'business as usual' message. The Journalism Department spread the word to its media contacts via e-mail and the university website proved an extremely useful resource to get this message across. Internally, the staff newsletter was used to strengthen the 'business as usual' message.

The lack of key staff made managing the incident more difficult. The positions of university secretary, director of personnel and a director of estates and facilities were either being advertised or were not due to be taken up until later in the year.

Furthermore, the Vice Chancellor had announced that he wanted to change the organizational structure of senior staff during the period from May 2001 to December 2001. It was planned to merge the two main planning committees to incorporate them much more deeply into the process of university strategy formation.

University culture and policies

The university employed more than 1200 permanent staff and numerous part-time staff. There were in excess of 14 000 students and every day hundreds of people visited the university, making it a logistical nightmare. Security staff were posted at every entrance and exit and routinely checked security cards.

In 1993 a 'No Smoking' policy was adopted and smoking was restricted to specifically designated areas. Fire alarm tests were performed weekly in addition to unannounced fire simulations at periodic intervals.

University risk assessment, management and contingency planning

Long before the fire, City University had crisis management plans which had been reviewed shortly before the fire by the Southern Universities Management Services organization. The plans worked well in the event but the university did not have a corporate business continuity plan.

The university generally took a proactive approach to risk assessment and management, pioneering this and taking a holistic view of the organization. A best practice document had been created, with a risk register divided into business domains, within which risks relevant to university strategies were listed and assigned a score reflecting the likelihood of their occurrence and the impact they would have. If a high score was assigned to both aspects, the controls that surrounded that risk would be assessed by the business domain manager to determine how it could be better managed. This practice is also being introduced at the individual school level within the university.

Every two years the University Finance and General Purpose Committee reviews its insurance cover to ensure its appropriateness and that it is up to date. This proved invaluable following the fire.

Objectives identified following the fire

Objectives to provide clarity and guidance for the clean-up and restitution were determined at the earliest opportunity. These were identified as:

- To continue to operate in all academic and support units directly affected by the fire and to support affected individuals as well as possible.
- To get the affected people back into decent accommodation as soon as was possible and to create the necessary teaching spaces for late September while restoring the damaged building.

- To obtain the entirety of the insurance entitlement to cover the damage.
- To maintain control of the entire operation, document it and learn from the experience while minimizing media-induced fallout and turning it to advantage wherever possible.
- To identify the cause of the fire and to take any appropriate management action to minimize the risk of a recurrence.

In addition, it was necessary to recreate a research area that had been lost. This was especially problematic as it had to be identical to the original including its size, colour, shape and layout so that the long-running research was not invalidated.

The emergency management team (EMT)

Membership of the EMT varied, reducing as the three-month period progressed, ultimately culminating in a small, focused team. Varying the membership as and when required capitalized on individual expertise and knowledge. The EMT met twice on the day of the fire and daily for several days after that. This reduced to approximately every week until all standard operational management lines were able to manage the EMT activities.

At every meeting, minutes were taken and circulated for action. These were sent to all of the affected senior managers. Recommended actions and problems were collated to form an archive with documentary evidence on the fire and decisions, including video footage and photographs. This proved useful when dealing with the insurers. The principle was that actions were agreed upon and those responsible made them happen, chased by the minute taker if necessary. The benefit of group working was clear as many actions interacted with each other and this was not always foreseeable if one was working in isolation. Group working was supportive and critical as and when required.

In the following weeks, the EMT oversaw many activities including establishing the extent of the lost space and the implications for teaching and other activities, as well as defining the losses involved.

Urgent tasks for the following day

Ten critical activities were identified to be necessary that day that related to relocating staff and students, learning about what happened and informing those affected.

- Rearrange affected examinations and inform students.
- Secure enough teaching space for lectures.
- Ensure site was safe.
- Relocate groups of staff.
- Inform insurers of the fire.
- Recover, and restore where necessary, information held in computer or paper files.
- Ensure that the media did not exaggerate the effects.
- Ensure that the quality of teaching and learning was not compromised.
- Manage staff fears and expectations.
- Manage the logistics of dealing with people.

Good communications were crucial to enable these activities to be successfully completed. It also allowed home-working by some staff, easing some of the problems.

Results of the fire

Staff obviously had an increased workload to compensate for the lack of expertise described earlier. To lessen this, external experts were used to help with the aftermath.

Although the insurers did cover the majority of the cost, the university had to cover the remainder, which meant that its available capital was depleted and it therefore incurred opportunity costs as the money was no longer available for investment elsewhere.

A great deal of management time also had to be spent working with the loss adjustors. The university also appointed their own loss adjustors. The benefits of this were two-fold: first, it was then possible to obtain expert advice immediately and, second, it protected the university's interests.

Despite the event, City University still met its target student numbers and survived as a functioning business and university.

Lessons learnt

Some staff did not back up their computer work and hence lost some of it in the fire. The School of Informatics did, however, create daily back-up tapes that were stored in the fire safe. This proved invaluable.

Effective, timely, frequent and consistent communications were vital and different media were necessary to convey messages. Face-to-face communications were crucial for those affected. The contributions from all those involved were recognized through formal letters of thanks, stories in the staff newsletter and a party. This helped to confirm the university's commitment and appreciation of staff and the efforts that they had made.

The EMT was very successful and, following the success of the relationships with external professionals, it was felt to be advisable to build longer-term relationships with those who had helped during the aftermath of the fire. It was also felt to be beneficial to make some formal arrangements with other nearby organizations to provide accommodation if it was ever needed. The interaction between problems made it harder to solve them and will be actively considered in the future.

The review of insurance every two years meant that it was generally satisfactory, with one exception. Some staff had paid privately for books that were used for teaching. They felt that compensation was due for those lost in the fire. An interim budget was allocated to cover immediate replacement and a small premium increase in the long term was arranged to cover this.

There is now a strong emphasis on maintaining teaching material in electronic form and procedures have been implemented to monitor the impact on teaching.

Two important elements were found to be missing from the organization. No business continuity plan existed, which would have helped the university to prepare for a major disaster. The information infrastructure was also found to be lacking, as was the availability of teaching space and staff. Consideration is being given to policies, practices and responsibilities, and whether the American university practice of fire marshals inspecting every room and having the authority to require staff to resolve any problems may be advisable at City University.

REFERENCES

AAIB (1990) Report on the accident of Boeing 737-400 C-OBME near Kegworth, Leicestershire on 8 January 1989. Aircraft Accident Report 4/90. London, HMSO.

Abt, C. (1970) *Serious Games*. Viking Press, New York.

Adams, J. (1988) Risk homeostasis and the purpose of safety regulation. *Ergonomics*, 31(4): 407–428.

Adams, A. (1992) *Bullying at Work*. Virago, London.

Adams, J. (1995) *Risk*. UCL Press, London.

Adams, J. (1999a) *Cars, Cholera and Cows*. CATO Institute, Washington.

Adams, J. (1999b) *Risky Business – The Management of Risk and Uncertainty*. Adam Smith Institute, London.

Alexander, D. & Walker, L. (1994) A study of methods used by Scottish police officers to cope with work-induced stress. *Stress Medicine*, 10: 131–138.

Alexandrou, A. (1999) Educating the police service of the future through a public private partnership. In L. Montanheiro (ed.), *Public–Private Partnerships: Furthering Development*. Sheffield Hallam University, Sheffield.

Andrusyszyn, M.A. & Davie, L. (1995) Reflection as a design tool in computer mediated education. www.oise.utoronto.ca/ldavie/reflect.html

ANSCI (1993) *Human Factors Study Group*, Third Report: Organising for Safety. London, HMSO.

Arbuthnot, K. (2001) The art of command. In R. Flin & K. Arbuthnot (eds), *Incident Command: Tales from the Hot Seat*. Aldershot, Ashgate.

Auf der Heide, E. (1989) *Disaster Response: Principles of Preparation and Coordination*. C.V. Mosby, St Louis, MS.

Ayres, A., Hays, R.T., Singer, M.J. & Heinicke, M. (1984) An annotated bibliography of abstracts on the use of simulators in training. *Research Product*, 84-21, US Army Research Institute for the Behavioural and Social Sciences, Alexandria, VA.

Backer, P.O.J. (1996) Stress and military performance. In J. Driskell & E. Salas (eds), *Stress and Human Performance*. Lawrence Erlbaum Associates, Mahwah, NJ, pp. 89–125.

The Bank (1995) *Bank Control Group Information Pack*, Version 1, October 1995, internal publication.

The Bank (1996a) *Business Recovery Information Pack* (Formerly Bank Control Group – Info Pack), Version 2, July 1996, internal publication.

The Bank (1996b) *Business Recovery Information Pack* (Formerly Bank Control Group – Info Pack), Version 2.1, August 1996, internal publication.

The Bank (1996c) internal memorandum, dated 10 July 1996.

The Bank (1997a) Project Consul – Phase 1 Debrief and Lessons, Version 1, 21 January 1997, internal publication.

The Bank (1997b) Project Consul – Phase 2 Debrief and Learnings, Version 1.1, 24 November 1997, internal publication.

The Bank (1998) Business Recovery Information Pack, Version 4.3 July 1998, internal publication.

Baudrillard, J. (1988) *Selected Writings*. Polity Press, Cambridge.

Bauman, Z. (1991) *Modernity and Ambivalence*. Polity Press, Cambridge.

Bawtree, D. (1995) Safety culture and our response to its failure. Paper presented at 3rd Emergency Planning and Disaster Management Conference, Lancaster.

BBC *News* (1999) 20 January.

BCI (2001) 10 Standards (On-line). www.thebci.org

Beck, U. (1992) *Risk Society: Towards a New Modernity*. Sage, London.

Belardo, S., Pazer, H., Wallace, W. & Danko, W. (1983) Simulation of a crisis management network. *Decision Sciences*, 14(6): 588–606.

Belbin, R.M. (1981) *Team Roles at Work*. Butterworth-Heinemann, Oxford.

Belbin, R.M. (1983) *Management Teams: Why They Succeed or Fail*. Butterworth-Heinemann, Oxford.

Bergman, D. (1993) *Disasters Where the Law Fails: A New Agenda for Dealing with Corporate Violence*. Herald Charitable Trust, London.

Bernstein, P.L. (1971) On the classification and framing of educational knowledge. In M.F.D Young (ed.), *Knowledge and Control*. Collier-Macmillan, New York.

Bernstein, P.L. (1996) *Against the Gods: The Remarkable Story of Risk*. John Wiley & Sons Canada Ltd, Ontario.

Bingham, T. (1997) Continuing to take fraud seriously. *Accountancy*, March.

Blockley, D. (1992) Engineering from reflective practice. *Research and Engineering Design*, 4: 13–22.

Blockley, D. (1997) Hazard engineering. In C. Hood & D. Jones (eds) *Accident and Design: Contemporary Debates in Risk Management*. UCL Press, London.

Bloom, B.S. (ed.) (1984) *Taxonomy of Educational Objectives, Book 1, Cognitive Domain* (original publication 1956). Longman, New York.

Boot, R. & Reynolds, M. (1983) Issues of control in simulations and games. *Simulation/Games For Learning*, 13(1).

Booth, R. (1993) Safety culture concept, measurement and training implications. Paper presented at the British Health and Safety Society Spring Conference, Aston University, April.

Booth, S. (1995) The *Braer* disaster: a virtuous crisis? – international responsibility and prevention of incidents at sea. *Journal of Contingencies and Crisis Management*, 3(1): 38–42.

Booth, S.A. (2000) How can organisations prepare for reputational crisis? *Journal of Contingencies and Crisis Management*, 8(4): 197–207.

Bonger, W. (1905 and 1969) *Criminality and Economic Conditions*. Indiana University Press, Bloomington.

Borodzicz, E.P. (1996a) Security and risk: a theoretical approach to managing loss prevention. *International Journal of Risk, Security and Crime Prevention*, 1(2): 131–143.

Borodzicz, E.P. (1996b) After disaster: risk communication for social services and voluntary agencies. Paper presented and included in the proceedings of 2nd International Conference Local Authorities Confronting Disasters and Emergencies, Amsterdam.

Borodzicz, E.P. (1997) Risky business: crisis simulations examined in the context of the safety people. PhD, London University.

Borodzicz, E.P. (1999a) Business continuity management: using simulations to 'facilitate' learning within risk situations. In D. Saunders & J. Severn (eds) *Simulation and Gaming Research Yearbook Volume 7, Simulation and Games for Strategy and Policy Planning*. Kogan Page, London, pp. 169–181.

Borodzicz, E.P. (1999b) The terminology of dangerous events: implications for key decision maker training. *International Journal of Police Science and Management*, 2(3): 348–359.

Borodzicz, E.P. (1999c) Facilitating partnerships during crisis: social, private and voluntary agencies. *International Journal of Public Private Partnerships*, 2(1): 71–80.

Borodzicz, E.P. (2000) Gestione della sicurezza aziendale: un totem post-modernista? In Balloni, A. (ed.), *Didattica in criminologia applicata: Formazione degli operatori della sicurezza e del controlo sociale*. Cooperativa Libraria Universitaria Editrice, Bologna, Milan.

Borodzicz, E.P. (2004) The missing ingredient is the value of flexibility. *International Journal of Simulation and Gaming*, 35(3): 414–426.

Borodzicz, E.P. & Pidgeon, N. (1996) Exercise ERM!: Emergency response management simulation. In A.G. Carbonell & F. Watts (eds), *Simulacion ¡ya!, Simulaion Now!* ISAGA '95 (International Simulation and Gaming Association), Diputacion Provincial de Valencia, Spain.

Borodzicz, E.P., Pidgeon, N. & Aragones, J. (1993) Risk communication in crisis: meaning and culture in emergency response organizations. Paper presented at the SRA (Europe) Risk Conference, Rome.

Borodzicz, E.P., Pidgeon, N., Turner, B. & Blockley, D. (1993) The King's Cross fire: a case study in modelling disasters. EC Interim Report STEP Project CT90-0094. Bruxelles.

Borodzicz, E.P. & Van Haperen, K. (2002) Individual and group learning in crisis simulations. *Journal of Contingencies and Crisis Management*, 10(3): 139–147.

Borodzicz, E.P. & Van Haperen, K. (2003) Learning and training: a reflective account of crisis management in a major UK bank. *Risk Management: an International Journal*, 5(1): 33–50.

Bramley, P. (1990) *Evaluating Training Effectiveness: Translating Theory into Practice*. McGraw-Hill, Maidenhead.

British Psychological Society (1988) *Ethical Principles for Research with Human Participants*. British Psychological Society, London.

Brody, H. (1987) *Living Arctic: Hunters of the Canadian North*. Faber & Faber, London.

Brown, J., Cooper, C. & Kirkaldy, B. (1996) Occupational stress among senior police officers. *British Journal of Psychology*, 87: 31–41.

Browning, L.D. & Shetler, J.C. (1992) Communication in crisis, communication in recovery: a postmodern commentary on the *Exxon Valdez* disaster. *International Journal of Mass Emergencies and Disasters*, 10(3): 477–498.

Button, M. (1998) Beyond the public – the exclusion of private investigators from the british debate over regulating private security. *Gaze: International Journal of the Sociology of Law*, 26: 1–16.

Button, M. & George, B. (1994) Why some organisations prefer in-house to contract security staff. In M. Gill (ed.), *Crime at Work: Studies in Security and Crime Prevention*. Perpetuity Press, Leicester.

Button, M. & George, B. (2000) *Private Security*. Perpetuity Press, Leicester.

Cadbury Report on the Financial Aspects of Corporate Governance (1992) Gee Publishing, London.

Cannon-Bowers, J.A. & Bell, H.H. (1997) Training decision makers for complex environments: implications of the naturalistic decision making perspective. In C.E. Zsambok & G.A. Klein (eds), *Naturalistic Decision Making*. LEA, Mahwah, NJ.

Cannon-Bowers, J.A. & Salas, E. (eds) (1998) *Making Decisions under Stress: Implications for Individual and Team Training*. American Psychological Association, Washington, DC.

Cannon-Bowers, J., Tannenbaum, S., Salas, E. & Volpe, C. (1995) Defining competencies and establishing team training requirements. In R. Guzzo & E. Salas (eds), *Team Effectiveness and Decision-making in Organisations*. Jossey-Bass: San Francisco.

Canter, D. (1987) *Behavioural and Psychological Aspects of the King's Cross Inquiry*. Her Majesty's Public Records Office, Box MT 141 336.

Canter, D., Comber, M. & Uzzell, D. (1989) *Football in its Place*. Routledge, London.

Capra, F. (1975) *The Turning Point: Science, Society and the Rising Culture*. Fontana, London.

Cecchini, A. & Frisenna, A. (1987) Gaming simulation: a general classification. *Simulation/Games For Learning*, 17(2): 60–73.

Chapman, C. & Ward, S. (2002) *Managing Project Risk and Uncertainty: A Constructively Simple Approach to Decision Making*. John Wiley & Sons, Ltd, Chichester.

Charlton, D. (1992) Training and assessing submarine commanders on the Perishers' course. Paper presented at the First Offshore Installation Management Conference: Emergency Command Responsibilities, Aberdeen, April.

Christopher, E.M. & Smith, L.E. (1987) *Leadership Training through Gaming: Power, People and Problem-solving*. Kogan Page, London.

Chryssides, G.D. (1993) *An Introduction to Business Ethics*. International Thompson Business Press, London.

Clarke, R. (1980) Situational crime prevention: theory and practice. *British Journal of Criminology*, 20: 136–145.

Claxton, G. (1997) *Hare Brain. Tortoise Mind. Why Intelligence Increases When You Think Less*. Fourth Estate, London.

Collier, K. (1998) Once more with feeling – identification, representation and the affective aspects of role play in experience-based education. In J. Rolfe, D. Saunders & T. Powell (eds), *Simulations and Games for Emergency and Crisis Management*. Kogan Page, London.

Comfort, L.K. (1988) *Managing Disaster*. Duke University Press, Durham.

Coote, A. & McMahon, L. (1988) Debriefing simulation games: personal reflections. In D. Crookall (ed.), *Simulation-Gaming in Education and Training*. Pergamon Press, Oxford.

Covello, V.T. (1991) Risk comparisons and risk communication: issues and problems in comparing health and environmental risks. In R.E. Kasperson & P.J.M. Stallen (eds) *Communicating Risks to the Public*. Kluwer, Dordrecht.

Covello, V.T., Von Winterfeldt, D. & Slovic, P. (1986) Communicating scientific information about health and environmental risks: problems and opportunities from a social and behavioural perspective. In V.T. Covello, A. Moghissis & V.R.R. Uppuluri (eds), *Uncertainties in Risk Assessment and Risk Management*. Plenum Press, New York.

Cox, S. & Tait, N. (1991) *Reliability, Safety and Risk Management: An Integrated Approach*. Butterworth-Heinemann, London.

Crainer, S. (1993) *Zeebrugge: Learning From Disaster*. Herald Charitable Trust, London.

Crego, J. & Harris, J. (2001) Simulating command. In R. Flin & K. Arbuthnot (eds), *Incident Command: Tales from the Hot Seat*. Ashgate, Aldershot.

Crego, J. & Spinks, T. (1997) Critical incident management simulation. In R. Flin, E. Salas, M. Strub & L. Martin (eds), *Decision Making under Stress: Emerging Themes and Applications*. Ashgate, Aldershot.

Crichton, M., Flin, R. & Rattray, W.A. (2000) Training decision makers – tactical decision games. *Journal of Contingencies and Crisis Management*, 8(4): 209–218.

Croall, H. (1992) *White Collar Crime*. Open University Press, Buckingham.

Crookall, D. & Saunders, D. (1989) Towards an integration of communication and simulation. In D. Crookall & D. Saunders (eds), *Communication and Simulation: From Two Fields to One Theme*. Multilingual Matters, Clevedon, PA.

Cunningham, C. & Teather, E. (1990) Black Christmas: a bushfire simulation game. *Simulation/Games For Learning*, 20(1): 173–179.

Czarniawska-Joerges, B. (1992) *Exploring Complex Organizations: A Cultural Perspective*. Sage, London.

Dake, K. (1991a) *Myths of Nature: Culture and the Social Construction of Risk*. Surrey Research Centre, University of California, Berkeley.

Dake, K. (1991b) Orienting dispositions in the perception of risk: an analysis of worldviews and cultural biases. *Journal of Cross-Cultural Psychology*, 22(1): 61–82.

Dake, K. (1991c) Technology on trial: Orienting dispositions towards environmental and health hazards. Doctoral dissertation, University of California, Berkeley.

Davidson, C.H. (1989) Towards a new discipline of security management: the need for security to stand alone as a management science. *Security Management*, 1(1).

Dicken, P. (1992) *Global Shift*. Paul Chapman, London.

Dobson, R. (1995) Starting as you mean to go on. A study of compliance with operational procedures during the first 10 to 15 minutes of incidents. International project report, Brigade Command Course, Moreton-in-Marsh, Fire Service College.

Dombrowsky, W.R. (1995) Again and again: is a disaster what we call 'disaster'? Some conceptual notes on conceptualizing the object of disaster sociology. *International Journal of Mass Emergencies and Disasters*, 13(3): 241–254.

Dorner, D. & Pfeifer, E. (1993) Strategic thinking and stress. *Ergonomics*, 36(11): 1345–1360.

Douglas, M. (1970) *Purity and Danger*. Routledge, London.

Douglas, M. (1985) *Risk Acceptability According to the Social Sciences*. Russell Sage Foundation, New York.

Douglas, M. (1994) *Risk and Blame: Essays in Cultural Theory*. Routledge, London.

Douglas, M. & Wildavsky, A. (1982) *Risk and Culture: An Essay on the Selection of Technological and Environmental Danger*. California University Press, Berkeley, CA.

Drabek, T.E. (1986) *Human Systems Responses to Disaster: An Inventory of Sociological Findings*. Springer-Verlag, New York.

Driskell, J. & Salas, E. (1991) Overcoming the effects of stress on military performance: human factors, training and selection strategies. In R. Gal & A. Mangelsdorf (eds), *Handbook of Military Psychology*. John Wiley & Sons, Ltd, Chichester.

Driskell, J. & Salas, E. (eds) (1996) *Stress and Human Performance*. LEA, Mahwah, NJ.

Dror, Y. (1988) Decision making under disaster conditions. In L.K. Comfort (ed.), *Managing Disaster: Strategies and Policy Perspectives*. Duke University Press, Durham, NC.

Drottz-Sjöberg, B.M. (2003) *Current Trends in Risk Communication: Theory and Practice*. Directorate for Civil Defence and Emergency Planning, Norway.

DTAS (1994) *Draft Standards of Competence for Management of Risk and Investigation*. Direct Training and Advisory Services, Wicklewood, Norfolk.

Duckworth, D. (1986) Psychological problems arising from disaster work. *Stress Medicine*, 2: 315–323.

Dunning, D. (1999) Postintervention strategies to reduce police trauma. In J. Violanti & D. Paton (eds), *Police Trauma*. C.C. Thomas, Springfield, IL.

Dynes, R. (1994) Community emergency planning: false assumptions and inappropriate analogies. *International Journal of Mass Emergencies and Disasters*, 12(2): 141–158.

Elliott, D., Swartz, E. & Herbane, B. (2002) *Business Continuity Management: A Crisis Management Approach*. Routledge, London.

Endsley, M.R. (1995) Toward a theory of situation awareness in dynamic systems. *Human Factors*, 37: 32–64.

Endsley, M.R. (1997) The role of situation awareness in naturalistic decision making. In C.E. Zsambok & G. Klein (eds), *Naturalistic Decision Making*. LEA, Mahwah, NJ.

Endsley, M.R. & Garland, D. (eds) (2000) *Situation Awareness. Analysis and Measurement*. LEA, Mahwah, NJ.

Evans-Pritchard, E. (1976) *Witchcraft, Oracles and Magic among the Azande* [1937]. Clarendon Press, Oxford.

Fallesen, J. (2000) Developing practical thinking for battle command. In C. McCann & R. Pigeau (eds), *The Human in Command: Exploring the Modern Military Experience*. Kluwer/Plenum, New York.

Fayol, H. (1916) *Administration Industrielle et Generelle* (trans. 1949). Pitman & Sons, London.

Fennell, D. (1988) *Investigation into the King's Cross Underground Fire*. Department of Transport, HMSO, London.

Filley, D. (1999) *Risk Homeostasis and the Futility of Protecting People from Themselves*. Independence Institute. http://i2i.org/article.aspx?ID=602

Flin, R. (1996) *Sitting in the Hot Seat: Leaders and Teams for Critical Incident Management*. John Wiley & Sons, Ltd, Chichester.

Flin, R. (in press) Selecting the right stuff: personality and high reliability occupations. In B. Roberts & R. Hogan (eds), *Applied Personality Psychology: The Interface between Personality and I/O Psychology*. APA Books, Washington, DC.

Flin, R. & Arbuthnot, K. (eds) (2001) *Incident Command: Tales from the Hot Seat*. Ashgate, Aldershot.

Flin, R., Salas, E., Strub, M. & Martin, L. (1997) *Decision Making under Stress: Emerging Themes and Applications*. Ashgate, Aldershot.

Flin, R., Wyn, V., Ellis, A. & Skriver, J. (1998) The effects of sleep loss on commanders' decision making: A literature review (Project report CHS7381). Defence Evaluation Research Agency, Farnborough.

Fredholm, L. (1997) Decision patterns in major firefighting. In R. Flin, E. Salas, M. Strub & L. Martin (eds), *Decision Making under Stress: Emerging Themes and Applications*. Ashgate, Aldershot.

Freud, S. (1950) *Totem and Taboo*. Penguin, London.

Friedman, M. (1962) *Capitalism and Freedom*. University of Chicago Press, Chicago.

Frisby, C.B. (1947) Field research in flying training. *Occupational Psychology*, 21: 24–33.

Frosdick, S. (1995) Organisational structure, culture and attitudes to risk in the British stadia safety industry. *Journal of Contingencies and Crisis Management* 3(1): 43–58.

Frosdick, S. & Sydney, J. (1997) The evolution of safety management and stewarding at football grounds. In S. Frosdick and L. Walley (eds), *Sport and Safety Management*, Butterworth-Heinemann, Oxford, pp. 209–220.

Fukuyama, F. (1999) *The Great Disruption: Human Nature and the Reconstruction of Social Order*. Profile Books, USA.

Gamson, W.A. (1966) *SIMSOC*. Collier Macmillan, London.

Gardner, H. (1987) *The Mind's New Science: A History of the Cognitive Revolution*. Basic Books, New York.

Garfinkel, H. (1967) *Studies in Ethnography*. Prentice Hall, Englewood Cliffs, NJ.

Geertz, C. (1973) Thick description: towards an interpretative theory of culture. In C. Geertz (ed.) *The Interpretation of Cultures*. Basic Books, New York.

George, B. & Button, M. (2000) 'Too little too late'? An assessment of recent proposals for the private security industry in the United Kingdom. *Security Journal*, 10(1).

Giddens, A. (1991) *The Consequences of Modernity*. Polity Press, Cambridge.

Gilbert, C. (1995) Studying disaster: a review of the main conceptual tools. *International Journal of Mass Emergencies and Disasters*, 13(3): 231–240.

Gillespie, J.A. (1973) The game doesn't end with winning. *Viewpoints*, 49: 21–27.

Ginn, R.D. (1992) *Continuity Planning*. Elsevier Science, Oxford.

Glazer, M. & Glazer, P.M. (1989) *The Whistleblowers: Exposing Corruption in Government and Industry*. Basic Books, New York.

Goemans, T. (1996) Policy exercises as a learning tool for crisis management. Paper presented at the 2nd International Conference: Local Authorities Confronting Disasters and Emeregencies, Amsterdam.

Goodman, P. (1971) *Compulsory Miseducation*. Penguin, Harmondsworth.

Graham, J. (2001) *World Trade Center Case Study*. Royal and Sun Alliance. www.thebci.org

Gredler, M. (1992) *Evaluating Games and Simulations: A Process Approach*. Kogan Page, London.

Green, J. (1997) *Risk and Misfortune: The Social Construction of Accidents*. UCL Press, London.

Hacking, I. (1975) *The Emergence of Probability: A Philosophical Study of Early Ideas About Probability, Induction and Statistical Inference*. Cambridge University Press, Cambridge, MA.

Hamblin, A.C. (1974) *Evaluation and Control of Training*. McGraw-Hill, London.

Hampel Committee on Corporate Governance (1998) *Final Report*. Gee Publishing, London.

Hansen, J. (1995) *Oklahoma Rescue*. Ballantine, New York.

Hayes, J.W. (1992) *River Safety: Report of the Enquiry into River Safety*. Department of Transport, HMSO, London.

Haynes, A. (1992) United 232: coping with the 'one chance-in-a-billion' loss of all flight controls. *Flight Deck*, 3 (Spring): 5–21.

Health, D. (1991) *Disasters: Planning for a Caring Response.* HMSO, London.

Hearndon, K. (1993) *Corporate Computing 1993: Key Business Issues.* Computing Services Association, London.

Hearndon, K. & Moore, A. (1999) *The Handbook of Business Security: A Practical Guide to Managing the Security Risk* (2nd edn). Institute of Directors, Kogan Page, London.

Heath, C. & Luff, P. (1998) Explicating face-to-face interaction. In N. Gilbert (ed.), *Researching Social Life.* Sage, Thousand Oaks, CA, pp. 306–326.

Heath, R. (1998) *Crisis Management for Managers and Executives.* Financial Times/ Pitman Publishing, London.

HEFCE (2001) *Risk Management: A Guide to Good Practice for Higher Education Institutions.* Higher Education Funding Council for England and Wales, London.

Heinrich-Jones, F. (1999) The Public Interest Disclosure Act 1998 (Whistleblowing): the implications for management. *InfoRM* (May/June).

Heinzen, B. (1996) *Crisis Management and Scenarios: The Search for an Approach Methodology.* Ministry of Home Affairs, The Netherlands.

Henwood, K. & Pidgeon, N. (1994) Beyond the qualitative paradigm: a framework for introducing diversity within qualitative psychology. *Journal of Community and Applied Social Psychology*, June.

Hermann, M.G. (1997) Conclusion, the multiple pay-offs of crisis simulations. *Journal of Contingencies and Crisis Management*, 5(4): 198–206.

Hidden, A. (1989) *Investigation into the Clapham Junction Railway Accident.* HMSO, London.

Hightower, H. & Couta, M. (1996) Coordinating emergency management. In R. Sylves & W. Waugh (eds), *Disaster Management in the US and Canada.* C.C. Thomas, Springfield, IL.

Hildreth, R. (1989) Portrait of a disaster. *City and County*, 104(12): 40–41.

Hilton, T. & Dolgin, D. (1991) Pilot selection in the military of the free world. In R. Gal & A. Mangelsdorf (eds), *Handbook of Military Psychology.* John Wiley & Sons, Ltd, Chichester.

Hodgkinson, P. & Stewart, M. (1991) *Coping with Catastrophe.* Routledge, London.

HMSO (1991) Report of the Chief Inspector of Marine Accidents into the collision between the passenger launch *Marchioness* and *MV Bowbelle* with loss of life on the River Thames on 20 August 1989. Department of Transport Marine Accident Investigation Report, HMSO, London.

HMSO (1992a) *Dealing With Disaster.* Crown Copyright, London.

HMSO (1992b) *Principles of Command and Control.* Home Office Publication, London.

HMSO (1997) *How Resilient is your Business to Disaster?* Home Office Publication, London.

HMSO (1998) *Protecting People and Property.* Home Office Publication, London.

HMSO (2003) *Dealing with Disaster* (revised 3rd edn). Crown Copyright, London.

HMSO (2004) *Civil Contingencies Bill: A Short Guide.* Civil Contingencies Secretariat, Crown Copyright, London.

Home Office (1997a) *Business as Usual: Maximising Business Resilience to Terrorist Bombings.* Home Office, London.

Home Office (1997b) *Dealing with Disaster* (3rd edn). HMSO, London.

Hood, C. & Jones, D. (1996) *Accident and Design; Contemporary Debates in Risk Management.* UCL Press, London.

Hood, C.C. *et al.* (1992) Risk management. In *Risk, Analysis, Perception and Management.* Royal Society Study Group, 135–192, The Royal Society, London.

Horlick-Jones, T. (1990) *Acts of God? An Investigation into Disasters.* Association of London Authorities, London.

Horlick-Jones, T. (1995) Modern disasters as outrage and betrayal. *International Journal of Mass Emergencies and Disasters*, 13(3): 305–315.

Horner, D. (1976) Disaster simulation. *Journal of the Society for the Advancement of Games and Simulations in Education and Training*, 7(1).

HSE (1991) *Major Hazard Aspects of the Transport of Dangerous Substances.* Crown Copyright, London.

HSE (1992) *Selecting a Health and Safety Consultancy.* HSE IND(G) 133(L) C500.

Hunt, I. (1982) Developing a design philosophy for business games. *Simulation/Games for Learning*, 12(3).

Hunter, S., Gundry, A.J. & Rolfe, J.M. (1977) *Human Factors Topics in Flight Simulation: An Annotated Bibliography.* AGARD report No. 656. NATO Advisory Group for Aeronautical Research Development, Neuilly sur Seine, France.

Hytten, K. & Hasle, A. (1989) Fire fighters: A study of stress and coping. *Acta Psychiatry Scandinavia Supplement*, 355(80): 50–55.

ICCARUS Project (1989) *'Intelligent' Command and Control: Acquisition Review Using Simulation Learning Technologies.* Report in collaboration with the Design Information Research Team, Portsmouth Polytechnic, West Midlands Fire Service and the Learning Technologies Unit, Employment Department.

Irwin, A. (1989) Deciding about risk: expert testimony and the regulation of hazard. In J. Brown (ed.), *Environmental Threats: Perception, Analysis and Management.* Belhaven Press, London.

Irwin, A. (1995) *Citizen Science: A Study of People, Expertise and Sustainable Development.* Routledge, London.

Jacobs, B. & t'Hart, P. (1992) Disaster at Hillsborough stadium: a comparative analysis. In D. Parker & J. Handmer (eds), *Hazard Management and Emergency Planning*. James & James, London.

Janis, I. (1982) *Groupthink: Psychological Studies of Policy Decisions and Fiascoes*. Houghton Mifflin, Boston.

Janis, I.L. (1989) *Crucial Decisions: Leadership in Policymaking and Crisis Management*. Free Press, New York.

Joldersma, C. (2000) Policy learning through simulation/gaming. In D. Saunders & N. Smalley (eds), *Simulation and Games for Transition and Change, Simulation and Gaming Yearbook Vol. 8*. Kogan Page, London, pp. 77–85.

Joyce, D. (1989) Why do police officers laugh at death? *Psychologist* (September), 380–381.

Kaempf, G., Wolf, S., Thordsen, M. & Klein, G. (1992) *Decision Making in the AEGIS Combat Information Centre*. Report for Naval Command, Control and Ocean Surveillance Centre, San Diego (Contract N66001-90C6023). Klein Associates, OH.

Kahneman, D. & Tversky, A. (1979) Prospect theory: an analysis of decision making under risk. *Econometrica*, 47(2): 263–291.

Keegan, J. (1987) *The Mask of Command*. Jonathan Cape, London.

Keeling, A. (2001) Military Commander: Royal Marines. In R. Flin & K. Arbuthnot (eds), *Incident Command: Tales from the Hot Seat*. Ashgate, Aldershot.

Keller, A. (1990) The Bradford disaster scale. In A. Keller & H. Wilson (eds), *Disaster Prevention, Planning and Limitation*. British Library, London.

Kerstholt, J.H. (1997) Dynamic decision making in non-routine situations. In R. Flin, E. Salas, M. Strub & L. Martin (eds), *Decision Making under Stress: Emerging Themes and Applications*. Ashgate, Aldershot.

King's Fund (1992) *Too Many Cooks*. King's Fund, London.

Klabbers, J.H.G. (1999) Three easy pieces: a taxonomy on gaming. In D. Saunders & J. Severn (eds), *Simulations and Games for Strategy and Policy Planning, Simulation and Gaming Yearbook Vol. 7*. Kogan Page, London, pp. 16–33.

Klein, G. (1993) A recognition-primed decision (RPD) model of rapid decision making. In G. Klein, J. Orasanu, R. Calderwood & C.E. Zsambok (eds), *Decision Making in Action: Models and Methods*. Ablex, Norwood, NJ.

Klein, G. (1995) Naturalistic decision-making: individual and team training. Seminar presented at the Offshore Management Centre, Robert Gordon University.

Klein, G. (1997) The current status of the naturalistic decision making framework. In R. Flin, E. Salas, M. Strub & L. Martin (eds), *Decision Making under Stress: Emerging Themes and Applications*. Ashgate, Aldershot.

Klein, G. (1998) *Sources of Power: How People Make Decisions*. MIT Press, Cambridge, MA.

Klein, G., Calderwood, R. & Clinton-Cirocco, A. (1986) Rapid decision making on the fire ground. Paper presented at the Human Factors Society 30th Annual Meeting, San Diego, CA.

Klein, G., McCloskey, M., Pliske, R. & Schmitt, J. (1997) Decision skills training. Paper presented at the 41st Annual Human Factors and Ergonomics Society Conference, Albuquerque, NM.

Knight, R. & Pretty, D. (1996) The impact of catastrophes on shareholder value. *Oxford Executive Research Briefing*. Templeton College, Oxford.

Kolb, D. (1984) *Experiential Learning: Experience as the Source of Learning and Development*. Prentice-Hall, Upper Saddle River, NJ.

Kon-TraG (1998) Kon TraG und Aktienoptionslplane 16, Lagebericht 300, und Risikomanagement 3, 6, 11.

Krimsky, S. & Plough, A. (1988) *Environmental Hazards: Communicating Risks as a Social Process*. Auburn, Dover, MA.

Kroeber, A. & Kluckhorn, C.K.M. (1952) *Culture*. Peabody Museum Papers, Kent.

Kroll-Smith, J.S. & Couch, S.R. (1991) What is a disaster? An ecological-symbolic approach to resolving the definitional debate. *International Journal of Mass Emergencies and Disasters*, 9(3): 355–366.

Kuper, A. (1987) *Anthropology and Anthropologists: The Modern British School*. Routledge & Kegan Paul, London.

Kuper, A. & Kuper, J. (1985) *Social Science Encyclopedia*. Routledge, London.

Lagadec, P. (1982) *Major Technical Risk: An Assessment of Individual Disasters*. Pergamon Press, London.

Lagadec, P. (1990) *States of Emergency*. Butterworth-Heinemann, London.

Lagadec, P. (1991) *Preventing Chaos in a Crisis*. McGraw-Hill, Maidenhead.

Lagadec, P. (1993) Ounce of prevention worth a pound in cure. *Management Consultancy* (June).

Lagadec, P. (1995) Learning processes for crisis management in complex organisations: high reliability/normal crisis dynamics. Paper presented at Institutional Vulnerabilities and Resilience in Public Administration meeting, Leiden, 30 November–2 December.

Lagadec, P. (1997) Learning processes for crisis management in complex organizations. *Journal of Contingencies and Crisis Management*, 5(1): 24–31.

Landy, R. (1991) The dramatic basis of role theory. *Arts of Psychotherapy*, 18: 29–41.

La Porte, T.R. & Consolini, P.M. (1991) Working in practice but not in theory: theoretical challenges of high reliability organizations. *Journal of Public Administration Research and Theory* 1(1): 19–47.

Larken, J. (1992) The command requirement and OIM qualification. Paper presented at the First Offshore Installation Management Conference: Emergency Command Responsibilities, The Robert Gordon University, Aberdeen.

Larken, J. (2001) Military Commander: Royal Navy. In R. Flin & K. Arbuthnot (eds), *Incident Command: Tales from the Hot Seat*. Ashgate, Aldershot.

Latour, B. (1993) *We have Never Been Modern*. Harvester Wheatsheaf, London.

Latour, B. & Woolgar, S. (1986) *Laboratory Life: The Social Construction of Scientific Facts*. Princeton University Press, Princeton, NJ.

Lee, T. (1993) Seeking a safety culture. *ATOM Journal*, 429: 20–23.

Leigh, E. (2003) What is expected of the facilitator of interactive learning? An answer based on consideration of facilitation of 'open' simulations. In *The International Simulation and Gaming Yearbook*, Vol. 11, pp. 9–18.

Lerbinger, O. (1997) *The Crisis Manager*. Lawrence Erlbaum Associates, Mahwah, NJ.

Levi-Strauss, C. (1962) *Totemism*. Merlin Press, London.

Lewin, K. (1936) *Principles of Topological Psychology*. McGraw-Hill, New York.

Lichtenstein, S., Slovic, P., Fischoff, B., Layman, M. & Combs, B. (1978) Judged frequency of lethal events. *Journal of Experimental Psychology (Human Learning and Memory)*, 4: 551–578.

Lievesly, S. (1995) *Security into the 21st Century*. The Risk and Security Management Forum, Police Staff College, Bramshill.

Lines, S. (1999) Information technology multi-media simulator training: outcomes of critical decision-making exercises. *Police Journal*, April, 96–108.

London Emergency Service Liaison Panel (LESLP) (1992) *Major Incident Procedure*. Published by Directorate of Public Affairs and International Communication, Metropolitan Police Service, New Scotland Yard, London.

Lopes, L.L. (1987) Between hope and fear: the psychology of risk. *Advances in Experimental and Social Psychology*, 20: 255–295.

Loveluck, C. (1994) Eight propositions and a proposal. Edited version of the keynote address given at the 1994 ABSEL/SAGSET Conference in Warwick.

Lupton, D. (1999) *Risk*. Routledge, London.

Lupton, D. (2004) Risk ritual and the management of control and anxiety in medical culture. *Crawford Health*, 8: 505–528.

Manunta, G. (1998a) Illegitimati Non Carborundum. *Intersec*, 8(2).

Manunta, G. (1998b) *Security: An Introduction*. Cranfield University Press, Cranfield.

Manunta, G. (2000) Defining security. Diogenes Paper No. 1. Cranfield Security Centre, RMCS, Shrivenham.

Martin, L., Flin, R. & Skriver, J. (1997) Emergency decision making – a wider decision framework? In R. Flin, E. Salas, M. Strub & L. Martin (eds), *Decision Making under Stress: Emerging Themes and Applications*. Ashgate, Aldershot.

Maslow, A. (1968) *Toward a Psychology of Being* (2nd edn). Van Nostrand, Princeton, NJ.

Mathis, R., McKiddy, R. & Way, B. (1982) Police emergency operations: the management of crisis. *Police Chief*, November, 48–52.

McCann, C. & Pigeau, R. (eds) (2000) *The Human in Command: Exploring the Modern Military Experience*. Kluwer/Plenum, New York.

McDonald, N., Fuller, R. & White, G. (1992) The design and evaluation of an emergency exercise. *Simulation/Games For Learning*, 22: 326–335.

McLennan, J., Pavlou, O. & Klein, P. (1999) Using video during training to enhance learning of incident command and control skills. Paper presented at the Fire Service College, Moreton-in-Marsh, Gloucester, November.

Meyers, K.M. (1993) *Total Contingency Planning for Disasters*. John Wiley & Sons Inc., New York.

Milgram, S. (1974) *Obedience to Authority: An Experimental View*. Tavistock, London.

Millar, D.P. & Heath, R.L. (2004) *Responding to Crisis: A Rhetorical Approach to Crisis Communications*. Lawrence Erlbaum, NJ.

Mintzberg, H. (1980) *The Nature of Managerial Work*. Harper & Row, New York.

Mitchell, M. (1999) A current view from the UK in post-incident care: 'debriefing', 'defusing' and just talking about it. In J. Violanti & D. Paton (eds), *Police Trauma*. C.C. Thomas, Springfield, IL.

Moore, T. (1985) Community disorder simulation. *Simulation/Games For Learning*, 15(2): 73–82.

Moore, T. (1986) Police training for crisis: The use of simulation. *Police Journal*, 61(2): 119–136.

Moore, T. (1988) The use of computer simulations for police training. *Simulation/Games for Learning*, 18(1): 40–49.

Moore, T. (2001) Police Commander (UK): The Notting Hill riot. In R. Flin & K. Arbuthnot (eds), *Incident Command: Tales from the Hot Seat*. Ashgate, Aldershot.

Moran, C. & Colless, E. (1995) Positive reactions following emergency and disaster response. *Disaster Prevention and Management*, 4(1): 55–60.

Morentz, J.W. (1985) Saving lives: the emergency management game. *Information Society*, 3(4): 371–82.

Morrell, B. (1994) Keeping the Queen's peace. *Metropolitan Police Journal*, 10 (July): 6–9.

Murray, A. (1994) Training for operational command. *Fire Professional*, 67–71.

Nalla, M.K., Christian, K., Morash, M. & Schram, P. (1995) Practitioners' perceptions of graduate curriculum in security education. *Security Journal*, 6: 93–99.

Nelken, D. (1994) White collar crime. In M. Maguire, R. Morgan & R. Reiner (eds), *The Oxford Handbook of Criminology*. Clarendon Press, Oxford.

New, B. (1992) Too many cooks? The response of health-related services to major incidents in London. Research report 15, King's Fund Institute, Intertype, London.

Newman, O. (1972) *Defensible Spaces: Crime Prevention through Urban Design*. Macmillan, New York.

Newman, O. (1976) *Design Guidelines for Creating Defensible Space*. Law Enforcement Assistance Administration, Washington, DC.

Noble, S., Fallesen, J.J., Halpin, S.M. & Shanteau, J. (2000) Exploring cognitive skills of battle commanders. Paper presented at the Fifth Conference on Naturalistic Decision Making, Stockholm, Sweden.

North, R. & Wilcock, D. (1991) Major incidents – chaos and communications. *Simulation/Games For Learning*, 21(2): 169–172.

Noy, S. (1991) Combat stress reactions. In R. Gal & A. Mangelsdorf (eds), *Handbook of Military Psychology*. John Wiley & Sons, Ltd, Chichester.

O'Connel, J.J. (1997) From benevolent dictator to constitutional monarch: simulating a European works council in a US classroom. In J. Wolfe & J.B. Keys (eds), *Business Simulations, Games and Experiential Learning in International Business Education*. International Business Press, New York/London, pp. 21–38.

O'Neill, B. & Williams, A. (1998) Risk homeostasis hypothesis: a rebuttal. *Injury Prevention*, 4: 92–93.

O'Riordan, T., Kemp, R. & Purdue, M. (1987) *Sizewell B: An Anatomy of the Inquiry*. Macmillan, London.

OECD (1987) *Nuclear Agency Chernobyl and the Safety of Nuclear Reactors in OECD Countries*. Organization for Economic Co-operation and Development, Paris.

Orasanu, J. & Backer, P. (1996) Stress and military performance. In J. Driskell & E. Salas (eds) *Stress and Performance*. LEA, Hillsdale, NJ.

Orasanu, J. & Fischer, U. (1997) Finding decisions in natural environments: the view from the cockpit. In C.E. Zsambok & G. Klein (eds), *Naturalistic Decision Making*. LEA, Mahwah, NJ, pp. 343–358.

Osgood, C.E. (1949) The similarity paradox in human learning. *Psychological Review*, 56: 132–143.

Otway, H.J. & Von Winterfeldt, D. (1982) Beyond acceptable risk: on the social acceptability of technology. *Policy Sciences*, 14: 247–256.

Paine, D. (1972) *Basic Principles of Industrial Security*. Oak Security Publications, USA.

Paradis, S., Treurniet, W. & Roy, J. (1998) Environment perception process in maritime command and control. Paper presented at the NATO Symposium on Sensor Data Fusion and Integration of the Human Element, Ottawa, Canada.

Parker, D. (1998) Reducing regulatory risk: the case for a new regulatory contract with the privatised utilities. *Public Money and Management*, 18(4): 51–57.

Parker, R. (1987) Acquired immunodeficiency syndrome in urban Brazil. *Medical Anthropology Quarterly*.

Pascual, R. & Henderson, S. (1997) Evidence of naturalistic decision making in command and control. In C.E. Zsambok & G.A. Klein (eds), *Naturalistic Decision Making*. LEA, Hillsdale, NJ.

Paton, D. (1991) Major incident and disaster stress in firefighters. *Disaster Management*, 3: 216–223.

Paton, D. (1997) *Dealing with Traumatic Incidents in the Workplace* (3rd edn). Gull Publishing, Queensland.

Paton, D. (1999) Disaster business continuity: promoting staff capability. *Disaster Prevention and Management*, 8(2): 127–133.

Paton, D. & Smith, R. (1998) Work-related psychological trauma: promoting quality of life in high-risk professions. *Bulletin*, 26: 18–23.

Paton, D., Johnston, D. & Houghton, B. (1998) Organizational responses to a volcanic eruption. *Disaster Prevention and Management*, 7: 5–13.

Pearson, M. & Smith, D. (1986) Debriefing in experience-based learning. *Simulation/Games for Learning*, 16(4).

Peltzman, S. (1975) The effects of automobile safety regulation. *Journal of Political Economy*, 83: 4.

Perrow, C. (1984) *Normal Accidents: Living with High-Risk Technologies*. Basic Books, New York.

Peterson, D.M. & Perry, R.W. (1999) The impact of disaster exercises on participants. *Disaster Prevention and Management*, 8(4): 241–254.

Petranek, C.F. (1989) Knowing oneself: a symbolic interactionist view of simulation. In D. Crookall & D. Saunders (eds), *Communication and Simulation: From Two Fields to One Theme*. Multilingual Matters Ltd, Clevedon, PA.

Petranek, C.F. (2000) Written debriefing: the next vital step in learning with simulations. *Simulation and Gaming*, 31(1): 108–118.

Piaget, J. (1972) *The Principles of Genetic Epistemology*. Basic Books, New York.

Pidgeon, N. (1991) Safety culture and risk management in organizations. *Journal of Cross-Cultural Psychology*, 22(1): 129–140.

Pidgeon, N. & Turner, B. (1997) *Man-Made Disasters*. Butterworth, London.

Pidgeon, N. *et al*. (1992) Risk perception. In *Risk: Analysis, Perception and Management*. Report to the Royal Society Study Group, London.

Pigeau, R. & McCann, C. (2000) Redefining command and control. In C. McCann & R. Pigeau (eds), *The Human in Command: Exploring the Modern Military Experience*. Kluwer/Plenum, New York.

Pliske, R., McCloskey, M. & Klein, G. (1998) Facilitating learning from experience: An innovative approach to decision skills training. Paper presented at the 4th Conference on Naturalistic Decision Making, Warrenton, VA.

Popplewell, O. (1985) *Committee of Inquiry into Crowd Safety and Control at Sports Grounds*. (Interim Report.) HMSO, London.

Posner, R.A. (1974) The theories of economic regulation. *Bell Journal of Economics and Management Science*, 5: 335–358.

Post, R.S. & Kingsbury, A.A. (1991) *Security Administration: An Introduction to the Protective Services*. Butterworth-Heinemann, London.

Poyner, B. (1983) *Design Against Crime: Beyond a Defensible Space*. Butterworth, London.

Quarantelli, E. (1988) Disaster crisis management: a summary of research findings. *Journal of Management Studies*, 25: 373–385.

Quarantelli, E. (1995a) Disasters are different, therefore planning for and managing them requires innovative as well as traditional behaviours. Paper presented at the 3rd Emergency Planning and Disaster Management Conference, Lancaster University.

Quarantelli, E. (1995b) What is a disaster? *International Journal of Mass Emergencies and Disasters*, 13(3): 221–229.

Quarantelli, E. (ed.) (1998) *What is a Disaster?* Routledge, London.

Radcliffe-Brown, A.R. (1952) *Structure and Function in Primitive Society*. Cohen West, London.

Ragland, S., Chambers, R.M., Crosbie, R.J. & Hitchcock, L. (1964) *Simulation and the Effects of Severe Turbulence on Jet Airline Pilots*. Report NADC-ML-6411, US Naval Air Developments Centre, Johnsville, PA.

Raphael, B., Singh, B., Bradbury, L. & Lambert, F. (1983) Who helps the helpers? The effects of a disaster on the rescue workers. *Omega*, 14(1): 9–20.

Ratti, O. & Westbrook, A. (1970) *Aikido in the Dynamic Sphere: An Illustrated Introduction*. Charles E. Tuttle, Tokyo.

Rayner, C. (1997) The incidence of workplace bullying. *Journal of Community and Applied Social Psychology*, pp. 199–208.

Reason, J. (1990) *Human Error*. Cambridge University Press, Cambridge.

Reason, J. (1997) *Managing the Risks of Organisational Accidents*. Ashgate, Aldershot.

Regester, M. & Larkin, J (1997) *Risk Issues and Crisis Management*. Kogan Page, London.

Rhind, D., Toop, F. & Tibble, J. (2001) *Project Phoenix: A Case Study of City University's Recovery from Fire*. Universities UK, London.

Rolfe, J. (1998) Being wise before the event: a training practitioner's view of emergencies. In J. Rolfe, D. Saunders & T. Powell (eds), *Simulations and Games for Emergency and Crisis Management*. Kogan Page, London, pp. 8–15.

Rolfe, J.M. (1992) Training transfer: the basis for validating effectiveness. *Simulation/Games for Learning*, 22(4): 249–259.

Rolfe, J., Saunders, D. & Powell, T. (eds) (1998) *Simulations and Games for Emergency and Crisis Management: The International Simulation and Gaming Research Yearbook*. Kogan Page, London.

Rosenthal, U. (1986) Crisis decision making in the Netherlands. *Netherlands Journal of Sociology*, 22: 103–129.

Rosenthal, U. (ed.) (1989) *Coping with Crises: The Management of Disaster, Riots and Terrorism*. Charles C. Pub. Ltd., Springfield, IL.

Rosenthal, U. (1996) Crisis management: second-order techniques. In T. Horlick-Jones & A. Amendola (eds), *Natural Risk and Civil Protection*. R.E. Casale & F.N. Spon, Leiden.

Rosenthal, U. & Pijnenburg, B. (1991) Simulation-oriented scenarios: An alternative approach to crisis decision making and emergency management. In U. Rosenthal and B. Pijnenburg (eds), *Crisis Management and Decision Making*. Kluwer, The Netherlands.

Rosenthal, U., Comfort, L. & Boin, A. (eds) (in press) *From Contingencies to Crisis Management: An International Perspective*. C.C. Thomas, Springfield IL.

Rouse, W.B., Cannon-Bowers, J. & Salas, E. (1992) The role of mental models in team performance in complex systems. *IEEE Transactions on Systems, Man, and Cybernetics*, 22: 1295–1308.

Royal Society (1992) *Risk: Analysis, Perception and Management*. The Royal Society, London.

Said, E. (1989) *Orientalism*. Routledge, London.

Salas, E. & Cannon-Bowers, J. (1993) Team performance and training in complex systems. In collected papers of the Fourth Offshore Installation Management Conference, Robert Gordon University, Aberdeen, April.

Salas, E., Cannon-Bowers, J. & Blickensderfer, E. (1995) Team performance and training research: emerging principles. *Journal of the Washington Academy of Science*, 83(2): 81–106.

Sarbanes-Oxley (2002) 107th Congress of the United States of America, H.R. 3763.

Sarna, P. (1984) Training police commanders and supervisors in the management of critical incidents. *Washington Crime News Training Aids Digest*, 9(12): 1–6.

Sarna, P. (2001) Police Commander (USA). In R. Flin & K. Arbuthnot (eds), *Incident Command: Tales from the Hot Seat*. Ashgate, Aldershot.

Saunders, D. & Smalley, N. (eds) (2000) *Simulation and Games for Transition and Change, Simulation and Gaming Yearbook Vol. 8*. Kogan Page, London.

Scanlon, J. & Prawzick, A. (1991) Not just a big fire: emergency response to an environmental disaster. *Canadian Police College Journal*, 15(3): 166–202.

Schmitt, J. (1994) *Mastering Tactics: Tactical Decision Game Workbook*. Marine Corps Association, Quantico, VA.

Schon, D. (1983) *The Reflective Practictioner*. Temple-Smith, London.

Schuffel, H. (1984) *The Interaction of Rate Movement Presentation with Ships' Controllability*. Conference on Maritime Simulation.

Schumacher, E.F. (1973) *Small is Beautiful: A Study of Economics as if People Mattered*. Harper Row, New York.

Senge, P. (1990) *The Fifth Discipline: The Art and Practice of the Learning Organisation*. Doubleday, New York.

Serfaty, D. & Michel, R.R. (1990) Toward a theory of tactical decision making expertise. Paper presented at the Symposium on Command and Control Research, Monteray, CA.

Serrie, H. (1992) Teaching cross-cultural management skills. *Journal of Teaching in International Business*, 3(3): 75–91.

Sevennson, O. (1996) Differentiation and consolidation theory. In R. Flin, E. Salas, M. Strub & L. Martin (eds), *Decision Making under Stress: Emerging Themes and Applications*. Ashgate, Aldershot.

Seymour, M. & Moore, S. (2000) *Effective Crisis Management*. Cassell, London.

Sharp, J. (1999) *Business Continuity Management Explained: Just Another Buzzword?* CBI Business Guide, London.

Shaw, R. (1997) Decision making under stress: forming effective police commanders. *Police Research and Management*, Autumn, 51–59.

Sheridan, T.B. & Hennessy, R.T. (eds) (1984) *Research and Modelling of Supervisory Control Behaviour*. National Academy Press, Washington, DC.

Sjoberg, L. (1995) *Explaining Risk Perception: An Empirical and Quantitative Evaluation of Cultural Theory*. Rhizikon Risk Reports, Stockholm School of Economics.

Skriver, J. & Flin, R. (1996) Decision making in offshore emergencies: are standard operating procedures the solution? Paper presented at the SPE International Conference on Health, Safety and Environment in Oil and Gas Industry, New Orleans, LA.

Skriver, J. & Flin, R. (1997) Emergency decision making on offshore installations. In D. Harris (ed.), *Engineering Psychology and Cognitive Ergonomics* (Vol. 2, *Job Design and Product Design*, pp. 47–54). Avebury, Aldershot.

Slapper, G. & Tombs, S. (1999) *Corporate Crime*. Longman, Edinburgh.

Slovic, P. (1987) Perceptions of risk. *Science*, 236: 280–285.

Slovic, P. (1992) Perceptions of risk: reflections on the psychometric paradigm. In S. Kimsky & D. Golding (eds), *Theories of Risk*. Praeger Publishers, New York.

Slovic, P., Fischoff, B. & Lichtenstein, S. (1980) Facts and fears: understanding perceived risks. In R.C. Schwing & W.A. Albers (eds), *Societal Risk Assessment: How Safe is Safe Enough?* Plenum Press, New York.

Smith, D. (2000) Crisis management teams: issues in the management of operational crisis. *Risk Management: An International Journal*, 2(3): 61–78.

Smith, D. (2004) For whom the bell tolls: imagining accidents and the development of crisis simulation in organizations. *Simulation and Gaming: An Interdisciplinary Journal of Theory, Practice and Research*, 35(3): 347–362.

Sorokin, P. & Merton, R.K. (1937) Social time: a methodological and functional analysis. *American Journal of Sociology*, 42: 615–629.

Stammers, R.B. (1983) Simulators for training. In T.O. Kvalseth (ed.), *Ergonomics of Work Station Design*. Butterworths, London, pp. 229–242.

Starr, C. (1969) Social benefit versus technological risk. *Science*, 165: 1232–1238.

STASYS (1998a) *DRG Support Study Report*, Version 2. October 1998, Internal Publication.

STASYS (1998b) *Training of Business Continuity and Disaster Recovery Personnel*, Version 2. October 1998, internal publication.

Staw, B.M., Barsade, S.G. & Koput, K.W. (1997) Escalation at the credit window: a longitudinal study of bank executives' recognition and write-off of problem loans. *Journal of Applied Psychology*, 82(1): 130–142.

Staw, B., Sandelands, L. & Dutton, J. (1981) Threat rigidity effects in organisational behaviour: a multi-level analysis. *Administrative Sciences Quarterly*, 26(4): 501–524.

Stephens, C. & Long, N. (2000) Communication with police supervisors and peers as a buffer of work-related traumatic stress. *Journal of Organizational Behavior*, 21(4): 407–424.

Stern, E. (1997) Crisis and learning: a conceptual balance sheet. *Journal of Contingencies and Crisis Management*, 5(2): 69–86.

Stern, E. (1999) Crisis decision making: A cognitive institutional approach. PhD thesis, Department of Political Science, University of Stockholm.

Sternberg, E. (1998) *Corporate Governance: Accountability in the Market Place*. Institute of Economic Affairs, London.

Stewart, E. & Flin, R. (1996) Taking action. *Policing Today*, December: 14–17.

Stokes, A. (1997) Aeronautical decision making. In C. Zsambok & G. Klein (eds), *Naturalistic Decision Making*. LEA, Mahwah, NJ.

Stretch, D.C. (2000) Simulation design. In D. Saunders & N. Smalley (eds), *Simulation and Games for Transition and Change, Simulation and Gaming Yearbook Vol. 8*. Kogan Page, London, pp. 33–46.

Sundelius, B. (1998) Conclusion: learning from crisis experiences. In L.M. Newlove (ed), *Coping with Value Conflict and Institutional Complexity: International Conference in an International Perspective*. ÖCB, Stockholm, pp. 117–120.

Sutherland, E. (1940) White-collar criminality. *American Sociological Review*, 5: 1–12.

Sutherland, E. (1945) Is 'white-collar crime' crime? *American Sociological Review*, 10: 132–139.

Sutherland, E. (1947) *Criminology*. Lippincott, Philadelphia, PA.

Sutherland, E. (1949) *White-Collar Crime*. Holt, Reinhart & Winston, New York.

Sutherland, E. (1983) *White Collar Crime: The Uncut Version*. Yale University Press, New Haven.

Swedish Emergency Management Agency, PO Box 599, SE – 101 31, Stockholm, Sweden. www.krisberedskapsmyndiget

t'Hart, P. (1993) Symbols, rituals and power: the lost dimensions of crisis management. *Journal of Contingencies and Crisis Management*, 1(1): 36–50.

Taylor, J.L. (1971) *Instructional Planning Systems: A Gaming-Simulation Approach to Urban Problems*. Cambridge University Press, Cambridge.

Taylor, J.R. (1979) *The Penguin Dictionary of Theatre*. Penguin Books, Harmondsworth, Middlesex.

Taylor, P. (1989/1990) *The Hillsborough Stadium Disaster* (Interim Report/Final Report). London, HMSO.

Thiagarajan, S. (1994) How I designed a game – and discovered the meaning of life. *Simulation and Gaming*, 25: 529–535.

Thiagarajan, S. (2003) Interactive lectures: 20 years later. In *The International Simulation and Gaming Yearbook*, Vol. 11, pp. 25–35.

Thomas, W.I. (1951) The four wishes and definitions of the situation. In M. Janowitz (ed.), *Thomas on Organisation and Social Personality: Selected Papers*. University of Chicago Press, Chicago.

Thompson, D.R. (1989) Transfer of training from simulators to operational equipment – are simulators effective? *Journal of Educational Technology Systems*, 17(3): 213–218.

Thompson, G.H. & Dass, P. (2000) Improving students' self-efficacy in strategic management: the relative impact of cases and simulations. *Simulation and Gaming*, 31(1): 22–41.

Thompson, M., Ellis, R. & Wildavsky, A. (1990) *Cultural Theory*. Westview, Boulder, CO.

Thorndike, E.L. (1903) *Educational Psychology*. Lemke & Buechner, New York.

Todhunter, I. (1865) *A History of the Mathematical Theory of Probability from the Time of Pascal to that of LaPlace*. Chelsea Press, New York.

Toft, B. & Reynolds, S. (1994) *Learning from Disasters: A Management Approach*. Butterworth-Heinemann, Oxford.

Trist, E.L. & Bamforth, K.W. (1951) Some social and psychological consequences of the Longwall method of coalgetting. *Human Relations*, 4(1).

Trist, E.L. *et al.* (1963) *Organisational Choice*. Tavistock Publications, London.

Tsuchiya, T. & Tsuchiya, S. (1999) The unique contribution of gaming/simulation: towards establishment of the discipline. In D. Saunders & J. Severn (eds) *Simulations and Games for Strategy and Policy Planning, Simulation and Gaming Yearbook Vol. 7*, Kogan Page, London, pp. 46–57.

Turnbull, N. (1999) *Internal Control: Guidance for Directors on the Combined Code*. Institute of Chartered Accountants in England and Wales, London.

Turner, B. (1978) *Man-Made Disasters*. Wykeham, London.

Turner, B. (1991) The development of a safety culture. *Chemistry and Industry*, 1(7): 241–243.

Turner, B. (1994) Flexibility and improvisation in emergency response. *Disaster Management: Journal of Contingency Planning for Large Scale Emergencies*, 6(2): 85–89.

Turner, B. (1996) Scenarios in emergency response simulations. In Crisis Management and Fire Service Directorate, *Crisis Management Reader Seminar: The Use of Scenarios for Crisis Management*. Ministry of Home Affairs, The Hague, Holland.

Turner, B. & Pidgeon, N. (1997) *Man Made Disasters*. Butterworth-Heinemann, Oxford.

Tylor, E. (1871) *Primitive Culture*. John Murray, London.

Valverde, H.H. (1973) A review of flight simulator transfer of training studies. *Human Factors* 15(6): 510–523.

van Ments, M. (2003) Magic: illusion and trickery. In *The International Simulation and Gaming Yearbook*, Vol. 11, pp. 19–24.

Vaughan, E.J. (1997) *Risk Management*. John Wiley & Sons, Ltd, Chichester.

VECTOR Command UK (1999) *Vector Command Training Simulation* (Version 02/06/00). www.vectorcommand.co.uk

Vinten, G. (1994) Whistleblowing – fact and fiction: an introductory discussion. In G. Vinten (ed.), *Whistleblowing: Subversion or Corporate Citizenship?* Paul Chapman, London.

Violanti, J. & Paton, D. (eds) (1999) *Police Trauma*. C.C. Thomas, Springfield, IL.

Von Bertalannfy, L. (1968) *General Systems Theory*. MIT Press, Cambridge, MA.

Vrij, A., van der Steen, J. & Koppelaar, L. (1994) Aggression of police officers as a function of temperature. *Journal of Community and Applied Psychology*, 4: 365–370.

Walsh, T.J. & Healy, R.J. (1987) *Protection of Assets Manual* (7th printing). Merritt Company, Santa Monica, CA.

Waring, A. (1992) Developing a safety culture. *Health and Safety Practitioner*, 10(4): 42–44.

Waring, A. and Glendon, A.I. (1998) *Managing Risk: Critical Issues for Survival and Success into the 21st Century*. International Thomson Business Press, London.

Weir, D. (1996) Risk and disaster: the role of communications breakdown in plane crashes and business failure. In C. Hood & D. Jones (eds), *Accident and Design: Contemporary Debates in Risk Management*. UCL Press, London.

Weisaeth, L. (1987) Mestring av lederstress under ulykker og kriseituasjoner [Control of leader stress during accident and crisis situations]. In S. Larsen, T. Skerveongen & L. Ostigaard (eds), *Handbok i Sikkerhetsstyring* [Handbook of Safety Management]. Norwegian Management Publications, Oslo.

Wells, C. (1993) *Corporations and Criminal Responsibility*. Clarendon Press, Oxford.

Wells, C. (1995) *Negotiating Tragedy: Law and Disasters*. Sweet & Maxwell, London.

Wickens, C.D. (1996) Designing for stress. In J.E. Driskell & E. Salas (eds), *Stress and Human Performance*. LEA, Mahwah, NJ.

Wilde, G. (1976) The risk compensation theory of accident causation and its practical consequences for accident prevention. Paper presented at the annual meeting of the Osterreicherische Gessellschaft fur Unfallchirurgies, Salzburg.

Wilde, G.J.S. (1994) *Target Risk: Dealing with the Danger of Death, Disease and Damage in Everyday Decisions*. PDE Publications, Ontario.

Williams, C.A., Jr, Smith, M.L. & Young, P.C. (1995) *Risk Management and Insurance* (7th edn). McGraw-Hill, New York.

Wilson, J.D. (1989) Evacuation procedures and system drills. *IEEE Transactions on Power Systems*, 4(4): 254–256.

Wilson, J.Q. & Slater, T. (1990) *Practical Security in Commerce and Industry* (5th edn). Gower, Aldershot.

Worsley, P. (1984) *The Three Worlds*. Wiedenfield & Nicholson, London.

Wraith, R.E. and Lamb, G.B. (1971) *Public Inquiries as an Instrument of Government*. Allen & Unwin, London.

Wynne, B. (1981) *Rationality and Ritual*. British Society for the History of Science, Chalfont St Giles.

Wynne, B. (1989) Frameworks of rationality in risk management: towards the testing of naive sociology. In J. Brown (ed.), *Environmental Threats: Perception, Analysis and Management*. Belhaven Press, London.

Wynne, B. (1992) Risk and social learning: reification to engagement. In S. Krimsky & D. Golding (eds), *Theories of Risk*. Praeger Publishers, New York.

Yates, F. (in press) Observations on naturalistic decision making – the phenomenon and the 'framework'. In E. Salas & G. Klein (eds), *Research, Methods and Applications of Naturalistic Decision Making Principles*. LEA, Mahwah, NJ.

Zsambok, C.E. (1997) Naturalistic decision making: where are we now? In C.E. Zsambok & G. Klein (eds), *Naturalistic Decision Making*. LEA, Mahwah, NJ.

Zsambok, C.E. & Klein, G. (eds) (1997) *Naturalistic Decision Making*. LEA, Mahwah, NJ.

INDEX